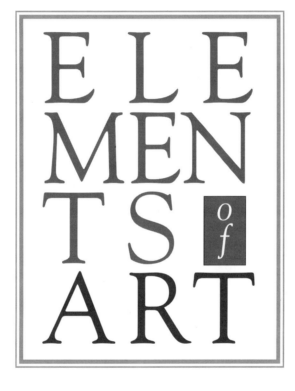

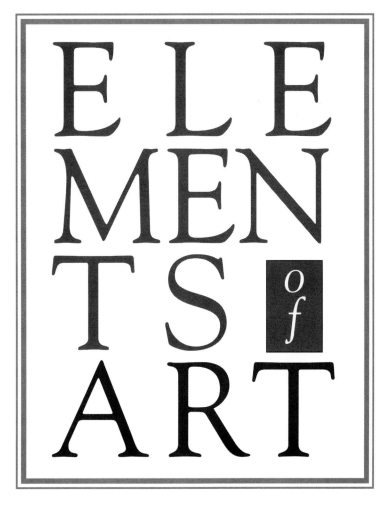

ELEMENTS of ART

RICHARD PUMPHREY

Lynchburg College

PRENTICE HALL, Upper Saddle River, New Jersey 07458

Library of Congress Cataloging-in-Publication Data
Pumphrey, Richard.
    Elements of art / Richard Pumphrey.
        p.   cm.
    Includes bibliographical references and index.
    ISBN 0–13–720376–4 (pbk.)
    1. Art—Technique.   2. Composition (Art)   3. Design   4. Art
appreciation.   I. Title.
N7430.P86   1996   94-36346
701′.1—dc20   CIP

Acquisitions editor: Bud Therien
Project manager: Alison Gnerre
Interior and cover design: Thomas Nery
Design director: Paula Martin/Leslie Osher
Manufacturing buyer: Bob Anderson

©1996 by Prentice Hall, Inc.
Simon & Schuster/A Viacom Company
Upper Saddle River, New Jersey 07458

Printed in the United States of America
10 9 8 7 6 5 4 3 2 1

ISBN 0-13-720376-4

Prentice-Hall International (UK) Limited, *London*
Prentice-Hall of Australia Pty. Limited, *Sydney*
Prentice-Hall Canada Inc., *Toronto*
Prentice-Hall Hispanoamericana, S.A., *Mexico*
Prentice-Hall of India Private Limited, *New Delhi*
Prentice-Hall of Japan, Inc., *Tokyo*
Simon & Schuster Asia Pte. Ltd., *Singapore*
Editora Prentice-Hall do Brasil, Ltda., *Rio de Janeiro*

CONTENTS

PROLOGUE

What is a design textbook? It certainly cannot be considered a "cookbook" for guaranteeing success in art. And a design textbook is not a rule book of rigid absolutes.

This design textbook is a guide to understanding the interrelationship of visual images produced by human beings from all the ages. Additionally, this design text is a guide to helping you find your place within this tradition of image making and discovering the common thread that unites your creative spirit with the creativity of those who have worked with different media to express themselves and their passions for thousands of years.

Those individuals who are involved in the arts in one way or another have probably always been involved in the arts. That involvement may have started off at a very minimal level, such as doodling in class notes and book margins, drawing in the sand at the beach, or shaping clay found at a river bank. What is interesting about each of these examples is that they demonstrate a conscious or subconscious desire and need for people to use a device other than oral communication for expression. There exists as part of human nature a subconscious drive

1. To bring to the surface one's emotions and passions from the intangible depths of the spirit, and
2. To give tangible form to those feelings. There is a need to give visual form to expression.

Perhaps what is most satisfying in this study of design is the realization that while there are some basic common denominators, or common threads, to visual expression—point, line, shape, value, color, and texture—there is an unlimited range of possibilities for the meaningful and unique arrangement/design of these

▶ Children Creating Images

common denominators. The way you selectively choose to use the common denominators, these components of art, is what makes your art unique.

> It is sensitivity to the arrangement of these same visual components which has defined the uniqueness of the works of art produced in both caves and cathedrals.

One of the biggest problems students of design generally have is being comfortable using a variety of media in the studio. While many students may feel comfortable with paper and pencil, having to use a lithograph crayon on matboard may be unnerving. On the other hand, some students are delighted and enthusiastic about the prospect of working with computer keyboards, programs, and printers to produce images. Significant learning and growth takes place in the design studio when students meet new challenges with a new sense of opportunity instead of a sense of dread; when "border experiences" are seen as occasions for further development.

In time, you will master the use of a variety of media as a result of your increasing familiarity with them. However, you may never become an artist if you neglect the implications of good design. You have undoubtedly visited craft shows and seen beautifully thrown pots or expertly woven fabrics. You have visited civic and corporate displays and observed masterly produced blueprints and schematic drawings. Quite simply, the woods are full of good craftspeople, those who handle their relative media and tools with expert skill. Yet, as you have observed, some of these images and items may have been disappointing due to their lack of visual significance—they have no punch, no real

importance. Many images are just disappointing regurgitations of other people's true art. While the images and forms may be well-made, they are not original in concept nor design. Good craftsmanship, alone, does not determine artistic credibility. A clean line, by itself, does not make art. Art requires a combination of good craftsmanship, design, and significance. In order to create art, all of these need to be understood, explored, and exploited!

Marketing devices such as "limited editions" seem to imply an elevated status to art objects that are reproduced on a limited basis. Unfortunately, however, an object offered "as one in a series" of a limited edition is not necessarily "art" merely because it may be relatively rare or hard to find. Rather, . . .

> Art is a visual form of meaningful expression.

In this definition of art, "Visual" emphasizes the fact that *art* does not represent another communication form—the visual arts are not just other forms of prose, nor are they historical narrations. "Meaningful Expression" involves purposefulness and a degree of uniqueness, and the necessity of communicating. "Meaningful Expression" necessarily includes taste and omits images considered trite, or even cute. Kenneth Galbraith wrote

> . . . the cutting edge of economic change in our time is not technology but design. The great expanding industries in our time are those that depend on good design, on artistic taste.

Therefore, a great deal of what we determine to be art will be based on values we develop and establish throughout our lives. The most significant ways to develop these values and refine our "taste" are to expand our experiences and acquire knowledge.

Throughout this text you will observe an emphasis on *the equal merits of various art forms, styles, and media.* This is a relatively contemporary concept which allows for artistic invention. You will find it interesting to compare this dominant theme of the text with some attitudes that have existed for centuries, as indicated in the first chapter, "The Finest of the Fine Arts—A Debate."

PREFACE: NOTES RELATED TO THE TEXT

▶ THE VOCABULARY

Terms relate to different fields of study in different ways. For example, in everyday language "slip" is something you do when you lose your footing. But in ceramics, "slip" is a mix of water and powdered clay which results in a medium which has the consistency of tomato soup. It is used for joining pieces of clay and casting ceramic objects. Another term, "contour," may be used in reference to plowing or drawing. Therefore, when art terms are introduced, do not take it for granted that you automatically know what the terms mean simply because you use them everyday—that assumption can get you into trouble. Surely you have used the terms LINE, SHAPE, VALUE, TEXTURE, and COLOR since you were about two or three years old, but can you really define them? And how do they relate to art as opposed to geometry or physics?

Terms may frequently overlap different disciplines. In this text, be alert to how specific terms will relate to their applications as determiners of a particular concept or property of *VISUAL ART*. Also, the definitions for the vocabulary words reflect the meanings in phraseology that has been determined useful to students.

"I'm sorry, but I can't carry on an intelligent conversation. I'm visual."

▶ Robert Weber / © *The New Yorker*

▶ THE PROJECTS

Studio projects are often approached by students with an overwhelming sense of dread, a dread that involves the assumption that all of the projects have to be completed within the absolute set of limitations provided in the assignment; that the projects are restrictive and do not allow for individual creativity. The suggested projects in this text outline a series of guidelines which are intended to carry you through various exploratory design situations.

Most importantly, the projects are not intended to limit your interpretation as to what the range of possible solutions to a problem can be. Rather,

> . . . the projects are a starting line, a place to begin your explorations of design and media; they are not a fence or a limit to your imagination.

Should you find that an idea in a project suggests a related but different approach or solution, you should consider this new direction in consultation with your teacher, as long as your direction incorporates the stated objectives of the project and adds something distinctive to it. Margarite Wildenhain states that . . .

> If one only puts out what he learns as opposed to exploring and making mistakes, he will not learn and grow . . .

In other words, push yourself. Be willing to go beyond what is safe in order to grow, to stumble before you walk. The child is delivered from the security and warmth of the womb just as the chick breaks out of the egg in order to grow. Growth is the natural order of living things, and *growth requires energy, effort and a willingness to dare.*

Worrying about how well one is going to do on the projects and how well one is going to handle the media are two of the major reasons students have problems with projects and media. Worrying is counterproductive, as it reduces energy and interferes with getting work done. Dr.

Robert Kriegel, a corporate consultant on strategies for dealing with change, notes that although people between the ages of 18 and 24 do more worrying than any other age group, most of what they worry about is beyond their control, and the more one worries, the worse things get.

However, there is no need for you to worry about the projects and media because these are things you can control. If you anticipate problems in one area or another, work through those problems. Practice with your media. As an athlete trains for a big event or as a lecturer practices a lecture, a student artist must practice and play with media before actual projects are produced. Dr. Kriegel says . . .

> Focusing on what you can control enables you to concentrate your energy and perform at peak levels.

▶ **THE ILLUSTRATIONS AND PLATES**

Examples

If you think about the sky, you can imagine it at least 365 different ways: a different way each day of the year. If you imagine a skeletal system you may see it as applicable to a human being, a dog, a bear, a snake, or an unlimited number of other species.

Similarly, to discuss an art concept and use just one or two examples to illustrate it is, at best, incomplete. Therefore, you are asked to understand that the examples provided in this text provide some of the possible interpretations of concepts, but certainly not all of the possible and valid solutions or ideas related to the concepts.

Interpretation

Similarly, there may exist many different ideas about the meaning of a particular image and whether it is successful or not. Throughout this text you will find various interpretations about the many images that are provided. These are based on the opinions of artists, critics, art historians, your author, and others. However, no interpretation of a work is presented as the *only* interpretation of that work. The brief analyses that are included are intended to stimulate your thinking about how particular art components can contribute to the significance of a given image. The discussions should provide a starting point for your own thinking, in addition to serving as the catalyst for classroom discussion.

> I find it a lot easier to enjoy a painting—and I value it more—when another opinion or interpretation is there . . . rather than just my own.

▶ TWO- AND THREE-DIMENSIONAL DESIGN

In this text you will study how the components of art are interrelated: how line relates to shape, how value relates to color, how repetition relates to movement, and the like. As these components of art are inseparable, so, too, are design considerations of two- and three-dimensional works. When we speak of line, we refer to both drawings and sculptures. When we speak of texture, we speak of paintings, drawings and sculpture. The same is true whether we are speaking of shape or balance.

Some special considerations are sometimes necessary when speaking of one art form as opposed to another, however. For example, concepts such as MASS, VOLUME, and TECTONIC—while being associated with SHAPE—are more three-dimensional considerations than two-dimensional. Still, ORGANIC and GEOMETRIC are shape considerations equally applicable to both two- and three-dimensional art forms. The difference between the illusion of SPACE in two-dimensional works, as opposed to a form's displacement of and movement in actual SPACE in a three-dimensional work, will also require special attention. Therefore, each chapter will first discuss its topic universally, then move on to relate it to a particular art form, as applicable.

The three art forms are

1. Two-dimensional art, such as painting, drawing, and graphic works;
2. Three-dimensional art, such as sculpture; and
3. Architecture.

Our study will focus on the two- and three-dimensional arts, and the chapter projects will include both two- and three-dimensional investigations in order to allow you the opportunity of exploring a wide range of media, techniques, and design considerations.

▶ Jacob Lawrence, *Cabinet Makers*, 1946
(Hirshhorn Museum and Sculpture Garden, Smithsonian Institution,
Gift of Joseph H. Hirshhorn, 1966)

▶ Le Corbusier, *Chappelle Notre Dame de Mont*
(Giraudon, Art Resource, NY)

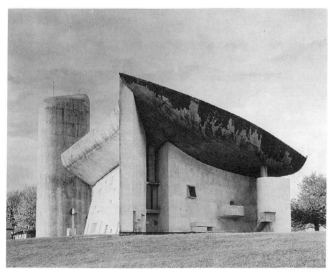

▶ Isamu Noguchi, *Black Sun*

▶ UNIT GLOSSARY

Art   A visual form of meaningful expression.

Craftsmanship   The skill and technical virtuosity with which one handles tools and media.

Craftspeople   Those who handle their media and tools with expert skill producing objects primarily for utilitarian ends.

Geometric shapes   Shapes which appear to have been mathematically constructed.

Mass   An area that appears to have bulk and density—a feeling of solidity.

Media   See "Medium."

Medium   The materials of which an art image is made, such as oil paint, charcoal, or marble. The plural form of MEDIUM is MEDIA.

Organic shapes   Shapes with undulating, free-flowing contours; frequently they resemble the shapes of living forms. Syn: BIOMORPHIC SHAPE.

Slip   A mix of water and powdered clay which results in a medium which has the consistency of tomato soup. It is used either for joining pieces of clay or casting clay forms.

Space   A limited or unlimited two- or three-dimensional area appearing to advance, recede, or extend in all directions, depending upon the visual clues provided by the artist.

Technique   Systematic use of tools and media to accomplish a task; the individual manner/style in which an artist manipulates a medium.

Volume   The actual space or area a 3-dimensional form displaces or circumscribes.

ACKNOWLEDGEMENTS

Institutions of higher learning, by the nature of their mission statements and goals, have different expectations of their faculty. I am fortunate to be employed by Lynchburg College in Lynchburg, Virginia, an institution which has traditionally placed quality teaching as the primary mission of its faculty. Toward this end, I am grateful that Lynchburg College has supported me in the writing of this text by the granting of a sabbatical leave, in addition to providing miscellaneous avenues of support, including staff, facility, and economic. *Elements of Art* grew out of the need to provide the college's art students with a foundation in design that would be applicable to their individual directions in art across the discipline, plus universal and timeless in its principles. Lynchburg College has been most generous in supporting this project to realize these goals.

However, institutions are not nameless. Many people here and elsewhere have facilitated the publication of *Elements of Art* in a variety of ways. My colleagues have been instrumental in providing motivation, ideas, and recommendations. Former College President, the late George Rainsford, and past Dean, James Traer, enthusiastically supported this project. My former teachers and teaching colleagues are also to be recognized for highlighting and enlarging upon the discipline they shared with me. Unfortunately, they are too numerous to list all, but those warranting particular attention are Virginia Davis, Patricia Kiblinger, Jane McCord, Bill Thompson, and the late Don Evans. Other colleagues to be noted are Thelma Twery and James Thompson. It was Virginia Davis, a noted author and accomplished educator and gallery director in her own right, who provided the catalyst to this text.

The preparation of materials for this text has involved the talents and skills of people from a cross section of areas of expertise. Facilitating the preparation of the text and providing a range of support services were Naomi Copes and Laurie Cassidy. Significant proofreading was done by Wendy Miles. Image research was most notably carried out by Elizabeth Henderson, in addition to Kristi Long, Catherine Dennison, and Eric deBruyn of Art Resources. Carol Hopchak was instrumental in making numerous photographs. My thanks is also extended to the numerous individuals at galleries, museums, private foundations, art centers, and the like, who worked to provide the many fine reproductions included in the text.

There have been countless individuals involved in the publishing of this textbook at Prentice Hall, far more than those with whom I have personally worked. Ms. Alison Gnerre deserves particular credit for having coordinated the project. Alison worked with skill and grace in the performance of all expected and unexpected services. Additionally, it cannot be understated how important everyone in the Humanities and Social Sciences division has been, including the College Division's editorial, design, and marketing departments. My initial contact at Prentice Hall was editor Bud Therien, who provided the constant programmatic and motivational support a project of this scope requires. His office was assisted by areas overseen by Lee Mamunes and Marisol Torres, to name just a few.

The publishers and I also would like

to thank the following reviewers for their valuable advice on this book: Marjorie Elliott Bevlin, Donald Cowan, and Patrick J. Shuck.

This textbook has not existed in offices, alone, however. For many years I have used drafts of it with my design students, soliciting their responses and recommendations. I am grateful for their ideas, sharing, and willingness to be used as "guinea pigs." I believe all of us have benefitted from the process.

Nor has *Elements of Art* existed just in classrooms. It has been the object of much discussion, exasperation, and joy at my home, as well. If it had not been for the regular interest and encouragement of my family to support me in my art and teaching, this book would never have been initiated. My wife, Kathryn, has been unselfishly ready to review any aspect of this project with me. Both of my children, Benjamin and Meredith, have contributed purposely and unwittingly in countless situations. Accordingly, their attention to *Elements of Art* has been both genuine and generous, and I love all of them for it.

Hopeful that no one has been omitted but understanding that someone undoubtedly has, I want everyone who assisted me on this project to know how appreciative I am for their enduring humor and sincerest efforts. It has been a collaborative project, intending to facilitate teaching and learning. I believe we have been successful toward that end.

ONE

The Finest of the Fine Arts

A DEBATE

HISTORICAL BACKGROUND

An age-old debate has been waged over the relative importance of the three different art forms we have noted: the two-dimensional and three-dimensional arts and architecture. This debate included Leonardo da Vinci and Michelangelo, artists who did not limit themselves to one art form or another (Figs. 1–1 and 1–2). Leonardo is noted primarily as a painter, yet his anatomical drawings, scientific investigations, and inventions are indeed noteworthy in the history of art and humankind. Michelangelo was skilled in painting and architecture, but he really preferred sculpture over painting. Yet each of these artists had definite feelings about the merits of the art forms.

For some people even today, the questions may still remain: which art form is the greatest and which artistic process or technique is most meritorious? From the notebooks of Leonardo da Vinci we observe his attitude:

> The one advantage which sculpture has is that of offering greater resistance to time.

In other words, sculpture lasts longer. Leonardo also went on to say . . .

> Sculpture is less intellectual than painting, and lacks many of its natural parts.

Would you dare say, as Leonardo did, that . . .

> Sculptural reveals what is with little effort; painting seems a thing miraculous.

▶ Figure 1-1   Michelangelo, *David*
(Alinari/Art Resource, NY, Accademia/Florence, Florence, Italy)

▶ Figure 1-2   Leonardo da Vinci, *Mona Lisa*
(Musée du Louvre, © Photo R.M.N.)

▶ Figure 1-3   Michelangelo, *Rebellious Slave* (Musée du Louvre © Photo R.M.N.)

Yet, many of Michelangelo's Florentine contemporaries saw his creations as almost godlike, and that Michelangelo, himself, was godlike for having created actual three-dimensional forms, not two-dimensional illusions. Some felt Michelangelo completed his works with a degree of perfection that could be attributed only to a god. As a result, these Florentines referred to Michelangelo as "*Il Divino*," meaning *the divine*.

If we learn that Michelangelo considered sculpture the finest of the fine arts, we also learn that he preferred one kind of sculpture over another. Michelangelo thought that stone carving was the finest form of sculpture, while modeling and bronze casting were secondary practices. Thus, the relative merits of the finest techniques were debated, in addition to discussions of the finest of the fine arts.

IMPLICATIONS

This Renaissance debate is known as the *Paragone*. Its objective was to define the best art form. This can never be resolved, however, because what may be best for one person may not be best for another, and what may be best for one political order, religious group, or country may not be best for others.

> **There is no universal truth about what is the best art form, style, or medium.**

Could we proclaim with equal assurance that no one particular tool or technique is of the most significance, most virtue? Is fine oil painting, for example, no "better" or no "more socially acceptable" than finger painting?

There is no place in today's art studios, galleries, or museums for the debate regarding which art style, technique, or medium is best, for it is generally understood that

> **The appropriate use of a medium depends on the expressive objectives of the artist.**

Working outside of traditional techniques, Helen Frankenthaler likes to spread a thin mix of paint onto a canvas which has been stretched across a floor. Jackson Pollock dripped his pigments from long sticks and tin cans with holes in them onto a similarly prepared canvas. In a continuing effort to explore the relationship between medium and technique, artists have thrown paint into the air behind revved-up jet engines thereby blowing the paint onto large canvases. They have also shot paint out of rifles onto canvas. Are these examples of inappropriate techniques, or are they modifications of "appropriate" ones, such as the airbrush?

Similarly, is a child's crayon an unacceptable medium because it is associated with a child's level of artistic skills? Are computer programs and laser printers unacceptable as tools for children's art because they took an adult's mentality to design the hard- and software? What would you say of the making of mud pies when compared to the techniques involved in ceramic art and clay sculpture? What of Robert Smithson's using unrefined natural materials, compared to a painter's using refined natural pigments, or his using a bulldozer to move earth for his sculptures, *Amarillo Ramp* (Fig. 1–5) and *Spiral Jetty?* Is not the bulldozer just a larger form of an artist's thumb?

Frequently we are inclined to consider an unfamiliar art-producing technique or style to be "inferior" to one we are more comfortable or familiar with. This is precisely when we should realize that we need to take more time—make more of an effort—to understand what the creator of an image is trying to communicate. Images produced by different techniques or unfamiliar cultures and depicting various styles warrant our full attention, as do the ones we have grown up with and become accustomed to. Differing degrees of familiarity with techniques,

▶ Figure 1-4   Donatello, *David*
(Alinari/Art Resource, NY, Bargello/Florence, Florence, Italy)

▶ Figure 1-5   Robert Smithson, *Amarillo Ramp*
(Gianfranco Gorgoni, photographer, John Weber Gallery)

cultures, and styles of art do not directly equate with differing degrees of the quality of art each effects; ease of recognition does not equate with better art.

Be careful not to judge the merits of a work of art on the merits of the medium or the sophistication and social acceptability of the style, tool, or technique alone. What you must be aware of is that the style, along with the tool, technique, and medium must be compatible with the overall expression of the image. All of these variables work together. If there is a change in one variable it affects the others, thus affecting the final visual image and its content.

> Those things which require significant effort to understand—which require more effort than you wanted to give—will often contribute a great deal to your growth as an individual and as an artist.

▶ Illustration 1-1   Student Work, *Computer Image*

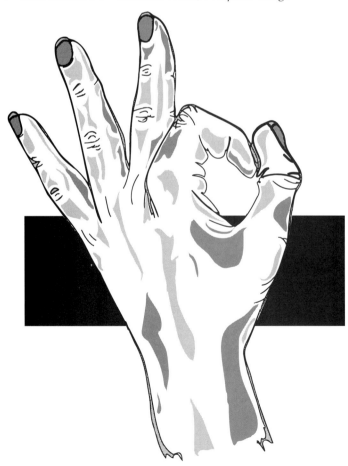

► **UNIT GLOSSARY**

Architecture   The art and science of designing and erecting space defining forms intended for human interaction.

Paragone   A Renaissance debate intended to determine the relative importance of the three different art forms: two-dimensional arts, three-dimensional arts, and architecture.

Style   Identifiable and characteristic trends associated with group movements or individual directions.

TWO

Design Background

THE BIG PICTURE

IN THE BEGINNING THERE WAS DESIGN

▶ PURPOSES OF ART

Art is a visual form of meaningful expression. This may include images that are made to glorify a political leader or a country. This may also include images that are made to emphasize a concept, such as speed or grace (Brancusi, *Mademoiselle Pogany,* Fig. 2–1). Not surprisingly, images and art have also served as expressions of larger, intangible concerns such as fertility and religion (Aztec *Birth Goddess,* Fig. 2–2). Sometimes the art was not made to be hung on a wall or put on a shelf. Originally, art—or more accurately, imagery—was made to play an integral role as part of a ceremony or ritual which complemented hunting, birth, or burial, as in many aboriginal societies.

Aboriginal art refers to the art native to or indigenous of a particular group of people. For us to consider aboriginal or any other culture's visual forms as art, the images produced must be visual forms of meaningful expression: an expression of something personal, private, public, or anything else that can be given visual significance.

In an effort to establish a definition of art that was applicable to all the art produced by humankind, a nineteenth-century attempt from a book entitled *Art and the Artists of All Nations,* reads:

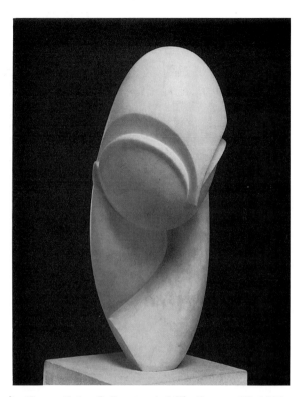

▶ Figure 2-1   C. Brancusi, *Mlle. Pogany III, 1930*
(Constantin Brancusi, Philadelphia Museum of Art: The Louise and Walter Arensberg Collection)

> What is *ART?* Who is an artist? What is it to produce an artistic work? The answers to these questions bring us close to the highest activities of the human mind and to the history of civilization. Savagery has no art,

▶ Figure 2-2   Aztec, *Birth Goddess*
(Tlazolteotl [B-71, Dumbarton Oaks, Trustees for
Harvard University])

The negative connotations and preju-
dices associated with terms such as *primitive* or *savage* art have hindered many
peoples' response to the merits and credibility of nonwestern art forms. *Primitive* or
savage implies technologically and/or culturally deprived societies and people
which lack the potential for aesthetic sensitivity, in addition to being of consider-
able antiquity. Yet the Mayans, for
example, were neither technologically nor
culturally deprived; nor was their culture
so very old, as they were active as recently
as eight hundred years ago. Conversely,
some contemporary cultures utilize Stone
Age technologies, such as the Txuka-
hamei Indians of Brazil or the Asmat of
New Guinea. The terms *primitive* and
savage, therefore, are not sociologically,
anthropologically, or descriptively accurate adjectives when generically applied
to a culture. They are disparaging terms
that should not be used to describe a society or its art.

▶ Figure 2-3   Stonehenge, c., 2000 B.C.
(Charles Gatewood/Art Resource, NY)

▶ VIEWER EXPERIENCE

When we look at *Stonehenge* (Fig. 2–3), believed to have been created around 2000
B.C. as a celestial observatory, most of us
respond to the images of the monolithic
stone slabs with a sense of awe and wonder; we are overwhelmed by the physical
size of the stones and the strict order in
which they were originally arranged. Yet
within this order and the now eroded and
broken fragments, we feel the energy of
the irregular surfaces and the distorted
edges. The resulting boldness of the verti-

cal and horizontal stones effect control and purpose.

It is interesting to compare *Stonehenge*—a work of *late* Neolithic people—to contemporary paintings by Robert Motherwell or Franz Kline [Figs. 2–4 and 2–5). We find in their paintings a similar, purposeful placement of forms; similar irregular contours; and similar strong contrasts between the foreground and background shapes that we saw in the monoliths and trilithons from Stonehenge.

Unfortunately, however, some of the same people who felt the energy of Stonehenge cannot feel the same or similar energy in the Motherwell or Kline paintings. While Stonehenge served a practical purpose which was complemented by a visually rewarding arrangement of forms, the Motherwell and Kline paintings do not provide a similarly satisfying viewer experience for many people. This may be because

1. The paintings appear to have no physical "use." Function and use—practicality—are often cited as factors in determining an object's value and credibility.

2. These paintings are not "of" anything (objective subject matter); perhaps they do not fit a preconceived idea as to what art "should" be (objective subject matter).

3. Stonehenge was a Neolithic shrine. That concept kindles the imagination and may be more satisfying than the stones themselves.

4. The photograph of Stonehenge is a reminder of something that is real, while the painted images do not exist beyond the surface of the canvases.

However, if we recognize that the Motherwell and Kline paintings and Stonehenge have the same basic visual and organization components, and if we acknowledge that Stonehenge appears powerful and meaningful, then are the Kline and Motherwell paintings just as powerful, as artistically valid?

▶ Figure 2-4   Robert Motherwell, *Eligy to the Spanish Republic #34*
(Albright-Knox Art Gallery, Buffalo, New York, Gift of Seymour H. Knox, 1957, © 1994 Estate of Robert Motherwell/VAGA, NY)

▶ Figure 2-5   Franz Kline, *Painting No. 7*
(1952, © The Solomon R. Guggenheim Foundation, New York, © 1994 Estate of Franz Kline/VAGA, NY)

▶ Figure 2-6   Willem de Kooning, *Woman I*
(1950–52, oil on canvas, 6′ 3⅞″ x 58″, The Museum of
Modern Art, New York, Purchase)

Leonardo da Vinci's painting of the *Mona Lisa* (Fig. 1–2) is easy for one to talk about in terms of its being "art" because it was painted by an accepted Renaissance "master" and has been popularly regarded as "art" for many centuries. In other words, the *Mona Lisa* does not serve as a challenge to existing values and perceptions of art. It has artistic credibility and has, as a result, contributed to a common understanding of what art is.

On the other hand, Willem de Kooning's *Woman* (Fig. 2–6) is not as easy for some to talk about. Does it display the characteristics associated with art? Has the artist's name benefited from a comparable test of time, and is that really important? Are you comfortable judging the merits of *Woman* for yourself?

One of the objectives of this text is that as a result of your study and the completion of the projects you will develop artistic and critical capabilities which will assist you in determining both the successful and unsuccessful images you find in galleries and studios.

COMMON DENOMINATORS

▶ VISUAL COMPONENTS

Although unapparent at first glance, the Leonardo and de Kooning paintings have a great deal in common:

1. Both artists have defined the subjects with particular *colors*. Leonardo's colors are mostly representational, that is, closer in harmony with actual appearances, whereas de Kooning's colors are more personalized, more subjective. Accordingly, the *Mona Lisa* is more traditional and, for many viewers, more acceptable than de Kooning's.

2. Each of these images is composed of a variety of *shapes*. Again, some are more representational than others.

3. The shapes in both paintings have edges which we refer to as contours, as *lines*.

4. Some areas of the compositions are lighter than others, and some are darker. And in some areas the colors are lighter or darker than others. This relationship of light to dark is referred to as *value*.

5. The painted surfaces' actual or implied tactile qualities are known as *texture*.

These visual components of art—*line, shape, value, color,* and *texture*—are observed to be components that all art from all time periods have had in common;

> the components of art are observed to be "universal."

Prince Sultan Slaman al-Saud, a Saudi Arabian astronaut aboard the space shuttle *Discovery* in 1985, observed . . .

The first day or so, we all pointed to our countries. The third or fourth day, we were pointing to our continents. By the fifth day, we were aware of only one earth.

The shuttle astronauts initially took comfort in the security of their relative corners of the earth. Then they realized how the individual parts were integral to the larger whole; they were aware of the infinite diversity of their planet and sensitive to how all of the earth's diversity was subordinate to its overall unity.

After you have acquired experience looking at and making art, you will recognize the significant diversity among the arts. However, you will also become profoundly aware of the similarities, the "common denominators," which make up the visual arts.

▶ Figure 2-7   NASA, The Earth

▶ Figure 2-8   Alberto Giacometti, *Diego*
(Tate Gallery, London/Art Resource, NY, 1959)

▶ Figure 2-9   Anonymous, African Mask

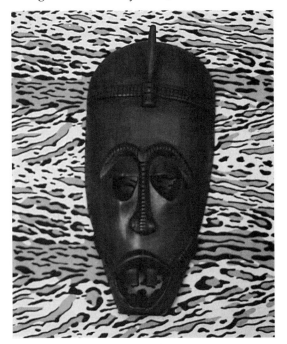

▶ **TECHNIQUE**

The technique employed by an artist should complement the subject and content of a created work. In reference to the manner in which the aforementioned images were painted, we observe that Leonardo da Vinci went to great lengths to have his image look nice and smooth—a fitting complement to the young and proper woman. On the other hand, de Kooning left the surface appearance of his painting looking more rough and ravaged—again, a fitting complement to his broad and brutal handling of the medium and an indication about his feelings toward the *subject matter.*

If we compare a portrait bust of Diego Giacometti (Fig. 2–8) by his brother, Alberto, to an African mask (Fig. 2–9), we observe that the makers of both images, separated by years and continents, have each incorporated the same visual components of art, yet vastly different sculpting techniques. The resulting visual effects are considerably different: The mask evokes a sense of quiet calm and control, while *Diego* evokes nervousness and similar afflictions. The makers of these images were working with their own individual sensitivities to image making, innate sensitivities—perhaps genetically determined—that are common among many individuals.

Why are there differences seen in each of these works if they incorporate the same visual components of art? In general, why do images look different from one another, even if the subject matter may be the same? You have probably already realized that the answer focuses on a variety of factors, but most conspicuously including

1. The nature of the artist: the artist's whole being—personality, emotional stability, hopes, and dreams;

2. The time and place in which the artist lives: environmental and cultural factors contributing to a determination of who and what the artist is; and

3. The artist's particular selection and arrangement of the visual components.

Of these three factors which contribute to determining the final form an image may take, you observe that the visual components (line, shape, value, color, and texture) are the only factors that are not variables; their arrangement or organization is the variable.

The arrangement of the visual components of art is referred to as design, and there are several *organizational components of art* which contribute to the overall design of a work.

In the following chapters we are going to take a closer look at the *visual* and *organizational components of art*, and we will study examples of how they work together to contribute to an artist's effective visual communication.

These *visual* and *organizational components* always work together, never independently, as you will see.

▶ Figure 2-10   Georges Braque, *The Table*
(1928, oil and sand on canvas, 70 ¾″ x 28 ¾″, The Museum of Modern Art, New York)

▶ Figure 2-11   Chardin, *Fruit, Jug, and a Glass*
(Image no. 741, National Gallery of Art, Washington, Chester Dale Collection, 1962)

"ISMS"

▶ Figure 2-12   Pablo Picasso, *Girl Before a Mirror*
(March, 1932, oil on canvas, 64 x 51¼″, The Museum of Modern Art, New York, gift of Mrs. Simon Guggenheim, © Jan. 11, 1994)

▶ Figure 2-13   Christo, *The Running Fence*
(Photographer, Wolfgang Volz, Copyright Christo 1976)

When one looks at a great hallmark of art, such as Michelangelo's *David*, and then compares it to Picasso's *Girl Before a Mirror* (Fig. 2–12), the question which is so often asked is "How can this type of art—this 'modern art'—be justified?" How can it be justified when one considers the rich tradition of art? Do images such as *The Running Fence* (Fig. 2–13) represent the work of incompetent lunatics who have lost their historical perspective? Do individuals who like and display works of this type have no discretion, no taste? Does the artists' individuality threaten accepted conventions about what art should be and has been?

▶ ART AS REACTION

Even the most casual glance at an art book will demonstrate that ideas about art seem to change a lot. However, as you look at the history of people from an anthropological, cultural, technological, or any other point of view, you observe that everything associated with humankind is in a state of change—nothing about our species or our world is constant or fixed. Accordingly, as we change, so too will our art. We react to everything that makes up the world in which we live.

To Life Forces

In order to understand the evolution of styles of art, of "isms," whether it be from Neoclassicism to Romanticism in painting or Modernism to Post-Modernism in architecture, one must realize that

1. All visual art is created as a reaction to something, and
2. Visual art is a meaningful expression of that reaction.

The Paleolithic (Old Stone Age) *Willendorf Venus* (Fig. 2–14), carved over 30,000 years ago, was created as a symbol of Paleolithic peoples' need to ensure fertility and the perpetuation of their species. The *Clay Bison* (Fig. 2–15) was inspired by similar concerns—a need to give a tangible symbol to a preoccupation with life forces.

To Society

Styles of art can evolve not only from society to society but within a society itself. For example, a cycle of changes in Greek cultural attitudes can be observed in Greek art, progressing from passive, formal symmetry to swelling, turbulent contours, evoking great *pathos* rather than *ethos*. Examples of the Greeks' changing attitudes can be seen in the *Thebes Apollo* (Fig. 2–16), *Tenea Apollo* (Fig. 2–17), and *Laokoon and His Sons* (Fig. 2–18). Over many years, the forms become more representational than idealized.

To Art

The dissonance of the Italian Mannerist style was a reaction against the perfection and order of the High Renaissance. Realism was partially a response to the alleged superficialities of Impressionism, and Op Art was a response to Pop Art. You see, art is not only a reaction to life and religion. Art is frequently a reaction to art, artists, and collectors of art, as depicted in Peter Breugel's *Artist and the Connoisseur* (Fig. 2–19).

Artists may also respond or react to more formal principles associated with art, such as the visual tension created between two shapes or the relationship between two colors. Any visual stimuli can elicit a response from an artist, including the visual and organizational components of art, themselves. For example, the subject matter of Josef Albers's *Homage to the*

▶ Figure 2-14 *Willendorf Venus*
(© by Prehistorische Abteilung Naturhistorisches Museum, Wien)

▶ Figure 2-15 *Clay Bison, Prehistoric Sculpture*
(Giraudon/Art Resource, NY)

▶ Figure 2-16

▶ Figure 2-18

▶ Figure 2-17

▶ Figure 2-16   Thebes, *Mantiklos Apollo*
GREEK, ABOUT 700 B.C., BRONZE
(Frances Barlett Collection, Courtesy Museum of Fine
Arts, Boston)

▶ Figure 2-17   *Tenea Apollo*
(Foto Marburg/ Art Resource, NY)

▶ Figure 2-18   *Laokoon and His Sons*
(Vatican Museums, Alinari/Art Resource, NY)

Square: Portal A (Fig. 2–20), is the nonfunctional, nondescriptive square—a specific shape, a visual component.

To Technology

As images and creative needs change, so do artistic techniques. These are complemented by ever-increasing advances in technology. No longer is the artist obliged to use traditionally acceptable techniques of making sculpture, such as casting images in bronze or carving forms from marble. There should be no societal repression of an individual artist or art object for the incorporation of a traditional or nontraditional medium or technique. With the advent of welding, for example, artists such as David Smith (Fig. 2–21) broadened the range of possible images and expression well beyond the traditional, "the safe," incorporating a new constructivist technique. Light—a nontangible vehicle to carry color—has been explored by technologies from neon to lasers and exploited by visual artists beyond functional applications. Many processes of technology which originally served industrial and utilitarian ends have become standard techniques of painters and sculptors.

▶ STYLE

Understanding that as people change, so, too, will their art, it is important to look at a few concepts which are applicable to variations found in artistic styles.

First of all, there may be (1) a dominant cultural or group style, such as Cubism; and (2) there may be a variety of artists working in a stylistic mode—such as Cubism—in their own personal manner of expression, or style. Braque and Léger (Fig. 2–22) may both be considered Cubists, for example, since they shared a

▶ Figure 2-19   Peter Breugel, *Artist and the Connoisseur* (Graphische Sammlung Albertina, Vienna)

▶ Figure 2-20   Josef Albers, *Homage to the Square: Portal A* (Yale University Art Gallery, Gift of the Artist to the University Press)

▶ Figure 2-21   David Smith, *Cubi XII*
(Hirshhorn Museum and Sculpture Garden, Smithsonian Institution, Gift of the Joseph H. Hirshhorn Foundation, 1972,
© 1994 Estate of David Smith/VAGA,New York)

common vision of the geometric ordering of forms, a synthesizing of several views of a form into one, flattening of spatial orientations, and the like. But most importantly, each had his individual approach to Cubism—his own *style*.

> Thus we observe style to be a two-part definition concerned with group and individual identifiable characteristics and trends.

▶ RESPONSES TO THE VISUAL WORLD

While we acknowledge that artists produce a fascinating breadth of imagery, it is perplexing to observe the narrowness of tolerance which many people have for images which are not strictly representational. A lot of people don't like Cubism, for example, because they don't easily recognize the geometricized and rearranged subjects they are looking at in many Cubist paintings and sculptures. In response to Cubism, one may hear someone say, *"I really prefer Realism—I like things that look realistic."*

This may mean two different things. It may mean that the person likes images that appear to be representational, that is, images having a visual resemblance to tangible subject matter, and that is all. Or it may mean that the person likes images which have a natural appearance *and* an underlying meaning—the definition of Realism.

If one takes delight in the simple recognition of actual subject matter, in being able to identify all of the natural forms in the image without a concern for anything other than surface appearances and subject matter recognition, what this person likes is Naturalism. But how does this differ from Realism? Realism incorporates Naturalism—it is dependent upon representational forms. Additionally, however, Realism has significance. In other words, there is a point to it all other than just the mimicking of nature.

▶ FOOLING THE EYE

Some artists copy subject matter with such exactitude that they fool the viewer into believing that what one is looking at is real as opposed to being an image, as did Raphaelle Peale in his painting *Still Life with Lemons* (Fig. 2–23, p. 22). In order to fool someone so convincingly, it would be necessary for the artist to accomplish several things. First, the artist would have to paint the forms on a scale that is the same as the subject matter. Secondly, all of the shapes and their contours would have to be in strict harmony with the subject. There would have to be absolute fidelity to all subtleties and nuances of shape. Also, the colors of the subject matter would have to be depicted as they appear to the human eye, and texture would have to be simulated as accurately as possible. For example, people would have to feel that they could get a splinter from a rough wooden object or taste the juice from a cut piece of fruit if those subjects were painted. To complement all of this, the indication of a light source would have to be convincing, causing shadows to fall in a plausible manner with forms shaded on their appropriate sides. Thus, the value relationships would have to be in harmony with the direction and intensity of a light source. In order to be successful in *Trompe l'oeil Art,* a style of art that has as its intent to "fool the eye," one needs to masterfully handle tools, technique, medium, and ground to depict a convincing

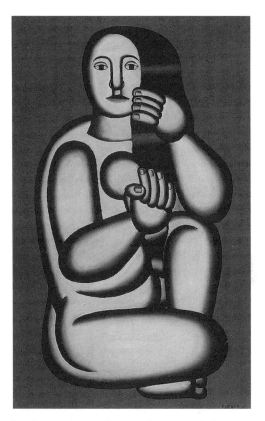

▶ Figure 2-22   Fernand Leger, *Nude on a Red Background*

(Hirshhorn Museum and Sculpture Garden, Smithsonian Institution, Gift of the Joseph H. Hirshhorn Foundation, 1972)

▶ Figure 2-23   Raphael Peale, *Still Life With Lemons* (Reading Public Museum)

▶ Figure 2-24   Harnett, *After the Hunt* (The Fine Arts Museum of San Francisco, Mildred Anna Williams Collection, 1940.93)

image. In other words, all of the visual components in the subject matter need to be simulated as closely as possible in the created image.

It is important to remember that a "convincing" reproduction of a subject, alone, is not enough for an image to be considered "art." A significant presentation based on a unique organization of the visual components is required—good design is a prerequisite. Many feel that displays of intricate detail determine what is or is not art, but that criterion, while an element of Trompe l'oeil Art, falls woefully short of defining art because it negates the aesthetic and the meaningful.

William Harnett is proclaimed to be the "master" of the Trompe l'oeil style, and his painting, *After the Hunt* (Fig. 2–24), of 1885, is a standard-bearer of that style. His accurate simulation of the subject matter is indisputable. In addition to Harnett's good technique, however, we observe that the organization of the visual components is compelling. We note the conspicuous emphasis on circular shapes contrasted against straight lines (variety and harmony, repetition and movement), in addition to other organizational delights, thus unifying and adding interest to the seemingly divergent subjects which make up the hunt.

The Staircase Group, by Charles Willson Peale (Fig. 2–25), is reported to have fooled George Washington enough to cause him to tip his hat in the presence of these painted figures as they appear to momentarily halt on the steps and acknowledge a passerby. Peale went so far to "fool the eye" as to include the actual wooden panels of the bottom step in the painting to facilitate the transition from the real world outside the painting to the unreal world inside. Harnett and others would also put real hinges on images of painted doors or attach actual window frames around paintings to facilitate their

▶ Figure 2-25   Charles Willson Peale, *Staircase Group*
(Philadelphia Museum of Art, The George W. Elkins Collection)

▶ Figure 2-26   Fontainebleau Hotel, Florida, Miami Beach, Florida
(Mural by Richard Haas)

▶ Figure 2-27   Duane Hanson, *Self With Model*
(Murray Spitzer, Photographer)

grand illusions. These represent early forms of *collage* art. It is nice to see that there is plenty of room for whimsy in art!

Trompe l'oeil Art is not a style relegated to the past. On an exterior wall of the Miami Beach Fontainebleau Hotel is painted a scene that causes pedestrians and vehicle operators to look twice (Fig. 2–26). This monumental mural simulates the appearance of water, sky, clouds, and architectural and sculptural forms so convincingly that it is difficult to tell where the actual building stops and the mural begins. Would it be as successful on a cloudy day?

The concepts and applications of Trompe l'oeil Art are applicable to painting and sculpture alike. Duane Hanson is noted for his fiberglass figures that appear so lifelike they look ready to walk and talk, and frequently people wait for them to do so [Fig. 2–27]! But as you respond to this and all art styles—all "isms," not just Trompe l'oeil—you have to ask yourself questions about their ultimate significance. When looking at some of the examples we have discussed, are you able to determine the art's "meaning": political, social, personal, or other? Trompe l'oeil Art is a style that depends upon representational simulation of natural forms, but it goes beyond that. Its function may be to fool the eye and challenge ideas about things we often take for granted. Duane Hanson said of his sculptures:

> I'm not duplicating life. I'm making a statement about human values. My work deals with people who lead lives of quiet desperation. I show the emptyheadedness, the fatigue, the aging, the frustration. These people can't keep up with the competition. They're left out, psychologically handicapped. . . . But there's a sad truth to them. Sad music, sad novels . . . the greatest art has been filled with melancholy.

► ABSTRACT ART

Understanding the differences among Naturalism, Realism, and Trompe l'oeil Art is a prerequisite to your understanding of the difference between art and the mechanical, noninterpretive copying of something. But now that you have a good understanding of the differences, you need to tackle the next biggest stumbling block in a discussion of art and "isms": "What is abstract art?" The same person who said, "I only like Realism" (and did not know what it meant) might also say, "I do not like abstract art," and not know what abstract means.

Consider, again, Leonardo's *Mona Lisa* (see Fig. 1–2), for example. It may be exemplary of great art, especially for a person who does not like abstract art. After all, Lisa looks like a nice lady and the setting she is seated in appears pleasing. Everything looks like it could be real. Now, stop right there—"looks like it could be real" does not mean that it is a naturalistic copy of the "real" environment. Although the work appears fairly representational, when you look closely at the background you observe that the right side does not really correlate with the left side. Leonardo has taken some liberties with the selection and proportional arrangement of the two landscapes.

If you look at Edward Hopper's *Early Sunday Morning* (Fig. 2–28), you observe that while the image looks about right, there is an oversimplification of the brick facade—of the brick color and individual character of the bricks. You might wonder what that thing is in the upper-right corner? What is casting that shadow on the wall by the top two windows on the left? Edward Hopper has structured his forms to arrive at a simplified representation of the overall setting that has a

► Figure 2-28   Edward Hopper, *Early Sunday Morning* (Purchase, with funds from Gertrude Vanderbilt Whitney, Collection of the Whitney Museum of American Art, New York)

▶ Figure 2-29   Theo van Doesburg, *Composition (The Cow)*

(Eight panel drawings, numbers 1, 2, 4, 5, 6, & 7: 4 ⅝″ x 6 ¼″, numbers 8 & 9: 6 ¼″ x 4 ⅝″. The Museum of Modern Art, New York, Purchase)

good design without an overt concern for details.

Having observed variations of naturalistic shapes, colors, textures, and values in these two paintings, you know that you cannot be talking strictly about naturalism. If an image is altered in any way *for the sake of artistic expression*, if there is any *personalization, stylization, rearrangement, or simplification of the form*—if the artist left out a couple of street lights or rearranged them so that they would look better—then the artist has abstracted his image (which was based on actual forms).

Of course, there is a great range of abstraction, from the basic simplification of subject matter—while maintaining a representational form—to the rendering of almost unidentifiable subject matter.

Both the Leonardo and Hopper images have elements of abstraction. In fact, you would be quite accurate in concluding that just about all art has some degree of abstraction.

Take another look at the *Willendorf Venus* (see Fig. 2–14). The maker of this image purposely emphasized some features while deemphasizing others. It has unusually large elements of the anatomy which are oriented toward reproduction and nursing, while the physical elements of the body unrelated to these functions are minimized.

> **You can see quite clearly that the origins of abstraction are in the origins of art itself.**

Makers of images have almost always sought to "streamline"—to abstract—their forms to allow them to communicate more effectively. The primary function of art is expression, and through abstraction one communicates more effectively. For example, if one chooses to shout instead of speak normally, this abstraction of speech allows the speaker to communicate more emphatically.

It is the artist's objective to respond to the world, not necessarily to copy it as it exists. People are more than recorders of things as they are; they imagine things as they could be or they interpret things as they seem to be. Artists, therefore, have their own, unique vision and are not limited by societal standards to a life of mindless copying. Abstraction is more the rule than the exception. Interestingly, some art historians have speculated that societies resort to *naturalism* in times of cultural sterility.

▶ OBJECTIVE AND SUBJECTIVE IMAGERY

Some of the difficulty in understanding the difference between art which is abstract and that which is not has something in common with the difference between the terms *objective* and *subjective*

- Subjective implies qualitative, personalized, and nonconformist concepts, whereas
- Objective implies standardization and adherence to observable, identifiable, quantifiable characteristics.

Abstract art is highly subjective, therefore, whereas naturalistic art involves an objective duplication of visual forms. Educator Ray Haas said:

> The qualitative aspects of life are more meaningful than the quantitative aspects.

Mr. Haas is emphasizing the personal and sensory aspects of life in general. Creating images based on our personal responses may be more significant and rewarding than the rote reproduction and recording of what is already around us.

While abstraction does have as its subject matter something actually observed or experienced, the imagery found in nonobjective art has no purposeful allegiance to anything actual or real in terms of subject matter, such as seen in Adolph Gottlieb's *Orb* (Fig. 2–30). Identifying the nonobjective artist's point of departure is difficult at best. Sometimes the image we see in a nonobjective work may actually remind us of something, but that may be coincidental and determined by the range of our own experiences, not necessarily the intention of the artist.

▶ Figure 2-30   Aldolph Gottlieb, *Orb*
(Dallas Museum of Art, Dallas Art Association Purchase)

Nonobjective art does not satisfy the object-oriented person since such an individual is conditioned to responding to representational forms. If representational forms are not given by the artist, the object-oriented viewer is frequently left feeling uncomfortable. The alert artist may choose to exploit that uncomfortable viewer sensation to make the message even stronger.

The intention of an artist is sometimes missed by a viewer because of differences in their experiences, sensitivities, knowledge, and so forth. It is not always necessary that the viewer perceive the exact intent of a work of art; rather, it is important that the work speaks to the viewer in a unique and meaningful way. Often the viewer sees things in a work that the artists did not intend, but that does not mean the viewer is wrong. Instead, it means that the work is capable of communicating on a variety of different levels, and that is very good.

▶ CONCLUSION

You may find that, in addition to relating to styles of art, some "isms" relate to a particular technique in the making of art images, such as pointillism: the application of paint in small dabs or dots of color, as seen in Seurat's painting, *Sunday Afternoon on the Grande Jatte* (see "Line and Dot," Fig. 6–20). In the end, you need to be sensitive to the fact that there are potentially as many "isms" (Neoclassicism, Romanticism, Formalism, and others) as there are possible directions art and individual artists can take, and to which identifiable characteristics can be observed and attributed. The twentieth-century French novelist and critic, Marcel Proust, wrote:

> Thanks to art, instead of seeing a single world—our own—we see it multiply until we have before us as many worlds as there are original artists.

▶ Figure 2-31   Brushes and Other Art Tools

▶ UNIT GLOSSARY

Aboriginal art   The art native to or indigenous of a particular group of people.

Abstract/Abstraction   A stylization, rearrangement, or simplification of form for the purpose of artistic expression. Abstract images are most often derivative of forms actually seen or experienced.

Design   The arrangement of the visual components of art.

Ethos   Dispassionate and objective response to circumstances.

Ism   Euphemism for a style of art; derivative from art movements such as Romantic*ism*, Impression*ism*, and Real*ism*.

Monolith   A large, single piece of stone.

Monolithic   A quality of massiveness and monumentality, either actual or implied, usually associated with a single stone used in sculpture or architecture.

Monumental   Having the (1) visual impression or (2) attribute of great size.

Naturalism   Objective recording of observed subject matter. (Note: Naturalism is not a true "ism"; rather, it is an artistic device.)

Neolithic   The "New Stone Age"; dates of practical usage vary somewhat, but usually begin around 8000 B.C., continuing to about 3000 B.C.

Nonobjective art   Nonrepresentational art; imagery is not based on anything observed or experienced.

Objective   Standardization and adherence to observable, identifiable, quantifiable characteristics.

Organizational Components of Art   Principles which govern the arrangement of the visual components of art, including dominance, proportion, balance, variety and harmony, repetition and movement, and economy. Syn.: DESIGN PRINCIPLES.

Paleolithic   The "Old Stone Age"; dates of practical usage vary somewhat, but usually begin around 30,000 B.C.., continuing to about 8000 B.C.

Pathos   Personalized and sympathetic response to circumstances.

Primitive   A disparaging term, implying technological or cultural deprivation, that should not be used to describe a society or its art. (Not to be confused with ABORIGINAL ART).

Realism   A style of art that depends on a high degree of representational imagery that yields an ultimate significance. This emphasis on ultimate significance, or "content," is what separates it most from "naturalism."

Representational   Images having a visual resemblance to tangible subject matter; ranges from objective to abstract imagery. (Not an ISM.)

Subjective   Qualitative, personalized, and nonconformist concepts.

Trompe l'oeil Art   Literally, "to fool the eye." A form of art that has as its object fooling the viewer into believing that what is painted is real.

Viewer Experience   The entire response of an individual to the circumstances involved in viewing a work of art: intellectual, emotional, physical, and so on.

Visual Components of art   Observable elements of an art form, including dot, line, shape, value, color and texture. Syn.: ART ELEMENTS.

THREE

Getting Started

MAKING CHOICES

Let's review one of the primary ideas presented in the previous chapters: The visual components—line, shape, value, color, and texture—can be arranged in different ways to communicate different things. When beginning to create an artistic image, we have to ask ourselves, *"What are we trying to say?"* and *"How are we going to say it?"*

Resolving these questions involves making choices about the selection and application of the visual components of art. We need to make decisions intended to enhance meaningful expression.

SUBJECT MATTER AND CONTENT

As we start to create an image, we work with subject matter as the seed of our expression. The subject matter gets our thought processes started and our creativity stimulated. Content is determined by the way the subject matter has been presented and by the sensitivity of the observer to perceive the merits of that presentation.

Consider Houdon's portrait of *George Washington*—objective subject matter (Fig. 3-2). The subject matter has the basic features and proportions associated with George Washington, but because of the erect body, tense brow and forehead, tight lips, and strong cheekbones, we see the sculptor was saying this image is "about" strength of character, mind, and body— that is its content.

Consider Jackson Pollock's *Autumn Rhythm* (Fig. 3-3). For Pollock, like Houdon, the subject matter is a starting point. Pollock's subject matter may be less tangible;

▶ Figure 3-1   Honore Daumier, *Two Sculptors*
(The Phillips Collection, Washington, D.C.)

▶ Figure 3-2 Houdon, *George Washington*
(Virginia State Library & Archives)

▶ Figure 3-3 Jackson Pollack, *Autumn Rhythm*
(Metropolitan Museum of Art, George A. Hearn Fund, 1957, 57.92)

it may be line and color, or it may be an idea such as the rhythm or path of falling autumn leaves. The subject matter may be the cyclic turning/returning/passing of the seasons. Quite possibly, the subject matter of *Autumn Rhythm* may be the subdued tones of the leaves of autumn or the delightful act of applying the paint in a physical rhythm with paint dripping from cans and sticks. Frequently, subject matter may not be identifiable; it may not make a reference to anything visually perceived in our world. Thus, the subject matter may be nonobjective. Even though you may not be able to identify or label what it is you are looking at, you should find "the viewing experience" to be unique and stimulating.

Content need not be resolved at the beginning of the creative process, but must be the result if the image represents "meaningful expression."

> Subject matter starts one thinking about something, and that "something" is the content of the work. Subject matter is the starting point; it is never the end.

MEDIUM

After one has been motivated by the subject (tangible or nontangible) to create an image, the question of what material to make the image out of—whether it be painted or sculpted—is a primary concern. A portrait painted in oil will be significantly different from one done in watercolor paints, or more profoundly different from one sculpted in clay or stone.

Therefore, the medium—the material of which the image is made—cannot be taken for granted. The artist usually makes a choice—consciously or subconsciously—when a medium is selected; a selection which the artist believes will most significantly complement the expressive objectives intended for the work. (See Fig. 3–4, Jose de Rivera's *Construction #107*).

The materials used for making two-dimensional and three-dimensional images may be natural or artificial (manufactured). Paints, for example, may have organic pigments suspended in water, or plastic compounds may be suspended in resins. Sculptors may carve stone or cast fiberglass. The natural or synthetic nature of a medium is not an issue, but its appropriateness to an image is. If the artist makes a poor selection regarding medium, it may visually weaken an image. Or, if an artist uses a medium in a way that is not in harmony with the physical properties of the medium, the integrity of the medium may be violated.

Maintaining the integrity of a medium is an objective of every student and professional artist. This is not to say that a medium has a clearly definable and predetermined range—quite the contrary is true. A medium's expressive scope is almost limitless. The last half of the twentieth century has seen dramatic and often

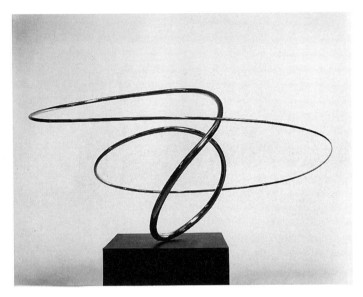

▶ Figure 3-4 Jose deRivera *Construction #107*
(Hirshhorn Museum and Sculpture Garden, Smithsonian Institute)

Many repair seams from numerous restoration efforts are evident. Questions which need to be asked about this sculpture are

1. Would the image of the *Laokoon* group have been compromised if it had been done in another medium, such as bronze?
2. Would there be any aesthetic or physical advantages if the *Laokoon* were done out of another medium?

Questions concerning the integrity of a medium are applicable to works done in oil, watercolor, terra cotta, or any other medium, and should be raised only in reference to a particular work. Theoretical cases seem difficult to resolve because one cannot project all of the different applications of a medium by different artists in all circumstances.

Regarding paintings by Rembrandt, Van Gogh, or Cezanne, you can imagine asking yourself whether or not the paint should be built up to such a degree that the surface of the canvas begins to take on the form of a relief sculpture. A hypothetical image might cause you to question the suitability of "painting" with clay on canvas.

> The aesthetic, expressive, and functional appropriateness of a medium are the final determiners regarding the integrity of a medium.

"Rules" associated with the appropriate use of media are written and rewritten every day, thus there are really no rules. Technologies and expressive needs change all of the time—change is the norm. You will not find a section on "The Rules of Art" in the back of this book. Do you think you should?

traumatic changes in art styles and techniques exploiting the full range of existing and newly discovered media. However, a single error in judgment regarding the (1) expressive or (2) physical use of a medium may cause the integrity of the artwork to be significantly weakened.

The carver of *Laokoon and His Sons* (see Fig. 2–18) may have been better advised to have used bronze instead of marble since the resulting atectonic form has been particularly vulnerable to shocks and forces during the passage of time.

TOOL AND TECHNIQUE

I f you go a step further with the concept of subject matter and medium having to be coordinated to produce a desired effect, you will realize that the tool the artist chooses with which to work a medium is also an important consideration in determining the visual effects of an image.

Fingers in oil paint have an effect different from a brush or palette knife. Welded and hammered steel, likewise, have different appearances. So, once a choice of subject matter has been made and you have determined what medium you want to work in, next you must decide in what manner you will work—technique—and what tools you will use. The use of one technique or another in a work of art does affect the viewing experience, thus contributing to the overall content of the work.

In the portrait entitled *Fanny/Fingerpainting* (Fig. 3–6), the entire image was created by Chuck Close actually stamping his inked fingerprints on the canvas to produce the lights and darks of the image. This places a human "touch" on the painting. The artist has removed the impersonal tool from his hand, thus closely coordinating his technique with the image's content. Are there any other reasons why Close may have used the "fingerpainting" technique?

There are many traditional and nontraditional techniques associated with the two- and three-dimensional arts. Any technique is affected by an artist's individual use of tools and the nature of a medium. The nature of a medium and the nature of an artist yield an identifiable

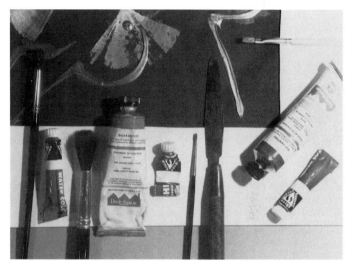

▶ Figure 3-5   Paint Media and Tools

▶ Figure 3-6   Chuck Close, *Fanny/Fingerpainting*
(National Gallery of Art, Washington, D.C., Gift of Lila Acheson Wallace)

▶ Figure 3 7   Helen Frankenthaler, *Mother Goose Melody*
(Virginia Museum of Fine Arts, Richmond, Gift of Sydney and Frances
Lewis)

▶ Figure 3-8   Pierre Daura, *Houses at St. Cirq-la-Popie*
(Daura Gallery Collection, Lynchburg College)

technique. This contributes to the artistic *style* that we discussed before.

Following are a few examples that demonstrate the range of techniques which some art forms employ.

▶ PAINTING

All paint is composed of three basic parts: pigment, vehicle, and medium.

Pigment is that part of paint which supplies the color. In its raw state, it may be a form of earth, a metal ore, an organic material, or a synthetic compound formulated by a chemist. Its raw form is that of a dry colored powder. It requires a binder to hold its particles in suspension so that it can be spread on in a film which will eventually harden to keep them permanently bound together and adhered to a surface. This binder is the *vehicle*. This vehicle, in turn, often requires something which permits it to vary in viscosity which thins it out. This substance is the *medium*. (In the case of a variety of graphic media such as some pastels, pencils, and charcoal sticks, however, there is usually no binder; the pigments are bonded together by pressure, unless a bit of oil or other binder is included for this purpose.)

The combinations of vehicles and media are numerous, but they are usually grouped in two families: aqueous and nonaqueous (those thinned with water and those requiring other thinners).

Recent years have seen the introduction of a number of plastic or synthetic paints. Educator Paul Lorenzi notes they are popular because they offer colors of extreme brilliance and they dry quickly and work easily. Among the most popular of the new paints are the polymer temperas having acrylic resins as medium and water as a vehicle.

Painting techniques, like other techniques, are most often dependent upon the particular painting medium and its characteristics. However, sometimes they are not. Oil paints, for example, as well as acrylics, can be applied thickly, creating a surface texture that is conspicuously built up. This technique is known as impasto. On the other hand, media such as oil paint, acrylics, and watercolor—to name just a few—may be applied thinly, in a diluted manner, creating a transparent film of a color or neutral, known as a wash. You will become familiar with other techniques such as glazing and scumbling in your painting classes.

▶ **DRAWING**

You will work with some introductory drawing techniques such as stippling and hatching (parallel line shading) later in this text, especially in the sections on line and value (in "The Visual Components of Art"). You may also find yourself using relatively unsophisticated techniques such as smearing and smudging soft graphic media, as with pencil or charcoal, using your fingers to get a subtle range of lights and darks. The proper technique when working with any medium is the technique that accomplishes your expressive objectives.

▶ **SCULPTURE**

There are a variety of techniques and processes employed by sculptors. The traditional sculptural processes are additive, subtractive, and substitutive. The additive process involves the building up, modeling, or assembly of a medium. In contrast, the subtractive technique involves traditional carving applications in stone, wood, or any other inspiring medium. The substitutive process involves changing the medium of a form from one material to another by way of molds and casting.

As with painting techniques, not all sculptural processes and media are limited to singular applications. We speak of clay as being a *plastic* medium, oriented to the additive process. And clay can also be cast. Plaster can be mixed and added to an armature and then carved into a particular shape. Working with plaster, therefore, embraces two techniques. Accordingly, we understand that

---

A single medium may have applications in a variety of processes.

The Production of Art

The additive process raises an important question about a process known as *fabrication*—the process of producing the final image, usually from sketches or maquettes, by welding, building, sewing, or other such assembly techniques.

In fabricated works, artists will most frequently work in collaboration with a subcontracting fabricator, such as a steel yard or plastics firm. The fabricator, however, may work independent of the artist. This could occur if the artist were now deceased or if another—such as a museum or private collector—owned the rights to a design or work of art.

Conspicuous questions arise when a work is fabricated, reproduced, or enlarged independent of an artist. Can artists claim something as their work if they

1. Do not actually make the final visual form, or
2. Do not contribute to all aesthetic decisions regarding the visual factors related to the final fabricated form?

Before you answer this, consider a symphony by Beethoven: If the symphony is performed by a particular symphony orchestra and directed by a conductor—in fact, brought to you by the orchestra—is the work any less a "genuine Beethoven"? Is a house, designed by an architect, any less that architect's work if a construction company builds it? A fabricator, workshop, or commercial printing company is obliged to produce a form in harmony with the aesthetic intent of the artist, as is the orchestra and building contractor. Otherwise, the integrity and authenticity of the produced art form may be challenged.

The question concerning the production of nonoriginal "originals," limited editions, and the like is not only associated with contemporary art. Ancient Egyptian, Greek, and Roman artists collaborated on great artistic accomplishments. The Romans are particularly noted for their masterful copies of Greek originals. In fact, if it were not for Roman reproductions, many images of Greek masterpieces would have been lost, such as the *Spearbearer* (Fig. 3–9), originally from fifth century Greece and copied by Romans centuries later.

Additionally, Peter Paul Rubens employed numerous artists to produce his designs and, in the end, Rubens would put the finishing touches on them. Gianlorenzo Bernini also employed many sculptors to help him realize the fabulous "Bernini Arcade" at St. Peter's in the Vatican. Phidias, the master sculptor of the Parthenon's sculptural program, directed and oversaw countless artists and artisans in order to complete the carvings which adorned that building on the Acropolis in Athens. Today we think of the works of Auguste Rodin, Andy Warhol, and Henry Moore when editions of works come to mind.

In conclusion, we see that technique involves two concepts. One is the generic process by which a form is created. The second element of technique involves the skill and technical virtuosity, or craftsmanship, with which an individual artist handles media.

▶ Figure 3-10   Andy Warhol, *Campbell's Soup Can*
(Alberto Ulrich, Milan, Collection/Photographer, Rudolph Burckhardt)

▶ Figure 3-9   *Spearbearer* (Doriphorus, after Policlete)
(Museo Nazionale/Naples, Alinari/Art Resource)

GROUND

▶ Figure 3-11   Miscellaneous Paper Grounds

▶ Figure 3-12   Georges-Pierre Seurat, *Seated Woman*
(Abby Aldrich Rockefeller Fund/The Museum of Modern Art, New York)

O n what surface are you going to work? Will it be paper, canvas, burlap, or something else? If you reply "paper," then what kind—drafting, charcoal, computer, watercolor? The term for any physical material on which a two-dimensional image is created is *ground*.

Grounds have varying surface textures. This quality of surface is often referred to as *tooth*. A single generic type of paper, for example, such as charcoal paper, may have varying tooth, ranging from smooth to coarse.

The selection of the type of material on which you are going to work is as important as the selection of the medium in which you are going to work, for the medium will work one way on one surface but quite a different way on another. Charcoal on smooth paper will produce an even, clean line, but on coarser paper the line will be irregular and vary in value. You note that Seurat (Fig. 3–12), for example, allows the ground to show through, becoming part of the resulting image. This occurs in paintings as well as other two-dimensional works.

The consideration of a ground is not usually a three-dimensional concern since sculptural forms are created *out of* a medium, not *onto* a ground.

▶ FIGURE-GROUND RELATIONSHIPS

Ground can be used two ways: It can be the *surface* on which an image is applied and it can be the relationship of a shape against the background (see the section on shape in "The Visual Components of Art"). Figure-ground relationships involve the way silhouetted shapes ("figures") appear when placed against a background (Illus. 3–1). For example, an image of a house placed against a background has a rather conspicuous and easily visualized figure-ground relationship (Illus. 3–2).

Sometimes a figure-ground relationship may not be clear-cut. For example, if a sphere is silhouetted against a ground, the sphere in silhouette may appear to be a filled-in circle or a hole (Illus. 3–3). Instead of looking like it is on the surface of the ground, the silhouetted circle may appear to be advancing or receding from the surface of the picture plane. The scale of a silhouetted circle also helps to establish its spatial location; if it is small it may appear farther away, but if it is large it may appear to be coming toward you (Illus. 3–4).

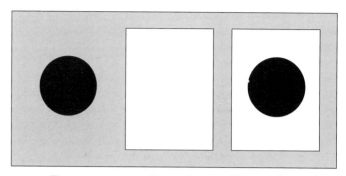

Figure   +   Ground   = Figure-Ground

▶ Illustration 3-1   Figure & Ground

▶ Illustration 3-2   Figure/Ground Relationship

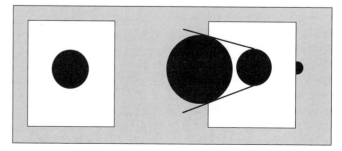

▶ Illustration 3-3   Sphere/Ground: Advancing and Receding Circle

In these illustrations there have been optical reversals of forms. The circle appears to have gone from a positive shape to a negative shape. This optical illusion is known as a *figure-ground reversal*. Military camouflage, for example, is a deliberate presentation of a figure-ground reversal intended to confuse optical appearances (Fig. 3–13). The classic example of this reversal is the faces/vase illustration (Illus. 3–5). Which do you see, the vase or the faces? Don't worry, the one you see first doesn't tell us anything important about your psychological makeup!

Referring again to the circle-and-square illustration (see Illus. 3–1), the area around the sphere, the empty shape, is also known as negative space, therefore, the space which is occupied is known as positive space. In this context, "space" and "shape" can be used as synonyms. Rogier van der Weyden's *Portrait of a Lady* (Fig. 3–14) has a dynamic positive-negative shape-space relationship. The change in direction of the head linen's

▶ Illustration 3-4   Size and Space

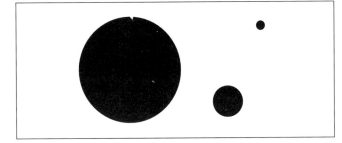

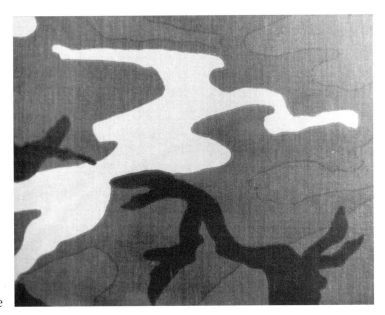

▶ Figure 3-13   Military Camouflage

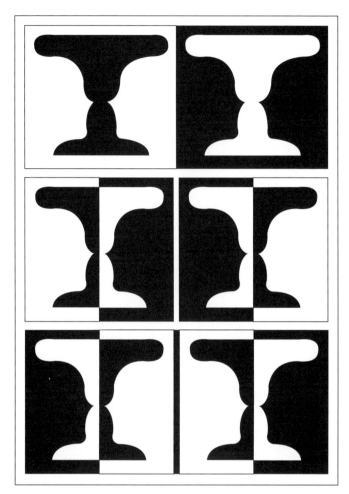

▶ Illustration 3-5   Ruben Vase

▶ Figure 3-14   Rogier Van der Weyden,
Portrait of a Lady
(National Gallery of Art, Washington, D.C./Andrew W.
Mellon Collection)

▶ Figure 3-15   Henry Moore, *King and Queen*
(The Henry Moore Foundation/Foto Marburg, Art Resource, NY)

edge at the top-center establishes a variety in line and energy to what would have been a very static silhouette. Van der Weyden intentionally introduced this line to keep the image "alive." He knew that dynamic negative shapes were as important to the composition as were dynamic positive ones.

The artist is responsible for designing both positive and negative spaces within the picture frame: the figure-ground relationships. There is no "leftover" space in a composition—everything is purposely designed.

FORMAT

▶ Illustration 3-6   Format Shapes: (A) Round/Tondo; (B) Rectangular; (C) Square; (D) Oval

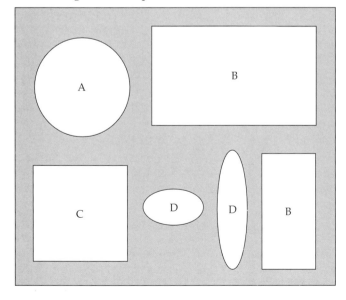

Not all grounds are rectangular in shape: Your ground may be square or irregularly shaped. Additionally, even though your ground may be one shape, you may want a picture with a different border shape.

The shape of the overall surface on which an image is applied is termed *format* (Illus. 3–6). The format may be square, rectangular, round (tondo), triangular, or just about any other configuration you can think of. If you are using frame shapes that do not resemble any known geometric or other shapes, then you may be utilizing a "free-form" format, such as Frank Stella's *Darabjerd III* (Fig. 3–16). Why would someone do this?

Some unusual examples of formats exist throughout the history of art (See

Fig. 3–17). For example, in Michelangelo's frescoes of the Sistine Chapel ceiling, various images are framed by actual or implied architectural boundaries. These individual areas have specific formats, and are identified as such in the accompanying diagram (Illus. 3–7). Note that the format in the ceiling's corner spans from one wall to another, thus producing a curved surface. There is no rule that says a picture's format must possess a flat surface. Painting on the irregular shape of the pendentives is as valid as would be painting on a basketball, a leather ceremonial shield as Castagno did with his image of *David* (Fig. 3–18), or tree leaves as seen in Figure 3–19 of a student's work. The appropriateness of the format is determined by the artist's expressive objectives.

▶ Figure 3-16   Frank Stella, *Darabjerd III*
(Hirshhorn Museum and Sculpture Garden, Smithsonian Institution, Gift of Joseph H. Hirshhorn, 1972/Art Resource, NY)

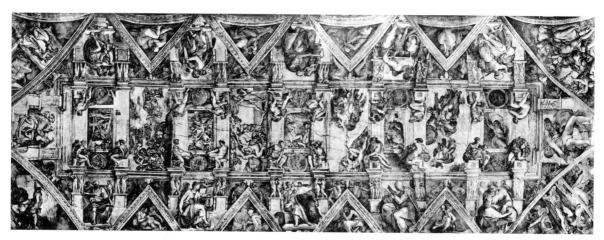

▶ Figure 3-17   Michelangelo, Sistine Chapel Ceiling
(Alinari/Art Resource, NY)

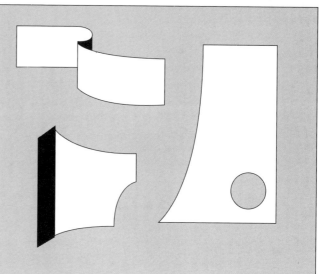

▶ Illustration 3-7   Free-Form Formats

▶ Figure 3-18   Andrea del Castagno, *The Youthful David*
(National Galery of Art, Washington, D.C., Widener Collection)

The frame of the format does not necessarily have to be the limit of the artist's image. It is not uncommon in print media to see an image appear to break out of the frame, overlapping it and progressing out of its "restrictive" area to get "closer" to you. In Baroque architecture, painted ceilings might actually have a sculpted, three-dimensional horse leg or human limb extending out of a painted image of the same. This heightens the image's drama and realism by advancing from its area into yours, metamorphosizing from a two- to a three-dimensional form.

Sometimes a painting may be made up of two, three, four, or more separate but related images instead of just one. Robert Campin's *Triptych of the Annunciation* (Fig. 3–20) is a three-panel painting celebrating the Annunciation. In this example, the images and organization of the outer panels complement the theme and design of the central panel. Also, you note that there are hinges between the panels, allowing them to be folded inward, thus protecting the painted surfaces. This format, known as a *triptych*, has its origins in Early Christian art where individuals

▶ Illustration 3-8   Architectural Format

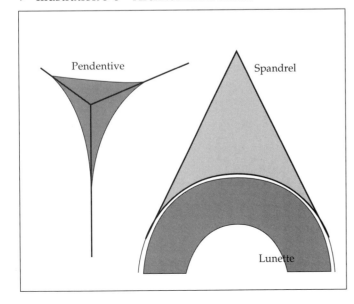

▶ Figure 3-19
(Wendy-Michele Laissue)

▶ Figure 3-20   Robert Campin, *Triptych of the Annunciation* (With Joseph in his Workshop [right] and Kneeling Donors [left]
(The Metropolitan Museum of Art, The Cloisters Collection, 1956 [56.70])

wanted small and portable altars. Paintings which are comprised of two separate but related panels are termed *diptychs*, and those with four or more are termed *polyptychs* (Illus. 3-9).

Today, the multipaneled format for paintings has been retained by some artists, although the function is frequently quite different. Additionally, the subject matter of these paintings may be either sacred or secular. In Max Beckmann's *Departure* (Fig. 3–21), he has even taken away the hinged format and made each panel relatively the same size. Yet, due to the interdependence of the three panels, it is still a triptych.

▶ PICTURE FRAMES AND PLANES

Understanding that the picture frame is the actual or implied outer limit of an image and that the artist is responsible for the form of everything within that picture frame, we are aware that there is an implied area or surface between all of the points of the picture frame. This area is referred to as the *picture plane* (Illus. 3–10). The picture plane is not the ground—it is not an actual surface; rather it is a reference point or area.

▶ PICTURE PLANES AND SPATIAL EFFECTS

When you look at some images it appears as though you are looking through a window frame into deep or receding space. Now you surely know you are not actually looking through the ground—you have not cut a hole in it to look through to the other side. Instead, you feel as if you are looking through an implied, transparent area—the picture plane—to a distance beyond (see the chapter on "Space").

▶ Illustration 3-9   Diptychs, Triptychs, and Polytychs

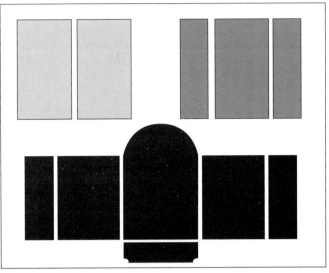

▶ Figure 3-21   Max Beckmann, *Departure* (1932–1933, oil on canvas, center panel 7 $\frac{3}{4}$″ × 45 $\frac{3}{8}$″ side panels each 7 $\frac{3}{4}$″ × 39 $\frac{1}{4}$″, The Museum of Modern Art, New York, given anonymously)

Picture Plane

▶ Illustration 3-10   Picture Plane

Or, you might feel as though the images on the ground do not appear to recede away from you, but stay flat on the area of the picture plane, adorning the surface in a more decorative manner like a checkerboard. This level of spatial reference is thus termed *decorative space*. Some images appear to jump right out of the picture frame, advancing toward you from the picture plane. This spatial reference is termed *advancing space*.

There are different types of receding, decorative, and advancing space, along with different ways to achieve each. Interestingly, compositions may simultaneously combine features of two or more types of space. We will more fully discuss these different types and applications when we consider "space" later in the text and observe how one can manipulate the visual components of art to create any desired spatial effect.

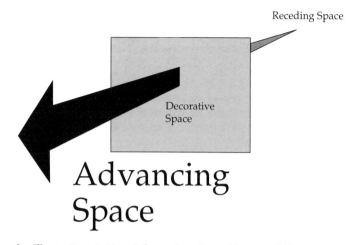

Receding Space

Decorative Space

Advancing Space

▶ Illustration 3-11 Advancing, Receding, and Decorative Space

COMPUTER-FACILITATED DESIGN CONSIDERATIONS

I n "easel arts," factors such as the tool, technique, medium, and ground equally affect the way an image looks. When one produces images using a computer, the same is relatively true. The tool is a combination of the keyboard, printer, software program, hardware, and mouse or graphics pen. The technique is the way you integrate these tools to produce an image. The medium is the image-producing material of your printer, and your ground is the actual type and color of paper used. Any variable in tool, technique, medium, or ground will affect your final image. As a result, these four factors

cannot be taken for granted. For example, your printer paper may appear to be white, but it may actually be buff or ivory. Pay attention to these types of variables because unfounded assumptions regarding any one of the image-producing factors can cause an unexpected visual effect which may or may not be in harmony with your aesthetic goals.

Traditionally, the hand of the artist is directly connected to the tool which produces an image: the pencil to draw with on the paper or the brush to paint with on the canvas. With pencil or paint, the image develops as a direct and simultane-

▶ Figure 3-22

ous response to the artist's manipulation of the tool. However, when using the computer keyboard or mouse as the hands-on element of the tool and the printer as another tool, the artist or designer finds the generated image twice removed: The image is first produced on the monitor and then generated in a final form by the printer.

While keyboard functions may remain relatively consistent, printer capabilities vary widely. A diagonal line, for example, on a dot-matrix printer will be "drawn" as a stepped, uneven mark. But the same line—drawn with the mouse in exactly the same way and looking exactly the same on your monitor—when printed with a sophisticated program on a laser printer, may produce a regular, even mark. Similarly, curves, circles, or rounded corners will be "stepped" or regular, depending on the capabilities of the program and printer.

It usually takes students a long time to get comfortable working with materials such as India ink or tempera paints. Sometimes media run or drip, and sometimes the ground—paper or canvas—is not well suited to a medium. A pen may leak or bristles may fall out of a brush. Of course, your printer can break down, the paper feeder can jam or get misaligned, or the program won't even run. Every tool and every medium has its own capabilities, liabilities, and limitations. Generally, however, craftsmanship is not a problem the designer encounters with computer-assisted images. Ink won't get smeared across the page or bleed underneath your ruler. Eraser marks won't be a factor. However, getting the image where you want it on the page—as opposed to where it looks like it probably is on your monitor's screen—may be a problem. Or making a change without wiping away from the computer's memory all of the work you have previously done may be a problem, too.

Using the computer to successfully assist you in the production of images is dependent upon practice and experience. These are the same determiners for excellence required of the more traditional art techniques.

SYNTHESIZING

When you have selected your subject matter, medium, tool and technique, and ground, it is time to get started. Squeeze out the paint or wedge the clay; sharpen your pencils or select the appropriate welding tips; select your software and printer type. You find yourself making lines, shapes, colors, and textures. You arrange these components of art according to your innate and developed sensitivities—this is the designing. You are making choices, consciously or subconsciously, about what you want your image to look like. You produce works of consequence with aesthetic merit: art.

Some choices may not be rigidly determined ahead of time—there may be a spontaneous relationship between you and the medium, tool, and ground as you progress which will cause you to alter some of your original ideas. This decision-making process, including the incorporation of the organizational components— dominance, proportion, balance, variety and harmony, repetition and movement, and economy—is sometimes purposeful and direct, sometimes spontaneous and insightful. Spontaneity is the result of practice and self-confidence, and should be encouraged and allowed to flourish.

Consider practice time spent on familiarization and experimentation with any tool, technique, medium, and ground, as time well spent: a good investment. Technique will come with time and practice. You don't always have to be creating "art" when you are working with art materials. Relax enough with tools and media so that you can play with them to learn their full expressive potential. Believe me, practice and play will save time

▶ Figure 3-23 Prehistoric Cave Paintings at Altamira. The Hall of Bulls, Altamira, Spain
(Giraudon/Art Resource, NY)

▶ Figure 3-24 Child's Art

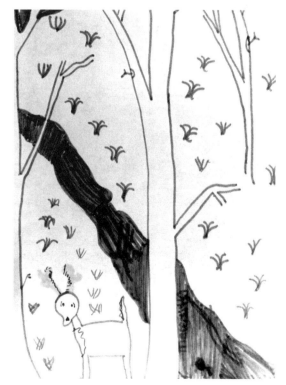

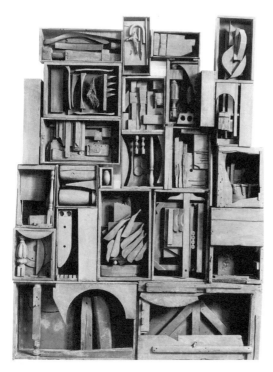

▶ Figure 3-25   Louise Nevelson, *Black Wall*
(Presented by the Friends of the Tate Gallery 1962, London)

in the long run and enhance creativity. Practice is as important to the artist as it is to the athlete, writer, or musician. Get to know your tools, media, and ground before you actually have to produce a given image for a specified purpose. Practice will help you to make the best choices to enhance meaningful expression.

> All of the people who create images called "art" have one thing in common: an innate sensitivity to the arrangement of the visual and organizational components of art. Continued study of the components of art will sharpen the sensitivities you already possess.

You may think it improbable that Paleolithic or Neolithic peoples went through all of these processes one by one, step by step, and you would be right. And when you made your first masterpiece at the age of three years (What your parents thought was a masterpiece!), you certainly did not go through these steps one by one, either. But as you look at all of the art produced from Paleolithic times to present, it is obvious that all art objects share common visual and organizational components, and decisions were made about their use. The visual result of the interaction of subject matter, medium, tool and technique, ground, along with the visual and organizational components of art, is termed *form*. The form of a work is the sum of its visual devices. The choices made regarding these components of art are what determines the uniqueness of a form.

▶ **UNIT GLOSSARY**

Additive Process   The building up, modeling, or assembly of a medium.

Advancing Space   Pictorial area which appears to advance toward the viewer from the area closest to the picture plane.

Binder   An agent which holds pigment particles in suspension so that the pigment can be spread on in a film which will eventually harden to keep them permanently bound together and adhered to a surface. Syn.: VEHICLE.

Constructive Technique   Related to the additive process, involves the joining of materials by mechanical means.

Content   The ultimate meaning or significance of a work of art.

Decorative Space   Pictorial area which appears to lie on the surface of the picture plane, neither advancing nor receding.

Fabrication   The process of producing a three-dimensional form, usually from sketches or models, by welding, building, sewing, or other such assembly techniques.

Figure-Ground Relationship   The shape relationship of subject matter against its background on the picture plane.

Form   The visual result of the aesthetic decision making process; the interaction of subject matter, medium, tool and technique, ground, and the visual and organizational components of art, and their resulting visual effects.

Format   The shape of the overall surface on which an image is applied, including square, triptych, rectangular, round (tondo), free-form, or triptych.

Found/Scrap/Junk Art   A misnomer. Art may be made from found, junk, or scrap materials, but the result should not be junk or scrap art! A more appropriate label is ART FROM FOUND MATERIALS OR ASSEMBLAGES.

Ground   The term for any physical material on which a two-dimensional image is created. This is not usually a three-dimensional consideration since sculptural forms are created out of a medium, not onto a ground.

Impasto   Paint applied thickly to a ground, creating a surface texture that is conspicuously built up.

Integrity of a Medium   The functional and aesthetic suitability of a material as applicable to a particular image.

Manipulative Process   Sculptural technique involving the shaping of a plastic medium, such as clay.

Maquette   A small, three-dimensional preparatory study for a sculpture, French term meaning "model."

Negative Shape   An area void of primary subject matter. Syn.: NEGATIVE SPACE. (See VOID.)

Picture Frame   The boundary of a two-dimensional image, either implied or actual. Every visual entity within the picture frame is the responsibility of the artist.

Picture Plane   An implied surface area spanning all of the points on the interior of the picture frame.

Plastic   Sculpturally, a medium which retains its shape after being shaped and modeled, such as clay. Generally, an entity's ability to be willfully modeled and/or altered, such as space or line.

Positive Shape   The area occupied by subject matter. Syn.: POSITIVE SPACE.

Receding Space   Pictorial area which appears to recede away from or behind the area of the picture plane.

Sacred   Of or relating to a particular faith.

Secular   Conspicuously omitting any reference to a particular faith.

Silhouette   The area described by a primary contour which is filled in with an even, overall value or color; no secondary contours are evident.

Subject Matter   The point of departure or idea stimulating the artist's imagery; may or may not be identifiable or representational.

Substitutive Process   Sculptural technique involving the changing of the medium of a form from one material to another by way of molds and casting.

Subtractive Process   Sculptural technique involving traditional carving applications on stone, wood, or any other appropriate medium.

Vehicle   See BINDER.

Wash   Media—such as oil paint, acrylics, and watercolor—applied in a diluted manner, creating a transparent film of a color or neutral.

FOUR

Designing: Theory and Practice

AN INTRODUCTION TO THE COMPONENTS OF ART

All makers of visual images are motivated by a sense of order which they feel is appropriate for their particular work. In studying the work of many millennia and many, many artists we have come to realize that all images of art incorporate these same components of organization: dominance, proportion, balance, variety and harmony, repetition and movement, and economy. How one chooses to organize the visual components will make that person's art as unique as the images of those artists who have lived at other times in other lands.

The individual components of visual expression have counterparts in other forms of expression, such as oral or written communication. In writing, for example, you have nouns, verbs, and other parts of speech. The organization of the words, or syntax, is what determines the meaning of a sentence. In visual communication it is the organization, or design, of the visual components that determines the particular meaning of an image. For example, it is the particular syntax of Shakespeare that separates him from Longfellow; and it is the form—the sum of all components in a work of art—that separates a painting by Andrew Wyeth from an Upper Paleolithic cave painting.

In introductory English classes you may have diagrammed sentences to visualize their separate parts and how the parts work together. In art, we can diagram the relationship of the components of visual expression to visualize how they work together. This is demonstrated in Illustration 4-4.

▶ Figure 4-1 Paintings from the Caves at Lascaux
(Giraudon/Art Resource, NY)

▶ Figure 4-2 Andrew Wyeth, *Young Bull*
(Photograph courtesy of the Wyeth Collection)

THE VISUAL COMPONENTS

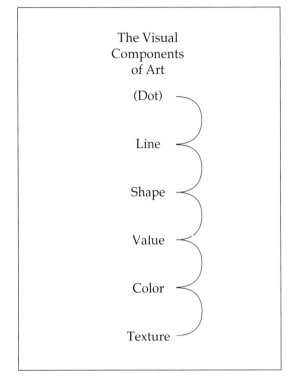

The Visual
Components
of Art

(Dot)

Line

Shape

Value

Color

Texture

▶ Illustration 4-1   Components of Visual
Expression

I t is important to recognize that the visual components do work together. It would be difficult, if not impossible, to speak of one visual component without making a reference to any of the others. You cannot talk about shape, for example, without considering line, for line is the outermost limit of a shape, its contour. We also see that line works with each of the VISUAL COMPONENTS. In fact, we realize that . . .

> Each one of the visual
> components can work with any
> and all of the remaining visual
> components.

The degree of variety and harmony which exists between the visual components in a particular work creates varying degrees of visual tension and energy.

THE ORGANIZATIONAL COMPONENTS

T he same parallels can be made when we discuss the relationship of the organizational components to one another. Let's again take line and use it in a conspicuously repeated manner. This repetition may create somewhat of a pattern and enhance our visual movement around the composition. Also, some lines are more dominant than others by size or grouping, thus affecting balance, but the composition may remain interesting because there may be variety and harmony in the handling of the line.

If we take this analysis a step further, we realize that we could say the same thing about color: A color can create dominance or affect balance depending on its usage. This is also true of shape, as it can be varied and contribute to the dominance of an area or concept due to the variety or harmony of its application. As we continue to make these relationships, we see that we can work with value and texture in a similar manner.

We appropriately conclude that

> Any one of the visual components can work with any one or all of the organizational components.

This unique relationship of the visual components to the organizational components is the design of the work. The relationship of the tool, technique, medium, and ground to the design results in the particular form of the work.

Can this same conclusion apply to the relationship of organizational components as it did to visual components? You can probably answer that for yourself now. You realize that if we take repetition, for example, we can have repetition of a line, shape, value, color, texture, or dot. And, we can affect the balance of a composition with line, shape, value, color, texture, or dot, too.

Therefore, we can make the same conclusion regarding the relationship of the design components to the visual components:

> Any one of the organizational components can work with any one or all of the visual components.

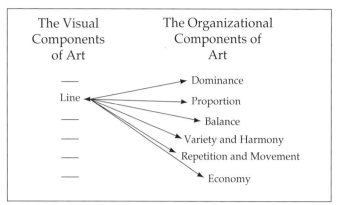

▶ Illustration 4-2

▶ Illustration 4-3

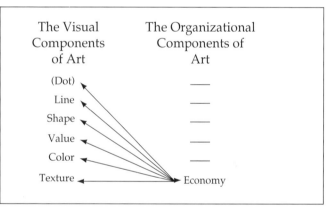

Components of Visual Expression

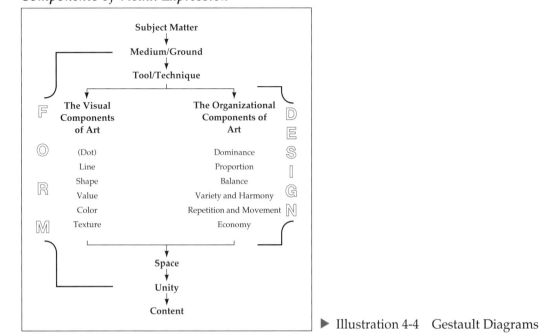

▶ Illustration 4-4   Gestault Diagrams

▶ Figure 4-3   Student Work, *Apples*

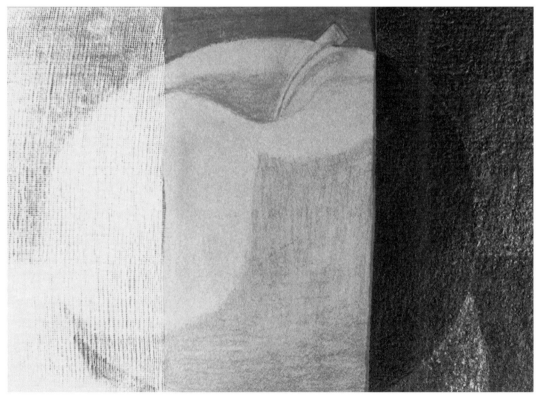

THE EFFECTS OF WORKING WITH THE COMPONENTS OF VISUAL EXPRESSION

▶ **SPACE**

One of the results of the application of the visual components to the surface of a ground (paper, canvas, board) is that there will be a spatial effect. Space is not used, spatial effects are created.

> Depending on the artist's objectives, a visual component may appear to lie in front of, behind, or on the visual picture plane.

The impression may be of looking through a window into deep, receding space or of having the image appear to advance toward you from the page.

In fully three-dimensional sculptural applications, forms will exist in or circumscribe space, providing meaningful viewing experiences from all vantage points: over, around, and through. Relief sculptures, which may have the visual effect of being more two-dimensional, can perpetuate the illusion of sculpted forms projecting from or through a window or opening (Figure 4-5).

▶ Figure 4-4   Louis Michel Eilshemius, *Study of Trees*
(Hirshhorn Museum and Sculpture Garden, Smithsonian Institution, Gift of Joseph H. Hirshhorn, 1966)

▶ **UNITY**

If an artist has been successful in handling the components of art on the ground, there is a resulting visual "rightness" to the work, or unity. The Greeks referred to this as eurythmy. Some images yield a psychological or symbolic sense of com-

▶ Figure 4-5   Donatello, *The Feast of Herod,*
Baptistry/Siena
(Alinari/Art Resource, NY)

(b)

▶ Illustration 4-5(a) & (b)   (a)

pleteness and total resolution from an incomplete or open-ended configuration of parts, known as gestalt. Thus, the unity may be clearly defined by the artist or felt by the viewer (Illus. 4–5).

▶ CONTENT

Ultimately, a completed visual image should have some expressive validity, some ultimate expressive significance to the artist, the artist's public, or the artist's time. This is the work's content, and it is the reason why any art is made in the first place. The content may be considered "deep," such as humans' relationship to one another or humans' relationship with nature; or it may be more personalized, such as the artist's delight in shape relationships or images of tension or joy. Whimsy, humor, politics, religion, education, philosophy, or anything else could be an element of a work's content: There is no proper or improper content. It is, however, improper to have a work that is void of content.

It is your job as the maker of art to have a purpose in the making of your images. It is your job as the appreciator of art to make the effort to understand the ultimate meaning of images produced by varying peoples of various cultures and periods. The form of the work, in addition to its cultural and historical perspective, is what determines its content.

If you sense the relationship of all the visual information provided by the artist and if you understand how the components of a work of art can work together, you have come a long way toward being able to determine the content of art objects, both the well-known and the relatively unknown. You have also come a long way in effectively directing the content of your own creations.

FIVE

The Organizational Components of Art

THE FOUNDATION OF DESIGN

DOMINANCE

When you look at a work of art, have you ever wondered how the artist gets your attention and holds it? How is your vision focused on a particular part of an image, and what makes one area or form more visually dominant than another?

▶ ASSOCIATION: FORM RECOGNITION

One of the most consistent means of getting a viewer's attention is to make an association with something the viewer would know. This is done by using images that relate to an invididuals's familiarity and experience with given subject matter. For example, you may not be inclined to study a tenth-century image from Madagascar if you have spent the majority of your life in the Americas. On the other hand, if you have painted landscapes in your art classes and walked down a hallway where some Winslow Homer or Andrew Wyeth paintings were hanging, you may be more inclined to really look at these because of your own experiences with the same subject matter; you are familiar with these types of images—you recognize them or can identify with them. *You are more comfortable with that which you know.*

Individuals tend to be attracted to images in art that are actually or reminiscent of something known or experienced, be it representational or abstract. You may have found yourself daydreaming, looking up into the clouds, and suddenly "seeing" an elephant or cartoon character in the shapes of the clouds. A rock configuration may have reminded you of the contour of a face, or sand in a sandbox may

▶ Figure 5-1   Student Work

remind you of sand dunes at the beach. Stylized or abstract fruit in a painted still-life or geometricized faces in portraits may be similar to the subject matter—even though not exact copies, reminding you of the subject. However, because of those similarities—because of the association with the original—you find yourself drawn to the images.

▶ ACCENT

A factor affecting how an artist gets you to look at or focus on something or some area of an image involves the *accent* of a particular part of the image. For example,

▶ Figure 5-2 Pierre August Renoir, *La Place Clichy*
(Fitzwilliam Museum, University of Cambridge/Art Resource, NY)

▶ Figure 5-3 Jack Levine/*Election Night* (1954)
(Oil on canvas, 63⅛" × 61½", The Museum of Modern Art, New York,
Gift of Joseph H. Hirshhorn, ©1994 Jack Levine/VAGA, New York)

a contrast in the visual components, such as line, shape, value, color, or texture may cause you to look at one area of a work more strongly than another. Also, the relative clarity of a form can direct your eyes. For example, in *La Place Clichy* (Fig. 5–2), Renoir directs your vision to the girl in the lower-right corner by having her in sharper focus than her surroundings. This is in harmony with the experience of vision, for we know that images get out of focus toward the edges of our direct vision, our peripheral vision.

▶ **GROUPING**

The eye (or brain) is inclined to recognize similar forms and associate them with one another, such as the bases on a ball field or the roundness of gauges on a dashboard. This grouping of forms can get your attention, too, because of their form relatedness: Groupings of similar, dissimilar, large, small, bright, dark, or any other combination of visual components can attract your vision provided there is contrast between a grouping and (1) other groups within the visual field, or (2) other components in the composition (Jack Levine, *Election Night*, Fig. 5–3).

▶ **PLACEMENT**

The placement or location of a visual component in a composition can affect dominance. We have all seen images where the subject matter is placed in the "bull's-eye" of the page; this is an obvious, logical placement to get one's attention. However, off-center placement of primary subject matter may be more unexpected and more jarring. This type of placement, when handled with the appropriate *accent*, can be particularly attention-getting. Conversely, if you don't want too much

▶ Figure 5-4 Katsushika Hokusai, *The Great Wave,* from the thirty-six view of Mt. Fuji (The Spaulding Collection, Courtesy, Museum of Fine Arts, Boston)

attention on a particular area, you may pull it off-center and "neutralize" its accent.

In the accompanying seascape (Fig. 5-4), you find your eye drawn in a clockwise rotation around the composition, along the contours and building shapes of the waves. You are carried around the center of the image, but not to the center. And, you see hidden in the valleys of the sea swells boats carrying oarsmen. The placement of the boats away from the center of the composition and the contrast of the scale and shape-types provide variety and interest. However, do the boats on the right provide enough contrast and interest to provide balance for the rising wave and calligraphy on the left? Do you feel viewing satisfaction even though the focal points are off-center? Finally, why would the artist arrange the composition in this manner?

▶ CONVERGENCE

Convergence is a technique that has been employed by artists for centuries to direct viewer attention and, therefore, control visual dominance. In the painting of the *Tribute Money* (Fig. 5–5), Masaccio used the converging lines of linear perspective as a device to define deep space and lead your eye to the primary figure, Christ. Also, the vanishing point of the receding/converging parallel lines lies behind Christ's head. Additionally, Masaccio incoporated a central (bull's-eye) placement for the primary figure. In Figure 5–6, you will also see that Leonardo uses perspective in the same manner in his painting of *The Last Supper.*

Converging lines do not always have to lead from near-to-far to direct your attention. They may also move horizontally or vertically to draw your attention across a composition as opposed to through one.

▶ Figure 5-5   Masaccio, *Tribute Money*
(S. Maria del Carmine/Florence, Italy, Alinari/Art Resource, NY)

▶ Figure 5-6   Leonardo, *The Last Supper*
(©1993 Fratelli Alinari)

PROPORTION

Proportion involves the visual agreement of relative parts. This includes tangible features with measurable ratios, such as the size of a mat compared to the size of a picture, or an individual's head size as compared to overall body length. But proportion also involves the agreeable relationship of intangible features, of felt sensations, such as the degree of intensity of red compared to green; it involves a feeling of balance among similar or dissimilar parts and other factors.

▶ "IDEAL" PROPORTIONS

There are some visual proportions that are considered "ideal" by different peoples of different times, such as the Golden Mean Rectangle (see Illus. 5–3). Many people consider "ideal" human proportions to contain 7½ head units for a body length (Illus. 5–1). Ideal proportions frequently represent national or cultural standards. Appropriate proportions, however, often relate to the visual agreement of relative parts in an image *regardless* of outside considerations. Ultimately, it is your presentation of the harmonious agreement of the visual components in a composition—two- or three-dimensional—which determines the appropriateness of proportions.

▶ CULTURAL FORMULAS

Some cultural interpretations of "ideal" proportions are really proportional relationships that are perceived by a culture as being agreeable. Egyptians from the third millennium B.C., the Old Kingdom, used a module of 24 units to establish the

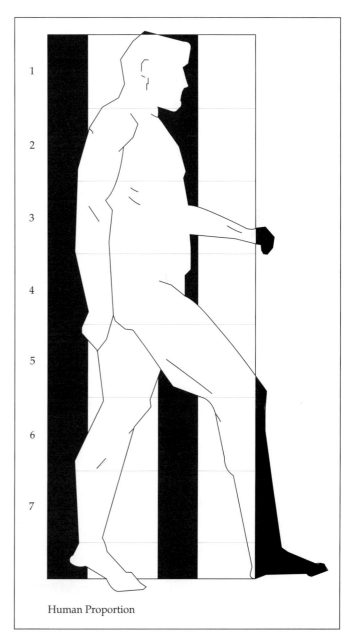

Human Proportion

▶ Illustration 5-1   Human Figure/Ideal Human Proportions

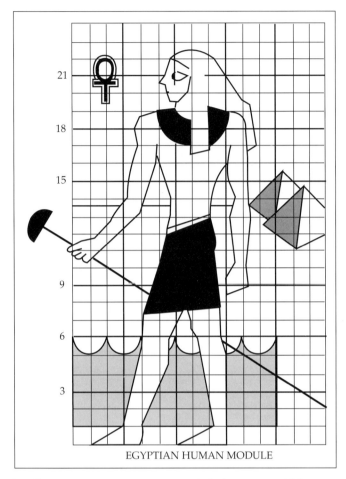

EGYPTIAN HUMAN MODULE

▶ Illustration 5-2   Human Module/Egyptian Old Kingdom

▶ Figure 5-7   Salvador Dali, *The Sacrament of the Last Supper*
(National Gallery of Art, Washington, Chester Dale Collection)

proper proportions of the human figure (Illus. 5–2). The Greek Polyclitus found 7½ head units to be ideal in the fifth century B.C. When examples of these two ideals are compared, it is interesting to discover that the Egyptian figure totals about 7½ head units also!

▶ GRIDS AND MODULES

Many artists of various times have found systems, modules, and grids to be meaningful frameworks in the development of their compositions. Greeks in the fifth century B.C. found the Golden Mean Rectangle (GMR) to be a satisfactory proportional system for the basis of the Parthenon. Twentieth century *surrealist* artist Salvador Dali also found the GMR applicable as an organizational system for his painting of the *Sacrament of the Last Supper* (Fig. 5–7).

In the Golden Mean Rectangle you observe the entire rectangle to be composed of a square and another GMR, and that GMR is made up of another square and GMR (see Illus. 5–3). This proportional progression—whether used in reducing or enlarging the GMR—always results in a Golden Mean Rectangle. Interestingly, when groups of people are asked to draw their impression of a well-proportioned rectangle, the results for the majority of the people surveyed are rectangles which have proportions similar to the Golden Mean Rectangle—there is a general feeling among most people that the proportions of the GMR are very agreeable.

When a line is drawn as to trace the construction of the GMR, we observe it has a shape that is similar to a nautilus shell; and we also observe this to be proportionally similar to the degree of curve of the volute on an Ionic capital.

On the other hand, John Dewey, author of *Art as Experience*, emphasizes individual design considerations over standardized formulas. He wrote:

> In order to be aesthetic, structure has to be more than physical or mathematical.

▶ NUMERICAL EQUIVALENTS

Photographers are often taught the "system of thirds": An image is divided in three equal parts vertically and three equal parts horizontally with the focal point being located at the intersection of one of the intersecting vertical and horizontal lines (Illus. 5–4).

Another position regarding mathematical proportions is that an odd number of visual components should be used in a composition as opposed to an even number, and if an image appears to "run off" the picture plane, outside the picture frame, then it should do so in at least three places. These are popular rules of thumb, but little else. The final determiner regarding how many of what to put into a composition, or how something may go beyond the limit of the picture frame is up to you—you are not limited by artificial rules of thumb. These rules are generalities which have been handed down over time—handed down by people who may or may not have known what they were talking about. Therefore, when it comes to what is right for your composition, you are the judge. You use your knowledge of design and the lessons from art history to make your judgments.

Mathematical considerations may be effective as part of and complementary to an overall composition. Mathematical equivalents for the arrangement of visual forms may be a help to some artists sometimes, but they are neither prerequisites to nor guarantees of successful art. You should not feel obliged to design a composition that is dependent upon a system.

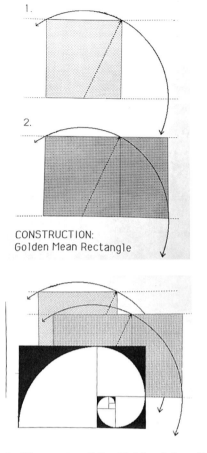

CONSTRUCTION:
Golden Mean Rectangle

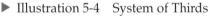

▶ Illustration 5-3   Golden Mean Rectangle

▶ Illustration 5-4   System of Thirds

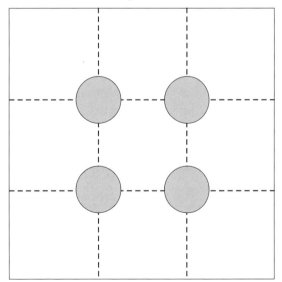

▶ Figure 5-9   Kathryn Meredith, Pencil
Drawing
(© Kathryn Meredith)

▶ Figure 5-8   Primitive, African (Nigeria), Plaque: King
Mounted with Attendants
(The Metropolitan Museum of Art, the Michael C. Rockefeller Memorial
Collection, Gift of Nelson A. Rockefeller, 1965 [1978.412.309])

▶ HIERATIC SCALE

Hieratic scale is a form of presentation
perceived to be an effective means of
showing the relative importance of figures within a composition. It may be used
equally well by societies or individuals to
depict the religious, political, or physical
importance of an individual featured in
an image.

As observed in Figure 5–8, a Niger-
ian bronze casting illustrating a king and
his attendants, we see the figure of the
chief to be central and largest. In hieratic
scale, a dominant human figure is also frequently presented as symmetrically frontal and placed higher in a composition or,
on a sculpture base, higher than other
forms and/or figures around it.

Compare this African example to the
child's drawing (Kathryn Meredith, Fig.
5–9) which shows an image of the child's
perception of God as larger than herself,
dominating the space, and protectively
standing over the child. (Also notice how
the same God-image is placed inside of
her, in the same gesture as the large God-
figure, symbolically showing the God-
presence in her in a personalized scale.)

> This example demonstrates that a
> predisposition to hieratic scale
> devices is innate and universal.

▶ CONCLUSION

Proportional relationships of various elements in a composition involve something looking "right" or "wrong": the Greek eurythmy which we spoke of before. It involves resolving visual tensions and contrasts between such components as shape (size, type), line, texture, value, and color in a composition. Look at Mondrian's *Composition in White, Black, and Red* (Fig. 5–10). If you were to change the width of a line or the size of the red shape the slightest bit or take away one of the horizontal white rectangles on the lower right-hand corner, you would drastically alter the overall sense of "rightness" of the composition because you have altered the overall proportions that Mondrian so painstakingly established. You observe that

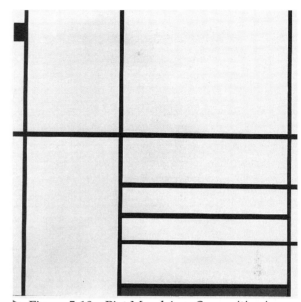

▶ Figure 5-10 Piet Mondrian, *Composition in White, Black, and Red*, 1936
(Oil on canvas, 40¼″ × 41″, The Museum of Modern Art, New York, gift of the Advisory Committee)

> Changing any single component of a composition changes the proportional relationships of all the parts, not just the one in question.

Your sensitivities to the tensions and harmonies between the parts will guide you in establishing appropriate judgments regarding proportions.

BALANCE

Balance is a concept that has many applications outside of the study of art. A child on a seesaw innately senses balance. An environmentalist is concerned about the balance of humankind and the natural world on this planet. The weights of a child and playmate at opposite ends of the seesaw need to be relatively equal. Or, the child senses that if the weights are somewhat unequal, the child or playmate can move closer to or farther away from the fulcrum point to maintain

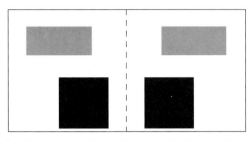

▶ Illustration 5-5   Symmetrical (Axial) Balance

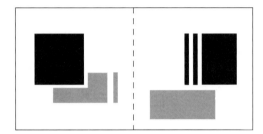

▶ Illustration 5-6   Approximate Symmetrical Balance

▶ Illustration 5-7   Asymmetrical (Occult) Balance

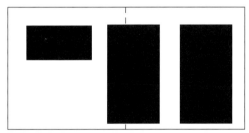

balance. The environmentalist does not have such easily definable components to move around, nor are the means of arriving at ecological balance as easy to define in an effort to strike an equilibrium of environmental forces that interact with one another. Minute changes in one part of an ecosystem may dramatically affect the harmony and balance of the entire ecosystem in the same way a minor shift of weight can dramatically affect the balance of a seesaw.

These examples exhibit principles of balance which are equally applicable to art.

> **An artist makes an effort to balance or arrange visual forces to maintain a feeling of visual harmony and equilibrium.**

An artist doesn't want a composition to visually fall off of the picture plane or sculpture stand. As the child won't "feel right" if the weight isn't balanced on the seesaw, the viewer of an art object won't "feel right" if the visual forces in a composition aren't in a state of equilibrium. (A sculptor may deal with *physical* equilibrium in mounting works on a base or balancing a mobile, but we are concerning ourselves with *visual forces* at this time, a component of two- and three-dimensional art alike.)

▶ TYPES OF BALANCE

Visual orientations to balance usually occur along the implied vertical axis of an image, through an area we imagine as the balancing or fulcrum point. An axis is a line which runs through the length, height, or width of a form at that form's center. For example, a bar through a rolling pin or the crease which results from a folded page could represent the locations of different axes. Usually, the axis is an implied line rather than an actual one.

When the visual components of one side are mirror-imaged on the opposite side of the implied central axis of the work, that is termed *symmetrical*, or *axial*, *balance* (Illus. 5–5). Symmetrical balance is not very often found in contemporary or western art, as many believe it yields monotony. Yet, in the mask illustrated in Figure 2–9, the symmetry yields formality, directness, and boldness—a controlled energy. Thus, one should not necessarily avoid symmetrical compositions.

Most frequently the components in a composition will not be symmetrically arranged; rather, they are approximately symmetrical. There may be a minor variation in the two sides of the image, yet the emphasis on a central axis can still be felt, and a similarity in the two sides can still be perceived. This is evident in Botticelli's *Birth of Venus* (Fig. 5–11) where the central axis runs from top to bottom, through the central figure, and the winged figures on the left are fairly *proportional* in size to the figure and tree grouping on the right.

Approximate symmetry avoids many of the perceptions of monotony that symmetrical balance may evoke. However, if an approximately symmetrical composition were poorly designed, it could be boring and monotonous, as well.

Salvador Dali's painting, *The Persistence of Memory* (Fig. 5–12), has a variety of images and shapes throughout the composition. Yet, while there is no clear central fulcrum point, there appears to be visual order—the work doesn't appear to want to fall off of the picture plane. In other words, while you would be hard pressed to find physical equivalents of

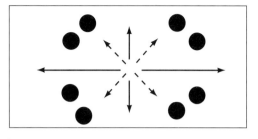

▶ Illustration 5-8   Radial Balance

▶ Figure 5-11   Botticelli, *Birth of Venus*
(©1990 Alinari Giraudon/Art Resource, NY)

▶ Figure 5-12   Dali, *The Persistence of Memory*, 1931
(Oil on canvas, 9½″ × 13″, The Museum of Modern Art, New York,
given anonymously)

▶ Figure 5-13   Charles R. Sheeler, Jr., *Staircase,*
Doylestown
(Hirshhorn Museum and Sculpture Garden, Smithsonian
Institution, gift of Joseph H. Hirshhorn, 1972)

equal weight on the right and left sides, the work feels right, and that is what counts. Thus, even though there is a lack of sameness on the right- and left-hand sides, there is an overriding sense of equilibrium. As a result, this work is termed *asymmetrically balanced*. A synonym for this is *occult balance.*

The examples we have been looking at have been concerned with balance along an implied vertical axis: balancing the left side with the right side. Additionally, it is important that a work not be too bottom- or top-heavy. Artists are concerned with balance along a horizontal axis also. When you look at Magritte's *Castle in Spain*, you observe that there is an emphasis on the vertical axis yielding approximate symmetry in addition to balance along an implied horizontal axis: The mass of stone at the top balances with the seashore at the bottom. Therefore, you see that qualities of balance can overlap with one another.

> There can be more than one type of balance in a composition.

A further example of one type of balance working with another is found in Charles Sheeler's *Staircase, Doylestown* (Fig. 5-13). Initially you perceive that the painting is divided almost in the middle by a vertical post and that there is a similar but unequal distribution of forms on each side of the post. Thus, the work is asymmetrically balanced. And, as you observe this asymmetry, you see that the ascending stairs appear to radiate from the center of composition quite dramatically, almost like a pinwheel. This emphasis on the distribution of forms and forces around a central point is termed *radial balance*, and is manifested in both two- and three-dimensional art.

VARIETY AND HARMONY

"Too much of a good thing isn't good" and "Variety is the spice of life" are cliches that are applicable to life and art alike. For example, we may take simple pleasure in the texture, color, and regularity of a single brick, yet a two-story brick wall is rather monotonous; a lot of bricks do not guarantee a nice wall. However, that same brick wall can become much more interesting and visually significant when punctuated with a variety of openings, such as doors and windows. If those openings are all rectangles, as are the brick shapes, then variety in size and proportion has been introduced while maintaining a harmony of shape. This enhances visual interest. Additionally, if the brick wall has been punctuated with a variety of openings that are nonrectangular, but may be circular or some other variation of shape, then variety of shape has been introduced without breaking the overall harmony of geometric shapes. When you look at variety and harmony, the components of line, shape, value, color, and texture are always considered.

Look at primitive artist Henri Rousseau's *The Dream* (Fig. 5–15). When considering harmony in this painting, we observe that both plant and animal forms have even-edged contours producing somewhat stylized and fanciful geometric shapes. The colors of most of the plant life have been simplified to a harmonious range of greens, and the textures of the vegetation are rather consistent, too, providing neither a foreboding nor overtly inviting tactile quality. The harmony, however, is not monotonous due to the introduction of a bit of variety which results

▶ Figure 5-14
(5-14b, Lynchburg, VA)

▶ Figure 5-15   Henri Rousseau, *The Dream*, 1910
(Oil on canvas, 6'8½" × 9'½", The Museum of Modern Art, gift of Nelson A. Rockefeller)

▶ Figure 5-16   Constantin Brancusi, *Torso of a Young Man*
(Hirshhorn Museum and Sculpture Garden, Smithsonian Institution, gift of Joseph H. Hirshhorn, 1966)

color value. Examples of variety are few yet can be found in the diameter and length of the two lower projections in contrast to the upper, in addition to a slightly tapering contour of the lower extremities. The bottom of the larger cylinder, instead of being severed, is intersected by the two smaller cylinders, thus introducing a triangular shape into the limited geometric order of the sculpture.

In each of these examples, the artists have purposely controlled variety and harmony to provide meaningful contrast.

Rousseau sought an image of a somewhat unreal world that was ultimately pleasing and satisfying.

Brancusi sought to emphasize the almost mechanical nature of the human figure while perpetuating subliminal references to antique art and connotations of fertility within the classic format of the human figure.

Variety and harmony are placed side by side under the organizational components because of their necessary orientation to one another. In a composition, variety and harmony can be utilized to varying degrees as we have seen, from overwhelming harmony to conspicuous variety. However, neither is "better," neither is more acceptable. Again, your expressive intent determines the amount of variety and harmony you will have in your compositions.

The tension that exists in the delicate balance between variety and harmony determines, to a large degree, whether or not the viewer will find the work to be visually alive and meaningful.

---

in visual interest and vitality. The geometricized shapes and hard-edged definitions of the plant life have been contrasted against the softer and more organic shapes in the lions, elephant, and reclining figure, which also have more naturalistic color and shading of their lights and darks.

Constantin Brancusi's sculpture, *Torso of a Young Man* (Fig. 5–16), has an overwhelming harmony of direct, uncluttered contours and rigid, geometric shapes; a slick, polished texture; and a uniform

REPETITION AND MOVEMENT

T he terms *repetition* and *movement* are not unique to the visual arts. We find examples of repetition in the alternating squares on a checkerboard and the pickets of a fence. We find movement in the waving of tree branches and the rolling of waves.

Repetition and movement have intrinsic connotations of energy, activity, and dynamics. These organizational components are equally associated with the arts of the museum and the arts of music and dance.

▶ REPETITION AND PATTERN

When one of the visual components (line, shape, value, color, or texture) is used often and placed in relatively close proximity to more of the same visual components so that similar parts are read together as a unit, we refer to that repeated unit as a pattern. The individual visual component which makes up the pattern is a motif, such as the square of a checkerboard. Andy Warhol created a pattern using the motif of a middle-aged woman in his work, *Ethel Skull 36 Times* (Fig. 5–17). What keeps this image more interesting than a checkerboard, however, is that Warhol gave varying degrees of *accent,* or emphasis, to some of the squares, thereby introducing some variety into the harmony.

Pattern does not always involve a rigid motif that is clearly definable. The common tree bark that you find on pines or maples is also irregular, yet due to the general similarity of growth directions, shapes, and textures, repetition and pattern can again be observed. If you look

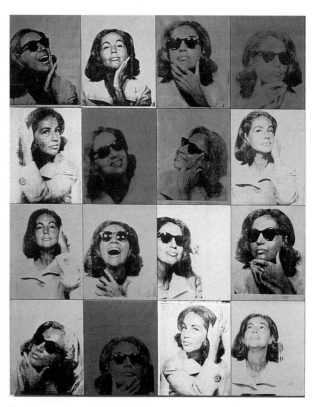

▶ Figure 5-17 Andy Warhol, *Ethel Scull-36 Times,* 1963
(One-third of the image has been reproduced, synthetic polymer paint and silkscreen on canvas, 36 panels, each 20 × 16", © 1995 The Andy Warhol Foundation, Inc.)

▶ Figure 5-18   Vincent Van Gogh, *The Starry Night*, 1889
(Oil on canvas, 29″ × 36¼″, The Museum of Modern Art, New York,
acquired through the Lillie P. Bliss Bequest)

▶ Figure 5-19   Millard Sheets, *Tenement Flats*
(National Museum of American Art, Smithsonian Institution, transfer from
the U.S. Department of the Interior, National Park Service)

very closely at the sky and other forms in Vincent van Gogh's *Starry Night* (Fig. 5–18), you will observe that his technique of applying paint in parallel directions creates a pattern of irregularly shaped and colored lines. Yet as these grouped lines are "stacked up," one upon another, you feel the pulsating repetition of the linear pattern. The repeated use of this linear pattern contributes to the overall unity of the composition as it provides harmony; repetition creates movement and unity.

▶ REPETITION AND MOTIF

A *motif*, the dominant visual element or theme conspicuously repeated in a composition, may or may not be involved in an individual pattern. In Sheets's *Tenement Flats* (Fig. 5–19) we observe a composition made up of a variety of shapes that are, essentially, slanting rectangles (parallelograms) of different sizes. These shapes are repeated enough to become the dominant visual component of the composition, clearly establishing themselves as the motif of the painting. The repetition of this motif contributes in a major way to drawing our eye around and through the composition, creating movement and energy.

Interestingly, if you took away from *Tenement Flats* the subject matter and tonal transitions, you would have a composition of severe geometric shapes that may remind you of images by Mondrian (see Fig. 5–10) or Van Doesburg (Fig. 6–49), which have the rectangles and diagonals as key components of their motifs.

Does the inclusion of identifiable subject matter in *Tenement Flats* make it "better" than the Mondrian or Van Doesburg? Does the comparison show that common sensitivities to organizational structure are innate? Also, does the inclusion of secondary organic motifs in *Tenement Flats* make it more successful by providing a visual relief to the geometric rigidity of the rectilinear shapes? Can you draw any conclusions about innate sensitivities to design after viewing these works and the work of seventeenth-century Dutch artist, Pieter de Hooch?

▶ REPETITION AND RHYTHM

The visual path your eye follows across, around, or through a composition is referred to as movement. Depending on the nature of the pattern and the accent of repeated components, your eye will "move" at different rates with different accents and pauses. The sculpture installation entitled *Stone Field Sculpture*, illustrated in the accompanying photograph (Fig. 5–21), encourages the visitor to actually move from stone to stone because of the various sizes of stones and differing spaces between them. Walking among the stones and seeing them in a photograph provides somewhat of a similar experience: When viewing the photograph, your eye moves around the images at a pace that changes according to the emphasis on the negative spaces and the size and accents of the various stones/*motif*. This particular pace combined with the visual path of movement is termed *rhythm*. The rhythm may be bold and staccato, as in the installation, or it may be smooth and fluid. (Also see Rousseau's *Sleeping Gypsy*, Fig. 5–22.)

▶ MOVEMENT AND ASSOCIATION

Movement doesn't always flow neatly across a pattern. Frequently, the artist causes your mind's eye to associate

▶ Figure 5-20   Pieter de Hooch, *The Bedroom*
(National Gallery of Art, Washington, Widener Collection)

▶ Figure 5-21   Carl Andre, *Stone Field Sculpture*, 1977
(Paula Cooper Gallery, NY)

▶ Figure 5-22   Henri Rousseau, *The Sleeping Gypsy*, 1897
(Oil on canvas, 51″ × 6′ 7″, The Museum of Modern Art, New York, gift of Mrs. Simon Guggenheim)

similar components to establish a more subliminal movement. In Henri Rousseau's *The Sleeping Gypsy* (Fig. 5–22), your eye skims across the moonlit highlighted contour of the lion's back, turns abruptly upward at the tuft on the tail, and then—this is where Rousseau is subtle—your eye moves back across the composition through the sky playing a connect-the-dot game with the stars.

Rousseau purposely arranged the stars to carry you around and back down into the painting. They are subordinate to many of the components in the composition, yet they are part of the motif—a small variation on the circular forms observed in the moon, vase opening, mandolin hole and keys, and even the Gypsy's toenails. It isn't coincidental that this motif exists and this movement occurs—Rousseau chose to paint those stars in those locations.

> Reminding ourselves that the artist is responsible for all of the designing—everything—within the limits of the picture frame, we observe that nothing should be coincidental. Everything Rousseau gives us to consider is purposeful.

▶ **PRIMARY VISUAL MOVEMENT**

In his painting *Raft of the Medussa* (Fig. 5–23), Théodore Géricault established several visual paths of visual motion, including

1. Paths through the directional thrust of various shapes (axes),
2. Paths along primary contour lines, and
3. Paths through groupings of similar forms.

You observe a tremendous swelling of bodies on the right, terminating with the dark-skinned fellow waving a banner in an attempt to hail the ship on the misty horizon. He is the apex of a triangle (Illus. 5–9) moving down from his left and right, a triangle which has at its base a line slanting from the right down to the lower left, sharing the contour of the beam on the raft's deck. This primary grouping is visually dominant since it has the greatest degrees of contrast of lights and darks (value), texture details, and gestural variations. The visual path along the perimeter of this group establishes the primary visual path.

▶ Figure 5-23   Théodore Géricault, *Raft of Medusa* (Musée du Louvre, © Photo R.M.N.)

▶ SECONDARY VISUAL MOVEMENT

Very closely associated with this is the polygon path established along the rigging of the makeshift mast and the contours of the raft. This is the secondary path of movement which is bisected by the mast forming two more triangles, establishing the triangle as a primary organizational consideration of *Raft of the Medussa*. (See Fig. 5–23).

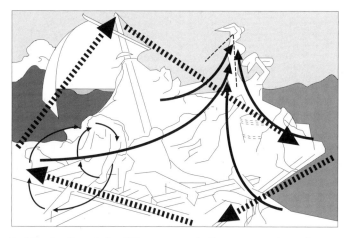

▶ Illustration 5-9   Diagrammatic Representation of Géricault, *Raft of Medusa*

▶ SUBORDINATE PATHS OF MOVEMENT

As you refer to Illustration 5–9, you see that there are several other subordinate paths of motion which follow other shapes, axes, contours, and value contrasts. Géricault used the visual components to "build" and populate his raft and to establish the seascape. He also arranged the components in a conspicuous manner to complement the drama of the image, thus complementing the content

▶ Figure 5-24   Beverly Pepper, *Thel*, 1975–77
(Steel, grass, 10⅛ × 135 feet, Hood Museum of Art, Dartmouth College, Hanover, N.H., purchased through the Fairchild Art Fund with a matching grant from the National Endowment for the Arts, Washington, D.C.)

▶ Figure 5-25   *Marcel Duchamp, Nude Descending A Staircase, No. 2*
(Oil on canvas, 58" × 35", Philadelphia Museum of Art, Louise and Walter Arensberg Collection)

of the work. Your eye immediately rises to the peak of action—you share in the drama of the moment.

> Movement serves to further the expressive objectives of the artist; to help communicate more effectively.

▶ MOVEMENT AND CLOSURE

These visual lines of movement in illustrations serve to "frame" most of the drama of the composition, except for the rise of humanity on the right. The concept of the implied boundary which keeps the grouping of visual forms in the composition from visually running off the picture plane is termed *closure*. It acts as a set of visual parenthesis to keep everything contained.

▶ MOVEMENT AND THE THREE-DIMENSIONAL ARTS

When applied to the three-dimensional arts, visual movement may be even more complex than previously outlined. In sculpture, for example, you are concerned with a form that occupies space and is visible from 360 degrees around, as well as from above. Therefore, in sculpture, movement is concerned with drawing the eye around, over, and through the piece, not just across it as in a two-dimensional work. All views and surfaces need to be visually rewarding, yet it is absolutely valid that there could be dominant and subordinate views—some sides of a sculpture may command more of the viewer's attention than others (Fig. 5–24).

▶ INDICATIONS OR IMAGES OF ACTUAL MOVEMENT

Earlier it was noted that "repetition and movement have intrinsic connotations of energy, activity, and dynamics." In reference to movement and its association with energy, we need to understand that there are two types of energy: *potential,* or energy at rest, and *kinetic,* or energy in action. Thus far, however, we have spoken only of visual movement, an implication of actual movement.

It is not uncommon for comic book artists to indicate the wagging tail of a dog or the path of a moving ball by selectively repeating some contours "behind" the tail or ball. This device for indicating actual movement on a static, two-dimensional plane was pioneered by the Futurists: early twentieth-century artists who wanted to capture the dynamics and activity of their increasingly mechanized world in art. In Duchamp's *Nude Descending a Staircase* (Fig. 5–25), the repetition of planes and contours represents actual movement. In fact, Duchamp was so successful in depicting action that some of his contemporaries subtitled this work "Explosion in a Shingle Factory."

▶ Figure 5-26   Jose de Rivera, *Infinity*
(©Smithsonian Institution, Washington, D.C.)

▶ KINETIC ART

Actual physical movement in art relates primarily to sculpture, although there are exceptions which we shall discuss shortly. At the simplest levels of kinetic art, a sculpture may be placed on a base that houses a motor, thereby turning the sculpture so that it reveals itself to the viewer and the viewer does not have to walk around it. The element of time, the fourth dimension, is thus involved: the time it takes for the image to present itself. Jose de Rivera's sculpture in front of the Museum of American History in Washington, D.C. (Fig. 5–26), incorporates such a motor and is, therefore, termed kinetic sculpture.

In some cases when a three-dimensional work cannot be easily seen from all sides, it is appropriate that it should revolve to maintain its full three-dimensional validity and enhance the viewing experience.

Few sculptors can be credited with inventing an art form, but Alexander Calder did exactly this. Trained as an engineer, it is understandable that he used wire and metal as his media. He found that when forms were suspended in air they would rotate according to the air currents; and when one form was suspended from another, it would also rotate according to the currents—sometimes in harmony with the first form, sometimes not. And the more forms you had, the more variables you had in terms of the movement directions and form relationships. These hanging, moving sculptures, termed *mobiles*, could take an infinite amount of time to present themselves. The hanging displays seen in many fast-food restaurants, grocery stores, and schools are variations on Calder's original invention.

The aesthetics of the mobile, while including continually changing and de-lightful shape relationships, involve a unity of visual components. This unity may center on a theme: All suspended elements may be related to a particular subject or concept. Or, the suspended elements and their supporting bars (the supports are part of the composition too, as they function like a sculpture stand) may be related by color or medium. In successful mobiles, there is a conspicuous visual unity of the visual components and their relationships.

An interesting outgrowth of the mobile and its orientation to visual dynamics is the inclusion of auditory elements in sculpture. Calder designed a mobile entitled *Red Gong* (Fig. 5–27) in which some of the rotating arms of the mobile would strike against plates of metal, also attached to the mobile, producing various

▶ Figure 5-27   Alexander Calder, *Red Gongs: Mobile*
(The Metropolitan Museum of Art, Fletcher Fund, 1955 [55.181a–f])

tones. Due to the variations in rotation, there would be corresponding variations in the arrangement of the sounds! Calder sought to expand the definitions of art by including time, motion, and sound as inherent characteristics.

The synthesis of kinetics and painting are two concepts that have remained relatively unexploited. Some artists have done paintings that have pieces cut out of them with moving images placed behind; some paintings are done in strips with contrasting strips moving behind. Even some billboard displays utilize vertical panels that rotate, collectively presenting different images on a single picture plane, according to what position the panels are in. While kinetics and two-dimensional art forms are not incongruous, they are concepts which have not been fully explored in relation to one another.

ECONOMY

Painters of landscapes seldom include every single tree. A painting or drawing of a tree seldom includes every leaf or limb. Similarly, most sculptors of portraits won't model every hair or every pore. Artists of two-and three-dimensional works employ selective vision, including what they feel is necessary while omitting what is not. All artists do this; they include what will best complement their expressive ends. This requires careful consideration of what is essential for the communication to be expressive and what is not.

> Economy implies a sense of thrift; nonessentials are avoided.

An image that employs severe economy is Kasimir Malevich's *White on White* (Fig. 5–28), a celebration of the extreme limits of pure form and tone in an image. Only two primary shapes are involved, a painted square on top of the square ground, and there is only the slightest value contrast of white to define the two squares. Why? Malevich wanted to strip through all levels of superficiality and nonessential imagery to communicate the most severe yet valid visual relationships he could imagine. Within this severity, the angular negative shapes, along with their varying values, establish a sense of tension and energy. He didn't feel he had

▶ Figure 5-28 Kasimir Malevich, *Suprematist Composition: White on White*, 1918
(Oil on canvas, 31¼" × 31¼", The Museum of Modern Art, New York)

▶ Figure 5-29   Arnaldo Pomodoro, *Triad*
(Donald M. Kendall Sculpture Garden at PepsiCo.)

to show bull fighters or street confrontations to arouse these emotions. Was he successful?

On the other hand, Jackson Pollock in his painting of *Autumn Rhythm*, which we have examined, has absolutely filled the picture plane with lines, shapes, values, colors, and textures. But, while the plane is filled, it is filled with *similar* lines, shapes, values, colors, and textures. Thus, Pollock has economically restricted his imagery to particular visual components, even though he has used them profusely. Economy yields harmony.

We see, therefore, that economy doesn't necessarily mean the use of the fewest possible visual components in a work: minimalism. Rather, in a larger sense,

---

Economy means the judicious choosing of what is and is not essential for effective communication: selectivity.

Arnaldo Pomodoro chose to leave some surfaces of his cylindrical sculptures (Fig. 5–29) solid and unbroken, whereas other surfaces appear broken, revealing a texturally rich and mechanized-looking interior seemingly subjected to ravaging decay. This economical use of solid as opposed to broken surfaces helps direct our vision and establish visual dominance and interest.

Renaissance architect Leon Battista Alberti believed that Classical beauty involved the perfect harmony of all visual parts; that nothing could be taken away from or added to a beautiful form without detracting from the form. This requires the judicious selection and application of visual factors: economy. Alberti's attitude is applicable to all art forms from all periods, not just the Classical.

Accent   Emphasis placed on an element in a composition by an artist to give that element particular visual significance. The relative visual prominence or dominance of a line as determined by its placement or location, attitude and direction, measure, and embellishment.

Approximate Symmetry   A minor variation of visual components from one side of a composition to the other while still maintaining a conspicuous similarity between the two sides.

Association   Relationship.

Asymmetrical Balance   A conspicuous, purposeful lack of sameness between the left and right sides of a composition that ultimately maintains a feeling of equilibrium. Syn.: OCCULT BALANCE.

Axis   A line (usually implied rather than actual) which runs through the length, height, or width of a form at that form's center. An axis may run through a volume, such as a rod through a rolling pin, or it may run across a surface, like a line across or down the middle of a page.

Balance   The arrangement of visual forces yielding a felt equilibrium.

Closure   The concept of the implied boundary which keeps the grouping of visual forms in the composition from visually running off the picture plane.

Contrast   Differences which are evident through comparison.

Convergence   A technique using lines or clusters of forms which proportionally diminish in scale or taper toward a common point located in the composition; most frequently, as forms get farther away they diminish in size, proportionally coming together toward a common point on or near the horizon line.

Dominance   Area or feature of a composition that is of primary visual importance thus commanding the attention of the viewer.

Economy   The judicious inclusion and exclusion of visual stimuli in a composition, usually involving a sense of thrift—nonessentials are avoided. Frequently yields the "essence" of a form.

Eurythmy   Proportional and other visual relationships in a composition that work well together and look "right." Syn.: UNITY.

Focal Point/Focus   Location on the picture plane to which the artist has directed your vision via artistic device which may include contrast, convergence, accent, or clarity of form.

Gestalt   A psychological or symbolic sense of completeness and total resolution yielded from an incomplete or open-ended configuration of parts.

Golden Mean Rectangle   A mathematically constructed rectangle with sides having a length-height ratio of about 5:8; considered by many cultures and individuals to have "ideal" proportions.

Harmony   Agreement of visual parts.

Hieratic Scale   A form of presentation perceived to be an effective means of showing the relative importance of figures within a composition; used by societies or individuals to depict the religious, political, or physical importance of an individual.

Kinetic art   Art that physically moves by natural or artificial (mechanical or nonmechanical) means.

Millennium   Period of one thousand years.

Mobile   Suspended sculpture that rotates according to air currents; invented by Alexander Calder.

Motif   A visual component conspicuously repeated in a composition; not necessarily involved in an individual pattern.

Movement   A path of visual direction that is determined by the artist's selective emphasis on and organization of various visual components.

Occult Balance   See ASYMMETRICAL BALANCE.

Proportion   The visual agreement of relative parts.

Radial Balance   The visual emphasis on the distribution of forms and forces around a central point.

Repetition   The recurrence of a visual component.

Rhythm   The viewing pace and movement along visual paths.

Rules of Thumb   Generalities which are handed down over time; usually taken for granted and not investigated or challenged.

Symmetrical Balance   The visual components on one side of a composition are mirror-imaged on the opposite side of the implied central axis of the work. May also be refered to as AXIAL BALANCE.

Tension   A strained relationship between the visual forces working in a composition and/or between the image and the viewer.

Unity   See EURYTHMY.

Variety   A simultaneous recognition of similarities and differences of visual parts.

DESIGNING: THEORY AND PRACTICE
UNIT PROJECTS

Appropriate media include any graphic or sculpture materials and their related processes that will yield a good visual presentation and last a reasonable amount of time in good condition. This may include traditional supplies, computer-assisted images, very good photocopying equipment, photography adaptations, and the like.

1. DOMINANCE AND ASSOCIATION

   a) Place a black circle in a picture frame along with other visual components, making that circle the most dominant visual element.

   b) In another frame of the same size, and placing the same black circle in the same location, make that circle subordinate to other more dominant visual elements. Don't let the circle be the focal point in the second composition.

   [Any media; mount both on a single page. Two- or three-dimensional.]

2. PROPORTION

   a) Compose a relatively simple composition of few lines and shapes in a particular format. Using that composition as your initial design, modify the proportions of its lines and shapes to accommodate two additional and significantly different formats of your choice.

   [Any media; mount all three on a single page.]

   b) Use the Golden Mean Rectangle as the proportional basis of an original composition. Leave the rectangle's lines of construction heavy—visually apparent—so that its structure can be seen in your composition.

   [May be objective or nonobjective; any media.]

   c) (1) Arrange a variety of geometric shapes and lines in a frame so that the visual proportions are satisfying.

   (2) In another frame, repeat the composition but greatly enlarge one visual compo-

nent beyond reason, keeping the rest of the composition the same as the first.

   (3) In a third frame, using the enlarged component as in the second frame, modify the rest of the composition to have satisfying visual proportions.

   [Any media; mount all three on a single page.]

3. BALANCE

   Create a composition that is *symmetrically balanced,* yet monotonous and boring. Then, repeating the same basic composition, elaborate on it while maintaining symmetry but making it stimulating and alive!

   [Any media; mount both on a single page.]

4. VARIETY AND HARMONY

   Mount many, many of the same item—nuts, bolts, acorn shells, pins, buttons, cotton balls—on a surface—board, tin, etc.—and, if desired, paint them one color to enhance their unity. In a second construction, using more of the same materials in relatively the same arrangement, add one or more different objects to add variety and enhance the resulting assemblage in a visually rewarding presentation.

   [Any media; any size.]

5. REPETITION AND MOVEMENT

   a) To compare the effects of movement in three repeated patterns, design a pattern that is based on the repetition of a single design unit/module (motif). Simplified shapes of everyday objects, numerals, letters, or shape relationships may be appropriate.

   (1) Do one version of the expanded pattern in *black and white;*

   (2) do a second version *reversing* the black and white (figure-ground); and

   (3) do a third version of the same pattern, using color.

   b) Arrange any images of three-dimensional solids so that their axial directions establish motion in a *circular* path that moves your eye from the outer edge to the inner area of a composition.

6. FIGURE-GROUND

Observing the dynamic effects of figure/ground reversals, design a composition where such reversals take place. Your subject matter may or may not be representational.

[Any media.]

7. KINETIC ART

Art that moves provides many challenging aesthetic and mechanical problems. Design an aesthetic form that is kinetic. (This may involve multiple parts.)

[Any media.]

8. MOTIF

Design a single shape and use it in a composition as the only motif as a positive and/or negative shape. It may be placed alone in some areas of the composition or in groups.

The motif may be repeated in the same or varying sizes. Create harmony and rhythm via the repetition of this motif.

[Any media.]

9. ECONOMY

On a single piece of paper, draw two picture frame borders.

a) Within one border design a fairly complex arrangement of lines and shapes.

b) In the second frame, selectively minimalize the visual elements of the first frame (in number, not size) while retaining the essence of the first composition's design.

[Any media.]

10. INDEPENDENT PROJECT

Write the instructions and provide the objectives for a project that is related to this chapter but not addressed in the aforementioned projects. Complete the project.

[Any media.]

SIX

The Visual Components of Art

CORNERSTONES OF EXPRESSION

The following figures/illustrations appear in the color insert: Figures 6-80, 6-101–6-105, 6-107, 6-110, 6-112–6-115, 6-116, 6-118; Illustrations 6-23, 6-25–6-30, 6-32–6-37, 6-39–6-41.

LINE AND DOT

▶ USAGE

As we begin our formal study of the visual components of art, let us remind ourselves that we are dealing with everyday concepts and vocabulary. Everyday vocabulary has a broad range of interpretations, however, which can complicate the assumed meanings of words. A line, for example, may call to mind something very mechanical and measured to one who is employed as a draftsman; yet to a writer a "line" of poetry may incorporate a full range of variables from the color of a rose to the utterings of a raven.

As part of the visual components of art, line and dot are considered together because of line's dependence on dot.

▶ OUR PERCEPTIONS OF LINE

Line may be perceived as a lot of different things, we have observed, such as the edge of a form or the expression of an emotion. Practically speaking, however, line does not exist in nature—it is a human invention. In contrast to what we may think, line is a conclusion, a result of our observation, not the natural starting point. It is an objective or subjective response to vision or experience.

> Line is a record of vision and feeling.

A tree limb, for example, is predominantly linear. We observe the direction of growth of that limb and interpret that direction with line. Also, a tree limb has a

▶ Figure 6-1
(Catherine Coburn)

▶ Figure 6-2 Amedeo Modigliani, *Head of a Woman* (National Gallery of Art, Washington, Chester Dale Collection)

▶ Figure 6-3 Odilon Redon, *Head of a Veiled Woman* (National Gallery of Art, Washington, Rosenwald Collection)

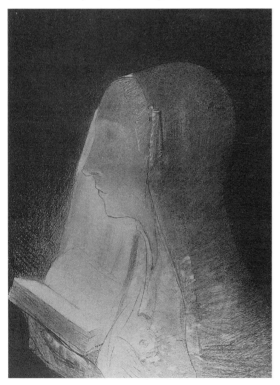

long shape—it is the edge of that shape we label as a line, or *contour*. We observe the limb and then look for the edge of that limb to draw the lines which we determine to make up the shape of that limb.

Therefore, a function of contour includes objectively describing a form by tracing its outline. Here it is known as a *primary contour*. Along the outside edge of the form the primary contour line is used to describe the meeting of positive and negative shapes which may be simple or may be complex (Fig. 6–2, Amedeo Modigliani).

Not all contours trace the very outside of a shape, however. Sometimes the contours of a form follow the outside and then move to the inside of a shape along another shape-edge known as a *secondary contour*. Additionally, within a shape there may be secondary shapes. Secondary contours may or may not share part of a shape's primary contour. Look at Odilon Redon's drawing entitled *Head of a Veiled Woman* (Fig. 6–3). Observe how the primary contour line of the forehead passes down over the nose to the upper lip, and then that line continues to the inside of the form, becoming a secondary contour where it defines the upper lip, and stops. Continuing down the neck, observe how the primary contour again moves inside the form. And in the open bodice of the dress there are several other shapes defined again by line—all defined by secondary contours.

The way you looked at contours in this example is very similar to the way you would draw using contour lines. One type of contour drawing is the *blind contour drawing*, which is done by looking only at the subject matter—not the page—during the drawing process. A *continuous contour drawing* is done without lifting the pencil from the page. There may be blind continuous contour drawings, too.

Contour defines not only the edges of shapes that meet, but also where value, color, and/or texture areas come together (Juan Gris, Fig. 6–4). The contour line defines the place of contrast. In this situation, the placement of contour is determined as a result of our observation, and your determination of where the line of contrast is may be different from someone else's. Therefore, you see that contour drawings can be highly personalized or subjective.

Sculptor David Smith used steel as his medium to "draw in space" and define the limits of the shapes of mountains, clouds, and sky in his *Hudson River Landscape* (Fig. 6–5). Again, you see how line is an invention of humankind.

▶ LINE AND MOVEMENT

Primary and secondary contours contribute significantly to visual movement over a form. They are arranged by the artist to keep you moving *through* a form, not just around it. The lines establish more than one visual path which is so very important to visual stimulation.

This relationship of primary and secondary contours can be seen in sculpture, as well. In observing Figure 6–6 (Max Bill), your vision has been directed through several paths of movement by the primary contour moving from the outside to the inside of the form, creating secondary contours.

Interesting and varied visual paths along contours can be found in many natural forms, as well. If you look at bones, for example, as Henry Moore did, you find the same relationship of the external to the internal.

> The primary contours move from the outside to the inside, keeping the form more interesting visually.

▶ Figure 6-4   Juan Gris, *Fantomas*
(National Gallery of Art, Washington, Chester Dale Fund)

▶ Figure 6-5   David Smith, *Hudson River Landscape*
(Purchase, Collection of Whitney Museum of American Art, New York, Photo by Geoffrey Clements ©1993, ©1994 Estate of David Smith, VAGA, New York)

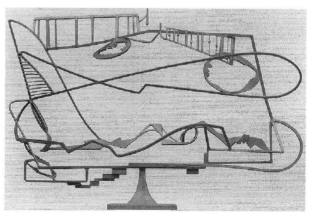

▶ Figure 6-6   Max Bill, *Monoangulated Surface in Space*, 1959
(©Detroit Institute of Arts, gift of W. Hawkins Ferry)

Seashells, water-eroded rocks, tree trunks, and driftwood also exhibit this relationship of contours. In an effort to understand what makes natural forms so dynamic, Moore observed this movement along contours and applied the principles to his own work.

Cross-contour is another concept regarding contour that shows line to be a result of our observations. Cross-contours usually appear to run perpendicular to the primary and/or secondary contours. They show the undulations of surfaces between contours, either actual—as in sculptures—or implied—as in Figure 6–7.

▶ GRAPHIC LINE

In the language of geometry, a line is the path of a moving point. But art deals with visual expression, so

> In art we must be oriented to line as the *visible* path of a moving point, such as the path of a pencil or pen, a plow on a field, or even an Etch-a-Sketch®.

A line made with a pencil on a page has definable length. And when you look very closely, you also observe a definable width. Therefore, we observe that a line is a long, narrow shape. When a long, narrow shape's length is conspicuously dominant over its width you have no problem referring to it as a line.

In some cases, such as the painting by Frank Stella (Fig. 6–8), there may be trouble defining some of the visual components as line or shape. Some of the shapes look like short lines and some of the short lines look like small shapes. Do not become unsettled about this dichotomy, however, as heroes are going to be neither made nor sacrificed regarding this particular problem of semantics. Observing this type of line-shape relationship is fun and demonstrates your responsiveness to varying yet similar visual characteristics of line and shape.

▶ Figure 6-7
(Photo by Grace Smith)

▶ WHAT LINE IS

Understanding that line is a human invention, we need to understand what line is and what it can do. As the visible path of a moving point, we realize that

▶ Figure 6-8   Frank Stella, *Sinjerli Variation I*
(Copyright ARS, NY, Art Resource, NY)

> There are as many different kinds of lines as there are implements which can make a point: your toe in the sand, a pen on a page, a brush on a canvas, and a chisel in stone, to name just a few.

The "point" is as much of a variable as is the kind of line or path it can make.

The path made by a moving point can be reduced to two basic line types: straight and curved. There are numerous examples in art of images that have many, many lines, such as Albrecht Dürer's *Melencholia I* (Fig. 6–9). But after an analysis of all the lines that one can see in Dürer's

▶ Figure 6-9   Albrecht Durer, *Melancholia I*
(Courtesy of The Fogg Art Museum, Harvard University Art Museums, gift of William Gray from the Francis Calley Gray Collections of Engravings)

▶ Figure 6-10   Eriko, 1993

engraving, one observes that there are still two basic line types.

Within this group of two line types, there are subtypes, the most notable of which is the *calligraphic* line that has its origins in the calligraphy of oriental masters. The nature of the oriental writing is carried over into oriental art (Fig. 6–10). Calligraphic lines are as variable and sensitively rendered in length and width in the paintings as they are in the writing. This calligraphic nature of the line is the result of the tool and technique used by oriental artists. Bamboo brushes with long bristles respond to the subtle pressures of the artist's hand. Used with ink, the brush records these variations very well.

As a calligraphic line changes in length and width, it appears to advance or recede in space: The bolder it is, the closer it appears; the thinner and more delicate the line becomes, the more it appears to recede (Illus. 6–1). Thus, you see how a line drawing can give the impression of a fully three-dimensional form. The calligraphic line can appear to sculpt the form as the shapes twist, turn, advance, and recede in space. When a calligraphic contour line appears to twist, turn, advance, and recede in space, we refer to it as modeling the form. The line defines the three-dimensionality of the form the same way that clay can be modeled to define a form—the line appears plastic. That is, the line appears to be a pliable or flexible form that can change its shape and direction and can hold that new impression. Also note that a straight line as well as a curved line can be calligraphic.

Producing a calligraphic line requires a drawing tool or medium that is very responsive to the hand. It needs to be flexible, broad, and soft so that more or less of the medium can make contact with the ground according to the pressure applied.

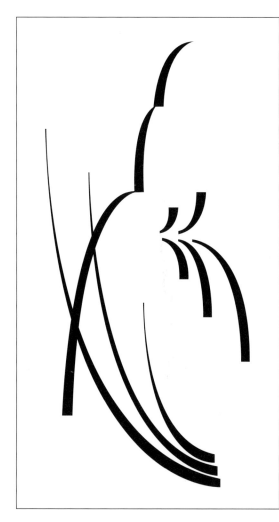

▶ Illustration 6-1 Calligraphic Lines

▶ Figure 6-11 Pablo Picasso,
Le Vieux Musicien (Source Unknown)

Technique will establish the identifiable character of a project or work of art, be it two- or three-dimensional. (Fig. 6–11).

It is necessary to apply a medium to a contrasting ground to make a line.

> **A line is not visible without contrast.**

▶ VARIABLES AFFECTING LINE

Line is dependent upon tool, technique, medium, and ground, and from the previous topic, "What Line Is," we see that the tool plays a significant part in the quality of the line. The line-producing tool can be any implement that

1. Will work in harmony with the selected medium, and
2. Will produce an image in harmony with the artist's expressive objectives.

However, variations on the traditional process of making marks on a page are also practical and expressive. Frequently one medium, when applied with a broad application over another, can be scratched or scraped through to reveal contrasting values or colors underneath (Fig. 6–56). This technique is known as *sgraffito*. If a medium to be scratched through is dry, the resulting line character may be ragged and course. On the other hand, a line may appear smooth and even if the upper medium is wet when scratched through.

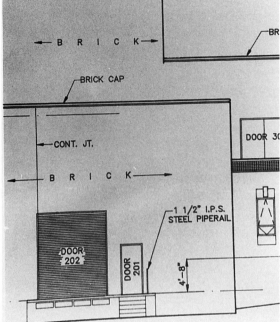

▶ Figure 6-12

While sgraffito is not suited for all work, especially computer assisted imagery, neither is casting in bronze nor carving in stone suited for all sculptures. Therefore, make choices concerning tool, technique, and medium that are purposeful and not taken for granted as paper and pencil too often are.

> A technique, tool, or medium is appropriate,* practical, or expressive if it works to complement the artist's expressive objectives in a composition.

*When describing the use of art media, avoid using the word *acceptable* as it implies nonart qualifiers in determining success.

▶ WHAT LINE CAN DO...

As an Objective Device

One of the primary functions of line as a component of visual communication is to convey information either by writing or by illustration (Fig. 6-12). That is, it is primarily a graphic device used to describe and define objective characteristics: shape, texture, and the like—and to serve as a record of vision. In a name, line forms the letters used to identify the owner of the name. From generalized outline drawings to detailed renderings and from stick figures to sophisticated hieroglyphs, line defines shape relationships.

As a Subjective Device

Line is considered the primary visual component because it not only has descriptive potential by defining shapes and communicating objective information, but it has tremendous expressive potential as well—it is considerably more than just a record of vision. A variety of considerations affect line's expressive nature (Fig. 6-13). You should be sensitive to these as you endeavor to make art a vehicle of your expression.

A factor that contributes to the interpretation of the meaning of a line is the emphasis an individual places on the line. Take a look at your signature. Take a look at someone else's signature. You see that there are some things that are similar and some that are different. Aside from the fact that one signature may be larger or smaller than another and the names are different, one of the basic differences between one signature and another is the distinctive quality of each individual's line. This distinctive quality is determined by the measure, type, direction, character, and accent of the line.

► PHYSICAL PROPERTIES OF LINE

Three properties of line affect the visual quality of a line. The first property—and the simplest to understand—is the dimension of a line, its *measure*, such as length and width. Another objective property of line is its type: straight or curved (Illus. 6–2). And the final property of a line is its character: edge quality, value, individual texture, and other visual effects that are extremely subjective and personalized, dependent upon the way the maker of the line applies the medium to the ground.

Line Character

Line character, whether observed in a signature or other graphic application, is partially determined by the nature of the artist: convictions, energies, passions, and mental and physical makeup. The tool an artist uses responds to the calm or anxiety of the artist; it reflects inner trembles and tumults. An artist's line may give something away about that artist's personality —line is autobiographical! Line, therefore, is a record of the artist's response to vision and sensation (Fig. 6–13).

Line Type and Direction

Not all line types are "read" the same way—each line is an individual component of expression, depending on how the artist or designer applies it to the page. Straight lines as compared to curved lines most frequently imply rigidity and sureness, whereas curved lines inherently evoke fluid motion and more ease than a straight line. However, the effect of a *type* of line is significantly dependent upon that line's direction.

    The direction of a line on the page, relative to the picture frame, can be a sig-

► Figure 6-13   Willem de Kooning, *Woman and Bicycle*
(Collection of Whitney Museum of American Art, New York, Purchase, Photo by ©1989 Geoffrey Clements, New York)

nificant factor in determining the meaning of a line. For example, a column, fence post, or soldier at attention implies unwavering stability and strength, resolution, and precision. If you were to draw the simple essence of the soldier, column, or post, you would probably draw a vertical, simple, regular straight line. Now consider a human runner, a sprinter: He attacks the air ahead of him on an angle with his head stretched way out ahead of his feet. Again, if you were to draw the essence of the sprinter—action—you would probably draw a simple diagonal line. All of the limbs of the runner might yield a series of angular lines producing a

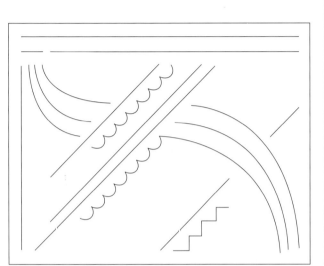

▶ Illustration 6-2   Line Types, Straight and Curved

▶ Illustration 6-3   Line Directions

▶ Figure 6-14   Alberto Giacometti, *Dog*
(Hirshhorn Museum and Sculpture Garden, Smithsonian Institution,
Gift of Joseph H. Hirshhorn, 1966; Tate Gallery, London/Art Resource,
NY)

▶ Figure 6-15   Frederic Remington, *The Stampede*
(The Thomas Gilcrease Institute of American History and Art, Gilcrease Museum)

zigzag effect which would enhance the effect of action and dynamics. If you wanted to convey the essence of calm or quiet, you can now see that a horizontal line (as in a calm ocean or a person at rest) would be quite appropriate, and it is clear how curved or wavy horizontal lines would accomplish this effect best. Thus, lines or shapes with vertical, diagonal, and horizontal directional thrusts are expressive because of their type and the directions in which they lie (see Illus. 6–3).

The pencil at the end of the hand is like the needle on a seismograph: The seismograph measures the dynamics of the earth's surface and the pencil responds to the whole personality of the artist.

▶ Figure 6-16   Lorrie Goulet, *Catalyst #2*
(The National Museum of Women in the Arts, Gift of Mr. and Mrs. Kenneth Prescott; ©1994 Lorrie Goulet/VAGA, New York)

▶ Figure 6-17   Jack Beal, *Girl Reading*
(Frumkin/Adams Gallery, Photo by Eric Pollitzer)

▶ **LINE ACCENT**

Another factor that contributes to the meaning of a line is its accent: the relative visual prominence or dominance of a line. Again, there is no formula for applying the right "amount" of accent, yet accent can be achieved by varying degrees of contrast between the line and its surroundings. Personal selectivity and subjective considerations determine how much visual accent is appropriate for a given expressive goal.

Elements which contribute to the visual accent of a line involve

1. The placement or location of a line on the picture plane;
2. A line's attitude and direction relative to other components in the composition and the picture frame;
3. A line's measure relative to other visual components in the visual field; and
4. The embellishment of a line, or how the artist has "dressed up" the line, giving it a particular visual identity. (Factors which affect embellishment include the degree of contrast between the line and its surroundings, such as value, color, and texture.

▶ DOT

Dot, along with its synonym, point, functions not only to provide the origin of a line, but also serves to enhance a composition. Therefore, "dot" is often perceived as subordinate to "line." A dot is the smallest visual component on a ground. It has only enough length and width to be visible.

▶ DOT AND CONTRAST: VALUE AND SHAPE

Individually, dots on a page or canvas are almost imperceptible due to their inherently small size, just as the pixels are on a computer monitor or TV set. To establish their presence, therefore, they need to be presented in significant contrast to their surrounding area—contrasting in value, color, or both. James Whistler's *Nocturne in Black and Gold: Falling Rocket* (Fig. 6–18) utilizes dots—lots of dots—of bright paint against a dark background to simulate fireworks displays. These dots charge the negative shapes with energy and add visual motion to the composition, drawing the viewer's eye up and around the composition.

In addition to value and color contrast, "dot" needs to become "dots" in order to establish a visual entity. This can be seen in an enlarged newspaper photograph (Fig. 6–19). Black dots are placed quite close together and even overlap one another to form dark areas. Similarly, they are placed farther apart to create lighter ones.

Thus, by their association with other dots, dots can collectively form images: the dots "mix" in your mind's eye, producing a full range of even gradations of value from light to dark. In drawing, this effect is produced by stippling.

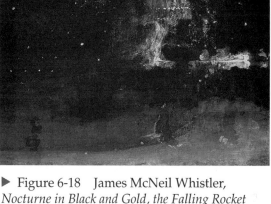

▶ Figure 6-18　James McNeil Whistler, *Nocturne in Black and Gold, the Falling Rocket* (Gift of Dexter M. Ferry, Jr., ©The Detroit Institute of Arts 1989)

▶ Figure 6-19

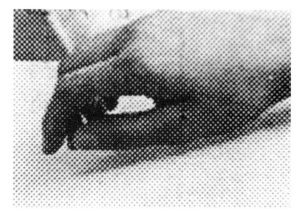

▶ Figure 6-20   Georges Seurat, *A Sunday on La Grande Jatte*
(Helen Birch Bartlett Memorial Collection, 1926, 224; Photograph ©1994, The Art Institute of Chicago, All Rights Reserved)

▶ Figure 6-21   Roy Lichtenstein, *Brushstrokes* 1967
(©Lichtenstein/VAGA, New York, 1985)

▶ DOT AND COLOR

Dots of various colors can be placed collectively so that they, too, can be read by your mind's eye as a gradually changing or even color. Whereas most artists have traditionally mixed different pigments on their palettes to form the desired hues before applying them to their canvases, the Post-Impressionists, such as Seurat, mixed their colors somewhat differently: They exploited the principle of the visual fusion of dots (Fig. 6–20). Seurat and other Post-Impressionists exploited the technique known as *pointillism*: the application of paint in small dabs or dots of color to a ground.

> The colors are intended to visually mix in the eye of the viewer as opposed to being physically mixed on the artist's palette.

Since then, other artists have taken this same principle of vision and made both objective and nonobjective works that are quite stimulating, visually. Richard Anuszkiewicz and Roy Lichtenstein (Fig. 6-21) have each oriented their use of colored "dots" to produce carefully orchestrated optical effects. Works that juxtapose vibrant colors and other components for heightened optical effects and negate traditional spatial references are examples of *Op Art*. Lichtenstein goes a step further by applying these principles to images from the "pop" culture, producing works in the style of "Pop Art."

▶ DOT AND LINE

One of the primary effects of using individual dots is suggesting lines. For example, we see the Big Dipper at night because the individual stars are bright, close enough together to suggest lines, and reminiscent of a familiar shape. In Rousseau's *Sleeping Gypsy* (see Fig. 5–22), we referred to movement across the sky being facilitated by the stars' positions. We associated this with a connect-the-dot game. Thus we see how dots can build implied shapes—gestalt—and direct visual movement.

You have observed how dot is very closely aligned with line. Dot is also closely related to shape, for by mathematical definition a dot has neither length nor width. However, like line, dot must have length and width to be visible. Therefore, if dots do have length and width they are two-dimensional; they are shapes. As you look back at most of these examples, you will observe that the dots really do look like shapes. This is especially true in sculpture.

Let us conclude that dot, while being an independent visual component, is almost never separated from line and shape, and that it can be affected by value and color. Used collectively, dots can effect a textural quality. Therefore, dot—like line—works with each of the visual components. While it may seem insignificant visually, it is not insignificant compositionally.

▶ Figure 6-22   Arnaldo Pomodoro, *Big Disc (Grand Disco)*
(Donald M. Kendall Sculpture Garden at Pepsi Co.)

▶ **SECTION GLOSSARY**

Accent   The relative visual prominence or dominance of a line as determined by its placement or location, attitude and direction, measure and embellishment.

Blind Contour Drawing   A contour drawing which is done by looking only at the subject matter—not the page—during the drawing process.

Calligraphic Line   A free-flowing line (curved or straight) which changes in length and width. Syn.: PLASTIC or MODELED LINE; See PLASTIC.

Character   Edge quality, value, individual texture, and other visual effects that are extremely subjective and personalized, dependent upon the way the maker of the line applies the medium to the ground.

Continuous Contour Drawing   A contour drawing done without lifting the pencil from the page.

Contour Line   A line which notes the edge of shape, color, texture, or value areas, and the change of direction of shape edges and surfaces.

Cross-Contour   A line which traces the undulations of a surface between two points of a primary and/or secondary contour.

Dot   The smallest visual component on a ground, having only enough contrast against the ground as to be visible. Syn.: POINT.

Line   The visible path of a moving point.

Measure   The length and width of a line.

Model   Able to be shaped at will, usually regarding a plastic medium. See PLASTIC.

Primary Contour   A line which describes a form by tracing its outline. Syn.: OUTLINE.

Secondary Contour   A line which describes changes of shape, color, texture, or value areas, and the change of direction of shape edges and surfaces which lie inside of the primary contour.

Sgraffito   One medium scratched or scraped through to reveal a contrasting value or color beneath it.

Stippling   A graphic process using small dots of varying proximity to one another for the purpose of making value gradations.

Tool   Any implement that will work in harmony with the selected medium to produce an image that is in harmony with the artist's expressive objectives.

Type   Straight or curved lines.

SECTION PROJECTS: LINE AND DOT

1. LINE: GRAPHIC DEVICE VS. RESPONSE TO DIRECTION

   a) Execute a carefully rendered contour drawing of a fairly complex tree branch that has no leaves, paying particular attention to subtle changes of direction of that branch.

   b) Next, using a soft watercolor brush, respond to the general shape of the branch, allowing yourself to "feel" the direction of its growth and letting that directional movement be apparent in your work.

   [Mount both on a single page.]

   Careful contour drawing requires very close observation of changes in the direction of a subject's edge; therefore, these contour projects—when done properly—will take a bit of time and may leave you somewhat fatigued.

2. PRIMARY AND SECONDARY CONTOURS

   a) Observing the hand you do not use to draw with, make a contour drawing of that hand incorporating the *primary contour* only; place the hand in an interesting position.

   b) Observing the same hand, draw the edge of the form and follow it to the inside when a shape-edge moves from the outside to the inside of the hand (*secondary contour*). Observe how this contributes to the impression of a three-dimensional, modeled form.

   [Ink or felt-tip on paper or Bristol board; mount both on a single page.]

3. CROSS-CONTOUR

   Line can further model the three-dimensionality of a form when cross-contours are drawn.

   Observing a relatively complex object, relate the three-dimensional quality of that form by drawing it with cross-contours. Establish the primary contour first, then add the cross-contours. Remember, maintain good visual organization of your subject matter on the page.

   [Ink or felt-tip on paper or Bristol board.]

4. BLIND AND CONTINUOUS CONTOUR

   A *blind contour* drawing is done by looking at the subject matter only, not the page. Although the finished drawing may be somewhat out of proportion, it will have accurate elements. *Continuous contour* involves drawing that subject with a single line that has only one beginning and ends when you finish the drawing. It requires that the artist draw slowly and carefully, noting the subtle changes of direction of edge and contour. The continuous line contributes to a feeling of movement and fluidity.

   Make a *blind, continuous contour drawing* of yourself—a self-portrait—using a good-quality felt tip pen. Be careful that your ground is not so porous that the ink bleeds when you are drawing slowly.

5. THREE-DIMENSIONAL—"SPACE DRAWINGS"

   a) Using a single length of wire, explore the three dimensions of space: height, width, and depth. Do so in a manner that is visually rewarding. If you are using a soft wire, you may consider hammering it in some areas to make the visual line (wire) have varying proportions, as in a calligraphic drawing.

   [Any wire-type yielding a final form about 14 inches in its largest dimension; mount on a base that complements the "maquette," unless the form is intended to be free-standing.]

   b) Using a single length of wire, execute a "space drawing" of your foot, noting primary, secondary, and cross-contours as they (1) define the form and (2) add visual significance to the resulting sculpture.

   (For variety and emphasis, consider using tissue paper to establish actual planes between some of the wire-contours.)

6. LINE TYPE

   One line type next to another line type emphasizes the differences between the two, a principle of contrast known as simultaneous contrast.

   Make a composition involving varying measures of one line type, then add a single line of any measure but of a different type for contrast.

   [Any media.]

7. LINE AND SHAPE

Exploiting principles of measure, complete two compositions to be mounted on a single page using lines of any type: the first being made up of long and short *thin* lines; the second composition being made up of long and short *fat* lines, trying to keep an emphasis on line as opposed to shape.

Don't forget that the negative shapes will contribute to variety. Utilize them as a compositional consideration.
[Any media.]

8. LINE AND SPACE

Imagine your signature being written in space and wrapped around an imaginary glass cylinder.

Draw that image, making the lines of your signature that are closer to you bolder and the lines that are farther away less bold, evoking the impression that the signature really does advance and recede in three-dimensional space. You might even want to use cast shadows to heighten the illusion.

Utilize the principles of *calligraphic line*.
[Any media.]

9. DOT

Dots which are close together in a linear arrangement direct visual motion. Dots which are gradually spread out along an implied line increase or decrease visual motion and rhythm.

Design a composition where the speed of the viewer's eye moving around an image is controlled by the spacing of dots. Your subject matter may be objective or nonobjective.
[Any media.]

10. SGRAFFITO

Sgraffito can yield interesting visual effects as the artist scratches through one medium and hue or value to reveal a contrasting hue or value beneath. Additionally, sgraffito can be fun, as the technique is not a traditional one and new experiences are usually rewarding.

Working in the sgraffito technique, design a composition that is dynamic and makes the sgraffito technique a dominant and meaningful part of the visual image. Experiment with your tools and media, perhaps involving those experiments in your image.
[Any media.]

11. INDEPENDENT PROJECT

Write the instructions and provide the objectives for a project that is related to this chapter but not addressed in the aforementioned projects. Complete the project.
[Any media.]

SHAPE

▶ **USAGE**

O ur world is filled with direct and indirect references to shape. We walk outside and see the shape of the clouds, trees, mountains, and buildings. People, animals, and all other living things come in quite a variety of shapes, as well. Yet, when we observe that there are countless variations on the shapes of things, we imprecisely assign the same, general shape characteristics to buildings, mountains, and people. We make lollipops

▶ Illustration 6-4   Shape Simplification, *Snap the Whip*

▶ Figure 6-23   Winslow Homer, *Snap the Whip*
(The Metropolitan Museum of Art, Gift of Christian A. Zabriskie, 1950 (50.41)

and trees, and tepees and mountains, look very similar—we call upon our left brain hemisphere to assign symbolic or generic shapes to these forms instead of relying on the particular skills of our right hemisphere to respond to what we actually see.

Additionally, our speech involves misleading references to shape. We speak of "the shape of things to come" and putting things "in shape"; we ask disobedient people to "shape up"; we define the condition of one's mental state as being in "bad" shape after the loss of a loved one or a person's physical condition as being "in" or "out" of shape. Shape, therefore, is a meaningful yet complex word used to describe our everyday world.

▶ OUR PERCEPTIONS OF SHAPE

Since we find shape everywhere around us, do we conclude that there are just about as many different kinds of shapes and shape relationships as there are objects that can be named? Is the shape of a door significantly different from the shape of a wall, and is the shape of a ball really so different from the shape of an orange or pea? Light bulbs and pears have similar shapes, as do piles of sand and piles of furniture. For hundreds of years, artists and scientists have concluded from their observations of our world that there are three basic shapes found in nature: the circle, rectangle, and triangle, Cezanne being one of the most recent artists to perpetuate this concept. Generally speaking, therefore, all forms in nature are

1. Circular, triangular, or rectangular—in other words, geometric shapes;
2. Combinations of these three shapes; and/or
3. Slight variations of them.

Interestingly, the same can be said of manufactured forms.

Rectilinear shapes are made up of straight lines, and *curvilinear shapes* are comprised of curved lines. If the world around us is primarily made up of these two classifications of *geometric* shapes, then what are the "slight variations" just mentioned? We know that all shapes are not necessarily symmetrical nor do they give the appearance of being mathematically constructed, as do most geometric shapes. Some shapes, such as lima beans and octopi or cumulus clouds and amoebas have gradually undulating and somewhat unpredictable contours which deny the precision of a drafting table. Forms such as these are termed *organic*. They may possess some regular curves, but their overall free-flowing contours and similarities to the shapes of living forms determines their organic shape classification (Miró, Fig. 6–24). It is easy to see why the term *biomorphic* is a synonym for "organic" when referring to shape.

> In art, it is not uncommon to have a single composition that contains both geometric and organic shapes.

▶ WHAT SHAPE IS

We can conclude from our observations that we are surrounded by shapes that are of two primary classifications: organic and geometric. These are the shapes we are used to; in most cases these are the shapes we can hold in our hands or physically touch. But many shapes are not physically separated from their surroundings. Instead, a smaller shape may be part of a larger shape, such as a nose on a face or a door on a house.

Additionally, there are more subtle considerations for a shape: One shape may stop where another starts without having any change in physical structure. For example, a patterned shirt or blouse has many lines and colors. The edge of one color area meeting another establishes the limit of that colored shape area.

> Shape is an area that has an actual or implied limit.

The actual limit may be a drawn contour line or the edge of a physical form. The implied limit may be the location of a visual contrast from one value, color, or texture to another (Braque, Fig. 6–25).

Shapes are created in a variety of ways. Two-dimensionally, they may be established by a drawn or painted contour. Or, if using a wide tool such as a litho crayon or broad paint brush, one stroke of the tool may establish an entire shape. Monet's *Rue St. Denis, Fête Nationale du 30 Juin, 1878* (Fig. 6–26) depicts many flags and many parts of flags painted with but a single stroke of the brush. What is particularly noteworthy is that the brush strokes give the direction and define the shapes of the flags. Monet's self-confidence and sureness allowed him to accomplish so much with a single stroke.

▶ SHAPES AND SPACE

The shapes we are surrounded by have both two and three dimensions. The differences among these shapes lies in the fact that two-dimensional (2-D) shapes have length and height, whereas three-dimensional (3-D) shapes have length, height, and width—sometimes referred to as depth (Illus. 6–5).

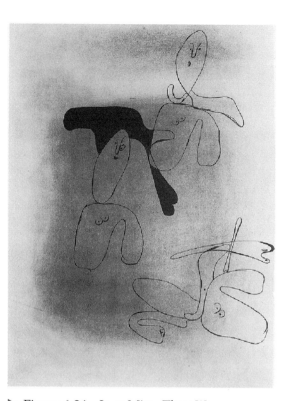

▶ Figure 6-24   Joan Miro, *Three Women*
(National Gallery of Art, Washington, Gift of Frank and Jeannette Eyerly)

▶ Figure 6-25   Georges Braque, *The Pink Tablecloth*
(Photograph Courtesy of The Chrysler Museum, Norfolk, Virginia, c ADAGP)

▶ Figure 6-26   Monet, *Rue St. Denis, Fête
Nationale du Juin 1878*
(Rouen, Musee des Beaux-Arts)

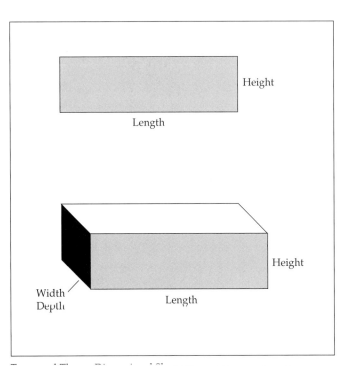

▶ Illustration 6-5   Two- and Three-Dimensional
Shapes

Two-Dimensional Concerns

A *plane* is an actual or implied, limited or
unlimited two-dimensional surface that
has no mass and which may exist in two-
or three-dimensional space. Planes may
be either *curvilinear* or *rectilinear* (see Illus.
6–6). A two-dimensional shape/plane
may appear to lie flat on the picture plane
or advance from or recede through the
picture plane. On a two-dimensional
ground, the spatial reference of a traditional rectangular plane will appear to advance or recede depending on a sense of
convergence as determined by the direction and emphasis of its parallel sides (see
Illus. 6–6; Fig. 6–27).

In mathematical applications, planes
have only implied surfaces. In art, however, we conceive of planes as being actual
and/or implied surfaces. Additionally, in
artistic applications it is perceived that
these planes may be flat and curved. Look
at a flat sheet of paper, for example, which
has the primary dimensions of length and
height. For practical reasons, negate the
consideration of its being a three-dimensional shape and consider it a plane, since
it has such a minimal edge (depth). In addition to being flat, the piece of paper—
the plane—may also have a curved surface, as in the form of a scroll: The rectangular plane rolls and changes direction,
but it is still a plane, nonetheless. And,
since the scroll does not come into contact
with any other shapes or planes and does
not define a volume, it is an open plane.
An open-ended cylinder, on the other
hand, has a curved surface, yet defines a

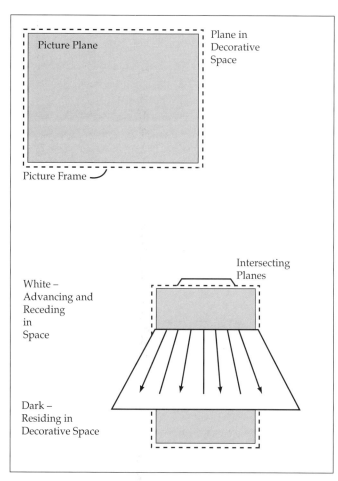

Picture Plane

Plane in Decorative Space

Picture Frame

White – Advancing and Receding in Space

Intersecting Planes

Dark – Residing in Decorative Space

▶ Illustration 6-6   Planes

▶ Illustration 6-7   Continuous Planes: Planes With Continuous Surfaces

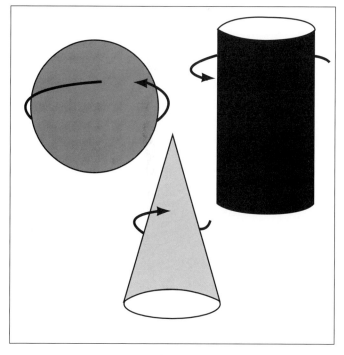

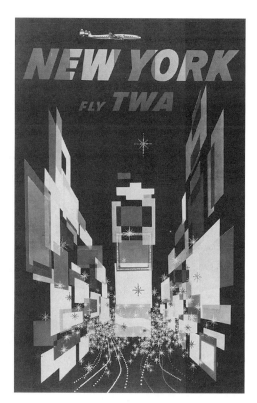

▶ Figure 6-27   David Klein, *New York, TWA*
(1956, Offset lithograph, printed in color, 40 × 25"
The Museum of Modern Art, New York, Gift of Trans World Airlines)

113

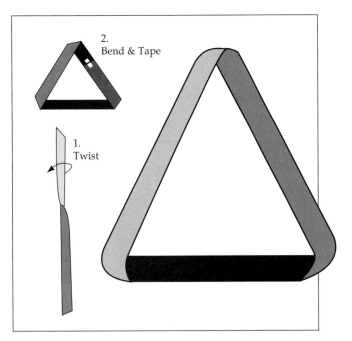

> ▶ Illustration 6-8   Mobius Strip: A Three-Dimensional Form With One Continuous Surface/Plane

volume—the actual space or area a three-dimensional form displaces or circumscribes. Thus, the cylinder is an example of a continuous plane, as would be a sphere or an open-ended cone: Continuous planes define volumes (Illus. 6–7).

A favorite trick of the physicists is to make a construction from a long, thin piece of paper—a long, thin plane. By giving the two-sided strip of paper a single twist and joining the ends with tape, a construction that has only one surface or plane is made, known as a Möbius strip (Illus. 6–8).

Therefore, don't have a mental image of a plane as having to be flat. A plane may twist, turn, advance, and recede in space. Depending on the direction of parallel sides, a plane may also appear to advance and recede in space, changing the space it occupies from a two-dimensional to a three-dimensional concern.

Three-Dimensional Concerns

If the shapes which make up a human face or body were simplified, you would see the face or body as a series of planes. The relationship of one plane to another—the planar relationships—define the form. If a plane is bent or creased, the crease—the abrupt change in the surface's direction—makes two planes by having established a limit to the shape. A diamond, for example, is faceted—it has many planes which establish its final form. Therefore, as seen in the diamond or the human face, a series of two-dimensional planes can construct a three-dimensional form.

Depending on the degree of convergence of the sides of a plane and/or its curvature, the implied space a plane occupies may appear infinite or very shallow. A plane, therefore, can "model" the degree of three-dimensional space it occu-

> ▶ Illustration 6-9   Planes Not Restricted to Flat Rectilinear Shapes

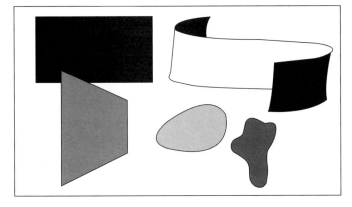

pies. Accordingly, space can be modeled—as shapes and lines can be, and we may refer to three-dimensional space as being plastic space (Illus. 6–10).

> We conclude that a plane can be a plastic shape and the space it occupies may be plastic, as well.

The two-dimensional arts show the three-dimensionality of a form by clearly defining planar relationships using contrasts of line, shape, value, color, and texture. Sculptors may actually build the planes which make up a form (Picasso and Kadisman, Figs. 6–28 and 6–29).

All sculptures are made out of media. Those made out of a physical medium, such as clay, steel, stone, bronze, and the like (as opposed to light and gas forms) involve a tangible material that can be manipulated—an actual three-dimensional substance. Many shapes made up of these substances appear to fill up a volume or displace space. In other words, they have *mass*. Mass implies a feeling of bulk and density—a feeling of solidity; "matter" between the contours. The surface of a form is the limit of its mass and the limit of its shape.

In painting, artists allude to qualities of massiveness by carefully shading their shapes to imply a three-dimensional solidity. In the nineteenth-century French painting of *Monsieur L. Bertin* by Ingres (Fig. 6–30), you observe weightiness, mass, and bulk by way of the significant and carefully controlled contrasts of light and dark over the form, in addition to the impression of the material of the jacket and vest being stretched over the swelling torso within.

A three-dimensional shape such as Rickey's *Four Lines Oblique Gyratory II* (Fig. 6–31), however, does not displace

▶ Illustration 6-10 Convergence Yields Shallow or Decorated Space; Converging Space Yields Deeper Space

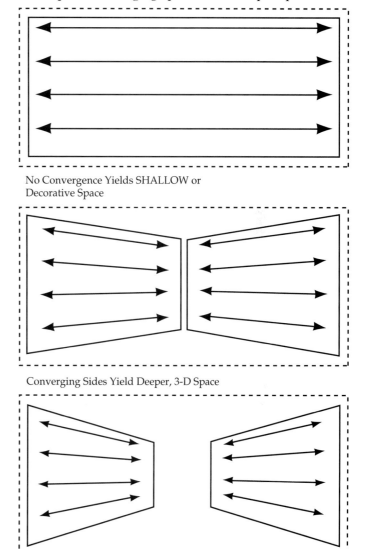

No Convergence Yields SHALLOW or Decorative Space

Converging Sides Yield Deeper, 3-D Space

▶ Figure 6-28 Pablo Picasso, *Woman's Head* (Fernande)
(Paris, Fall 1909, Bronze, 16¼ × 9¾ × 10½″; The Museum of Modern Art, New York, Purchase)

▶ Figure 6-29 Menashe Kadishman, *Suspended*
(Storm King Art Center, Mountainville, NY, Gift of Muriel & Philip I. Berman, Photography by Jerry L. Thompson)

▶ Figure 6-30 Ingres, *Monsieur L. Bertin*
(Musée du Louvre, © Photo R.M.N.)

▶ Figure 6-31 George Rickey, *Four Lines Oblique Gyratory II*
(Edition of 3. Collection of the artist. Photo © 1985 Ivan Dalla Tana)

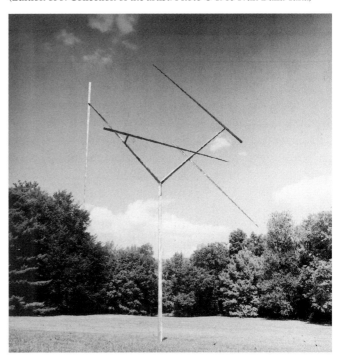

much of the space it occupies, but it does define a limit of space—a volume—that it occupies. Volume, therefore, is associated with

1. The actual space a three-dimensional form displaces, and
2. The combined positive and negative shapes involved in a single form presentation.

In other words, a volume is a displaced or circumscribed area.

You may have heard how engineers measure volumes which are irregularly shaped, such as car trunks. They determine how many golf balls (or similar objects) it takes to fill a box that measures 1 foot by 1 foot by 1 foot: a cubic foot. Then, after determining that number, they fill the trunk in question with golf balls. They add up all of the golf balls it took to fill the trunk and divide the total by the number of golf balls in a cubic foot. The result is the number of cubic feet of space that exists in that particular trunk. The car trunk is a definable area circumscribed by a border defining the volume.

The accompanying sculpture by Barbara Hepworth emphasizes volume and may be referred to as *volumetric*, whereas Auguste Rodin's *Balzac* (Fig. 6–33) emphasizes mass. The *Balzac* is also a "tight" form—there are no appendages nor protrusions into space from the primary mass. Since it is "tight" and emphasizes its mass and bulk, we refer to it as *tectonic*, unlike Antonio del Pollaiuolo's *atectonic Hercules and Antaeus* (Fig. 6–34) which has significant protrusions into space, deemphasizing its mass and bulk.

Sometimes a sculpture may be penetrated with voids—negative shapes.

Functions of the void in a sculpture include

1. Providing a visual path through the sculpture;
2. Revealing the mass and density of the sculpture;

▶ Figure 6-32   Barbara Hepworth, *Curved Form*
(Albright-Knox Gallery, Buffalo, New York, Gift of Seymour H. Knox, 1958)

3. Revealing the sculpture's opposite side;
4. Lightening the visual load of an area to remove visual heaviness and massiveness as necessary; and
5. Providing a focal point for the viewer's attention.

The latter is, perhaps, the most conspicuous function of a void. Through contrast of positive and negative shapes, plus other design factors, the artist can draw the viewer to a particular area of the work by using a void or voids (Figs. 6-35 and 6-36).

> **Voids are not "leftover" areas of the scupture, but are significant and purposeful compositional factors associated with shape.**

▶ NONTRADITIONAL PRESENTATIONS OF SHAPE

Early Cubist artists sought to redefine the way three-dimensional shapes were presented. For example, artists have traditionally looked at a still life or figure from one point of view and painted it from that view. An artist must be sure that the subject is painted from the same position every day so that the vantage point will not change. But this presents limitations, too. For example, if an artist likes more than one view of a shape, should the resulting image be confined to just one view or can more than one view be included, and can they overlap? The Cubists chose to do this, simultaneously presenting in their compositions more than one view of the objects, as seen in Juan Gris's *Breakfast* (Fig. 6–38). This style of presentation is appropriately known as simultaneous perspective.

Interestingly, the guiding principles of simultaneous perspective are thousands of years old. The Egyptians combined several views of humankind in one image, as seen in Figure 6–39, for example. The head is in profile but the eye is in

▶ Figure 6-35   Pamela Soldwedel, *Ishtar* (1990)
(Commissioned by Gosnell Properties, Pamela Soldwedel Sculptures)

▶ Figure 6-36   Alexander Archipenko, *Woman Combing Her Hair*
(National Gallery of Art, Washington, Ailsa Mellon Bruce Fund)

▶ Figure 6-37
(A. Fisken)

119

▶ Figure 6-38   Juan Gris, *Breakfast*
(1914, Cut-and-pasted paper, crayon, and oil over canvas, 31⅞ × 23½", The Museum of Modern Art, New York, acquired through the Lillie P. Bliss Bequest)

▶ Figure 6-39   False Door of Hesire, Sakkara, Wood 3rd Dynasty, Hesire Standing
(Egyptian Museum, Cairo, Foto Marburg/Art Resource, NY)

full view; the shoulders are square, but the front and back of the chest profile, too. Additionally, the figure has two of the same feet. The Egyptians combined all of these views because it was more descriptive of an ideal human: all-seeing, powerful, and active. This imagery in Egyptian art is referred to as descriptive perspective.

The use of simultaneous perspective is an abstraction of shapes as we know them. It involves breaking the shapes up into parts. Thus, this type of imagery is also known as *fractional representation*. These abstracted shapes are often complemented by broken value relationships, as well as altered color and textural qualities. Simultaneous perspective is a won-

derful means of exploring some of the more decorative potential of image making; producing images that are visually stimulating but not objectively imitative.

▶ CROPPING

Two-Dimensional

Perhaps one of the most interesting challenges the artist of two-dimensional images has when working from nature or designing original forms is determining how to limit what shapes will or will not be included in the composition.

In Rogier van der Weyden's *Portrait of Saint Luke Drawing the Virgin* (Fig. 6–40), you see the artist (van der Weyden, alias Saint Luke) drawing on a tablet in front of Mary and her child, inside of a large room. Yet, the artist is not drawing everything in the room. Rather, it appears that he is focusing on the primary subjects. Limiting the subjects from their environment by the picture frame is a concept known as "picture-framing" or *cropping*.

Artists are not required to paint or draw all of the objective shapes which they have seen in a still life or landscape. By way of cropping, artists limit the vastness of the field of view, making it a particular shape because of the limit of the top and side edges of the frame. The picture frame gives all shapes contained in it new and dynamic relationships.

Since there is so much in nature that can be chosen to draw or paint, introductory drawing students frequently use a 4-by-6-inch note card with a rectangular—or any other format—hole cut out of it to hold up in front of themselves like a camera's viewfinder to limit their vision and select what they want to draw. Although

▶ Figure 6-40   Rogier van der Weyden, *Saint Luke Painting the Virgin and Child*
(Gift of Mr. & Mrs. Henry Lee Higginson; Courtesy, Museum of Fine Arts, Boston © 1992; All Rights Reserved)

▶ Illustration 6-11   Viewfinder Format Cut-Outs

▶ Figure 6-41   Viewfinder

▶ Figure 6-42　Albrecht Durer, *Draftsman Doing Perspective Drawings of a Woman*
(The Metropolitan Museum of Art, Gift of Felix M. Warburg, 1918 (18.58.3))

Albrecht Dürer illustrated using the string grill to establish proportions in *Draughtsman Making a Perspective Drawing of a Woman* (Fig. 6–42), the illustration shows the artist using the grill's frame to establish the limit of vision that he has indicated on his paper. Roy Lichtenstein has severely cropped his image of the *Girl in Mirror* (Fig. 6–43) to show a dazzling relationship between the oval of the head and the mirror, in addition to the color and direction of the hair in each.

Three-Dimensional

When considering the human figure in art, one is reminded of the titans by Michelangelo or the sensuous bronzes of Rodin. Many Greek and Roman marble sculptures are known to us today as mere fragments of their original forms. Heads, arms, noses, and hands have been lost to the ravages of nature and humankind (Fig. 6–44).

Maillol's sculpture entitled *Female Torso for Chained Action* (Fig. 6–45) depicts a human torso. Purposely modeled without

▶ Figure 6-43　Roy Lichtenstein, *Girl in the Mirror*
(© Roy Lichtenstein)

▶ Figure 6-44 *Belvedere Torso*
(Archivi Alinari/Art Resource, NY)

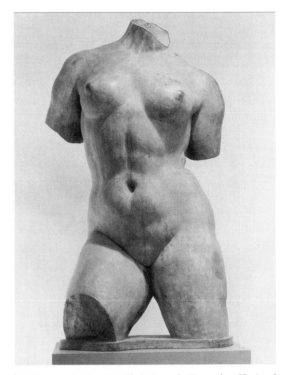

▶ Figure 6-45 Maillol, *Female Torso for Chained Action*
(Negative no. 74814, Metropolitan Museum of Art, Fletcher Fund, 1929 [29.138])

As artists became conditioned to looking at "amputated" classical relics, they became sensitive to the power of the incomplete form. Artists came to realize that a sculpture without a head is, perhaps, more universal than one with a head. Without a head, for example, a sculpture may be any one from any time or any race.

the limbs by Maillol, the omission emphasizes the powerful swelling forms of the torso while representing a power associated to womankind in general. This is especially apparent when Maillol's *Torso* is compared to the anatomically complete and slender *Young Girl with a Sheaf of Wheat* (Fig. 6–46) by Camille Claudel, which seems delicate and fragile in contrast.

When looking at these types of abstracted figures, you must ask yourself whether or not you miss the limbs or other body parts not shown; if included, would the parts have diminished some aspect of the form's content, or could they have helped? If you really do miss the parts, then the work has a weakened Gestalt and compromised overall significance. Would you agree that the omission of expected body parts allows room for the viewer to become involved in the piece? Do the omissions allow room for the individual's imagination to "complete" the work, thereby contributing to the personal significance of the sculpture?

▶ Figure 6-46   Camille Claudel, *Young Girl with a Sheaf of Wheat*
(The National Museum of Women in the Arts, Gift of Wallace and Wilhelmina Holladay)

▶ ## WHAT SHAPE CAN DO

As an Objective Device

Shape is usually perceived as an uncomplicated visual component of art. The shapes of things can be dutifully recorded by artists as an historical record or record of vision. Shape may also be used as an international visual language, such as in traffic control signs (Illus. 6–12).

> Shape meaning transcends written or oral communication.

Individual identifiable shapes serve as building blocks in forming a composition and the resulting content of an image. The depiction of easily recognizable shapes should be subordinate to an image's overall expression.

As a Subjective Device

As a visual component, shape may also be highly personalized. The artist must exploit shape's three properties to make it expressive. The three physical properties of shape are the same physical properties of line: *measure*—a shape's physical dimensions; *type*—geometric and organic, and *character*—the individual nature of a particular shape.

What is it that gives a shape an "individual nature," its character? What makes a shape stand out to the eye? In addition to recognizing variations in measure, type, and character, the human eye is oriented to (1) *familiarity*—those things with which you are acquainted and (2) *similarity*—related shapes within the visual field. As we discussed regarding dominance and association:

Our experience—our familiarity with shapes—is a primary determiner in how we respond to shape.

In Charles Demuth's *The Figure 5 in Gold* (Fig. 6–47), an image based on a fire engine company's number painted on a fire engine, you find your eye attracted to the largest "5" because of its size, location, color, contrast, and your familiarity with the shape of the "5." Your eye quickly picks up the other "5s" because of the *progression* of size in the repetition and their similarity to the first "5." You observe the smaller circular forms because of their similarity to the circle which makes up part of the large "5."

Our experiences direct us in forming conclusions, such as that organic shapes are "soft" and geometric ones are "hard." Thus, based on these perceptions about shape, we might conclude that a landscape or seascape with flowing shapes "feels" peaceful, whereas a mountainscape of jutting rocks and angular canyons might appear challenging.

Nonobjective or severely abstracted shapes may also evoke particular sensations and ideas because they relate in one way or another to your experiences.

Even though an image may contain shapes that are difficult to recognize or may not be "of" anything you have seen or experienced, they can be thought-provoking and meaningful.

Georgia O'Keefe's *Light Coming on the Plains, III—1917* (Fig. 6–48) may or may not remind you of familiar shapes. In essence, the image contains a primary

▶ Illustration 6-12   International Symbols

shape which has an undulating contour and is filled with colored shapes that are separated by diffused contours. The overall shape relationships may evoke softness and calm. Do they for you?

Psychological responses to shape are not dependent upon the viewer's being presented with familiar, representational shapes.

▶ DYNAMIC AND STABLE SHAPES

In the previous section on line, we spoke of a line's direction as contributing to its expressive effects. There are similarities regarding *shape* and direction, too. Shapes that have horizontal bottom edges appear

▶ Figure 6-47   Charles Demuth, *The Figure 5 in Gold*
(The Metropolitan Museum of Art, The Alfred Stieglitz Collection, 1949
(49.59.1))

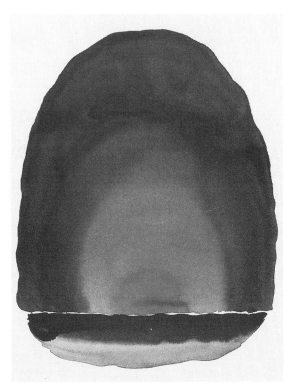

▶ Figure 6-48   Georgia O'Keeffe, *Light Coming on the Plains III*
(Courtesy Amon Carter Museum, Forth Worth Texas)

▶ Illustration 6-13   Diagram of Hard and Soft Shapes

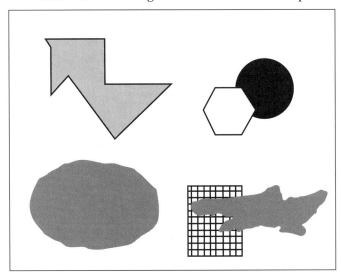

more stable, as opposed to those that have diagonal bottom edges or appear to rest on a single point (Illus. 6–14). These shapes that appear unstable are not necessarily weak elements of a composition, however. Because of their resulting diagonal edge and shape relationships, and the variety of negative shapes they may create, the unstable forms are more properly labeled *dynamic* shapes because of the visual energy they evoke (see Mondrian, Fig. 5–10, and Van Doesburg, Fig. 6–49).

Shapes will appear either stabile or dynamic, depending on

1. Their orientation to a base line, or deviations from true verticality or horizontality;
2. Relative symmetry;
3. The nature of the edge character; and
4. Their *attitude* or relative orientation to other shapes (Bellini, Fig. 6–50).

▶ Illustration 6-14   Stable and Dynamic Shapes

▶ SHAPE AND FIGURE-GROUND RELATIONSHIPS

An additional way to make a shape visually dynamic and bold is to make the entire form a silhouette against its background (Matisse, Fig. 6–51) or vice versa, making the silhouetted shape a light value against a dark negative shape. While emphasizing shape, this also emphasizes the shape's contour and the variety it may have. Asymmetry also contributes to the energy of the shapes.

Artists have also found that having a composition broken up into a fairly even ratio of positive and negative shapes adds visual energy and activity. A checkerboard, for example, has a fifty-fifty ratio of positive to negative shapes, as does Escher's *Prince on Horseback* (Fig. 6–52). The proportion of positive to negative shape areas—the alternation within the repetition—(in addition to the energetic color

▶ Figure 6-49   Van Doesburg, *Simultaneous Counter Composition*
(Stedelijk Museum, Amsterdam)

▶ Figure 6-50   Giovanni Bellini, *Christ Carrying the Cross*
(The Toledo Museum of Art, Gift of Edward Drummond Libbey)

▶ Figure 6-51   Henri Matisse, *Venus* (National Gallery of Art, Washington, Ailsa Mellon Bruce Fund)

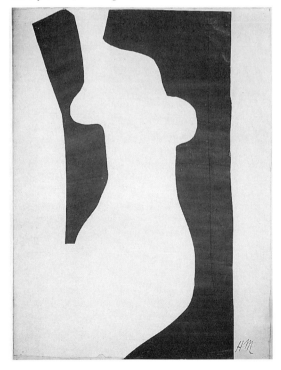

and diagonal orientation of the shapes) is what contributes to the energy felt in these works.

Psychologist Rudolph Arnheim wrote in *American Scientist* (1988):

> The most important development during the twentieth century in the psychological study of artistic expression has been the realization that sensory experience endows stationary objects with dynamic force.

And Arnheim notes:

> . . . the carrier of visual dynamics is the perceived form, not the material of which an art object is made.

He goes on to say:

> It was not by coincidence that the first theoretical acknowledgement of visual dynamics came from a scholar whose psychological interest was directed toward the arts . . . for it is particularly evident to persons whose minds are geared to the expressive qualities of what the eyes see; and these qualities are apprehended, emphasized, and sharpened in works of art.

There are several ways artists can add accent and character to the shapes they create. One of them is creating a tension in the dynamic forces of stabile and nonstabile shapes. Rudolph Arnheim summarizes his observations on the relationship between dynamic forces by stating,

> The key to expression in visual art is the rendering of dynamic forces in fixed images.

Sensitivity to the expressive potential of shape is important not only to the designer of a composition, however, but to the viewer of a work, as well. Studying the principles of dynamic and stabile shapes as depicted in the works of others will not only enhance one's understanding of the work, but will help one become a better artist.

The viewer of art must have the willingness to study obvious as well as subtle shape qualities in order to perceive the expressive objectives of the artist.

▶ Figure 6-52   M.C. Escher, *Horseman*
(© 1946 M.C. Escher/Cordon Art-Baarn-Holland)

▶ EXPRESSIVE USE OF SHAPE

Fortunately, artists—as creative beings—are allowed to create shapes of their own liking within a frame or on a modeling stand. They don't have to paint or draw objective copies of forms seen in nature. Lyonel Feininger's *Zirchow VII* (Fig. 6–53), a painting of a church in the suburbs of Berlin, depicts some architectural, landscape, and other miscellaneous shapes that are recognizable yet simplified geometrically. To further dramatize the scene, Feininger extended some of the contours of the positive shapes into the emptiness of the negative shapes, creating new geometric shapes. Then he gave these framed areas of negative shapes different values and colors for further visual significance and to have the total image relate more to the format (rectangular shape) of the entire image. Does this geometricized abstraction of the setting take something away from the work, or does it infuse the setting with energy and individuality, with dynamics?

Salvador Dali combines abstracted shapes with more naturalistic ones in his Surrealist paintings. By painting the sky, rocks, and water so convincingly, as seen in Figure 6–54, he has made the sagging clocks and ant-infested watches jarring, yet convincing. This is a common feature of Surrealist art: taking typical images of known objects and juxtaposing them with atypical images. Because the forms are

▶ Figure 6-53   Lyonel Feininger, *Zirchow VII*
(National Gallery of Art, Washington, Gift of Julia Feininger)

▶ Figure 6-54   Salvador Dali, *The Persistence of Memory*
(1931, oil on canvas, 9½ × 13". The Museum of Modern Art, New York. Given anonymously.)

▶ Figure 6-55   Edvard Munch, *The Scream*
(Photo J. Lathion, Nasjonalgalleriet, ©NG 1992)

easily recognized, you get drawn into the painting based on your own mental associations and experience with similar shapes. When you observe some minor variation which contradicts your experience it becomes more visually intriguing. Additionally, the image may also become jarring and thought-provoking.

Edvard Munch in *The Scream* (Fig. 6–55) gives you a painting filled with shape variations in his composition of a figure standing on a bridge which crosses a Norwegian fjord. The swirling forms of the sky and water, in addition to the strong diagonals of the bridge, evoke a passionate involvement in the setting as opposed to a pastoral depiction of water and land. The figure grabbing his head emphasizes the state of the mind as being the focal point of the work. The mind is neither stable nor calm in this case, not without anxieties, as Munch has expressed it through shape relationships. Art critic Robert Hughes writes of this work:

> Nothing that did not speak of strong feelings found a place [in Munch's work].

Feininger, Dali, and Munch have each used shape. However, because of each artist's unique expressive objectives and personalities, the effects of their shape presentations are quite different. Each has exploited the objective and subjective expressive potential of shape according to his own needs.

> **All artists of significance have been willing to go beyond the "safe" to experiment, to learn, and to grow for the sake of making their art more meaningful to themselves and to their viewers.**

▶ SECTION GLOSSARY

Atectonic A three-dimensional form which has significant protrusions or extensions into negative space, deemphasizing mass and bulk, while extending the form's energy.

Attitude One form's physical orientation to another.

Biomorphic Shapes See ORGANIC SHAPES.

Cropping Limiting the vastness of the field of view (limiting the subjects from their environment) by altering the shape and/or dimensions of the picture frame. Syn.: PICTURE FRAMING.

Curvilinear Shapes Shapes made up of curved contour lines.

Fractional Representation See SIMULTANEOUS PERSPECTIVE.

Geometric Shapes Shapes which appear to have been mathematically constructed.

Mass An area that appears to have bulk and density—a feeling of solidity.

Möbius Strip A looped strip of material constructed to have only one surface or plane.

Organic Shapes Shapes with undulating, free-flowing contours; frequently they resemble the shapes of living forms. Syn.: BIOMORPHIC SHAPES.

Picture Framing See CROPPING.

Planar Of or related to planes.

Plane An actual or implied, limited or unlimited two-dimensional surface that has no mass and which may exist in two- or three-dimensional space. Planes may be either curvilinear or rectilinear.

Plastic Shape See PLASTIC.

Rectilinear Shapes Shapes made up of straight lines.

Shape A two- or three-dimensional area that has an actual or implied limit. The limit may be a drawn contour line or the edge of a physical form. The limit may also be the location of a visual *contrast* from one value, color, or texture to another.

Tectonic A three-dimensional form having no appendages or protrusions into space from the primary mass, emphasizing its mass and bulk.

Void A penetration through a three-dimensional shape which yields a negative space/shape. Syn.: NEGATIVE SHAPE.

Volume The actual space or area a three-dimensional form displaces or circumscribes.

Volumetric Emphasizing volume.

SECTION PROJECTS: SHAPE

1. SHAPE IN NATURE

   Observe a landscape, rock outcropping, or other natural setting and draw it, reducing and simplifying the forms to the basic shapes found in nature: circles, rectangles, and triangles. If your work is done from a photograph, mount that photo on one part of the page and complete your composition in a framed format on another part of the page.

   [Shading may be used; any media.]

2. ORGANIC SHAPES

   Draw a bone (cow, horse, chicken), paying particular attention to how the contours of this organic shape move from the outside to the inside of the form. Embellish the *line drawing* with shading and texture as warranted. One of the delights of studying bones is that they demonstrate a full range of the visual components and their properties. Be sure your drawing fills the page.

   [Pencil or charcoal on Bristol board.]

3. PLANES

   a) Construct a replica of your hand or foot using heavy paper, cardboard, or matboard, reducing the form to a series of planar relationships. Keep visible indications of glue, staples, or tape to an absolute minimum—bend along scored or firmly creased lines.

   [A little larger than life size.]

   b) Paint a still life without line—using white paint with a wide brush on blue, black, or green paper—so that the *direction* of the brush strokes will imply the direction of the planes of the subject. Avoid drawing contours and using the brush for shading.

   [Tempra; "drybrush" may be most effective.]

4. POSITIVE AND NEGATIVE SHAPES

   a) Given a medium of predetermined measurements—polystyrene, wood, plaster, or the like—develop a three-dimensional organic or geometric form incorporating voids.

   [Rasps, saws, glue, etc.; apply a finish as desired.]

   b) Design an asymmetrically balanced composition that is visually dynamic due to an even distribution (fifty-fifty) of positive and negative shapes. (This is not a repeating pattern/motif project.)

   [Objective or nonobjective subject matter; tempera paints: black, or any single primary color, and white.]

5. VOLUME AND MASS

   a) Using strips—any measure—of heavy paper, aluminum, or similar material, construct an objective or nonobjective three-dimensional volumetric form.

   b) Draw a natural tectonic form, emphasizing its mass and bulk with exaggerated shading effects. Omit superfluous details as necessary.

6. CROPPING

   a) Select a photograph from a magazine, or one of your own, that measures about 5 inches by 7 inches. Determine how it could be made into a more stimulating composition if it were cropped, featuring an area of the photo of significant shape relationships.

   b) With any appropriate media, draw this new cropped image to a scale that is about the same size as the original uncropped photograph. Simulate values and colors as closely as possible.

   [Black-and-white or color photograph is appropriate; use an enlarging-reducing grid, if necessary. Mount the photo and your drawing on a single page.]

7. SHAPE AND MOTION

   a) Motion and Balance: Visual energy can be created by emphasizing unstable shapes, in addition to making new shapes from overlapping forms. Draw a frame around your 11-inch by 17-inch page. Place a piece of paper cockeyed over this and trace the part of its border that is inside of the frame. Do this two, three, or fifty times, again tracing the part of its border that is inside of the frame, allowing the forms to overlap. (This may or may not involve transparency.) Selectively fill in some of the new shapes with black or solid areas of color. Vary the measure of the contours for emphasis, if desired.

[Tempera paint, India ink, or colored marker.]

b) Motion and Space: Shapes that overlap one another create a sense of near to far and, if similar shapes are overlapped in a series, they add motion and some drama.

Using *opaque* planes, create motion around and through the picture plane.

[Media may include gouaches, tempera paints, and India ink.]

8. SIMULTANEOUS PERSPECTIVE

As the Cubists and Egyptians did, observe a series of still-life items, human figures, or buildings in a landscape and arrange them on your picture plane in a manner which represents different views presented at the same time—*simultaneous perspective*. This will involve significant overlapping, some transparency, unnatural shading, color, and textural effects, in addition to *incomplete* forms.

[Any media.]

9. SHAPE MEANING

Understanding that some symbols are universally understood, as in traffic and pedestrian signage, design/invent your own "international symbol" or sign. Keep color and clarity of shape in mind as you work, as well as the format of the sign.

[Any media.]

10. INDEPENDENT PROJECT

Write the instruction and provide the objectives for a project that is related to this chapter but not addressed in the aforementioned projects. Complete the project.

[Any media.]

TEXTURE

▶ USAGE

W hen traveling from one part of a country to another, one notes different textures of life and surroundings: The people in one region may seem hard and rough when compared to people in another region who appear soft or delicate. Some individuals speak sharply and others softly. Urban life may be felt to be coarse and abrasive in contrast to rural life. The surface of a lake may be choppy or smooth as glass, and mountains may appear rugged, craggy, and jagged. Trees may look bushy, and bushes may look nappy; clouds appear fluffy, and lawns look velvety.

More than anything, texture brings to mind the sense of touch. Something that relates to the physical sense of touch is *haptic*. An object or surface may have satisfying or unsatisfying haptic qualities. So, concepts such as rough or smooth, or coarse and abrasive have haptic connotations in addition to psychological ones.

> How one feels about something and how something actually feels can equally be related to perceptions of texture.

▶ OUR PERCEPTIONS OF TEXTURE

Sight is our primary sense when perceiving art. In the making of art, sight and touch work together. Vincent van Gogh wrote:

> What a queer thing touch is, the stroke of the brush.

Artists working in clay, stone, and paint can create their own manufactured or *artificial textures*. A sculptor models clay or carves stone and a painter, such as Van Gogh, may actually build up his paints. Artificial textures are physical and tangible, thus *actual*, and would also include the texture of a concrete cinder block or the plastic case of a stereo cabinet. Actual textures range from the very rough to the very smooth.

Artificial textures, such as modeled hair or the impasto in paintings, are manufactured. Natural textures, such as blades of grass or coarse sandy beaches and tree bark, are not. Yet, both are three-dimensional.

▶ Figure 6-56

Additionally, artificial textures can be made from natural media if a person carves into wood or casts stone to make concrete.

> A willful alteration of a natural surface—a natural texture—produces an artificial texture.

▶ WHAT TEXTURE IS

We are exposed to texture two different ways: through sight and touch. From our daily contact with surfaces, we encounter a variety of haptic sensations. These sensations are imprinted in our minds over time. We know that when we touch cotton it will be soft; we know that when we drape a wool blanket around ourselves it will feel scratchy. We are conditioned by experience to expect particular sensations when our skin touches tactile-stimulating materials. Thus, we know that wood may be rough and paper may be smooth. When we look at wood, we don't have to touch it to be aware of its roughness, nor do we have to rub the surface of typing paper to be aware of its smoothness; we do not have to touch something to "feel" it. Our sight—backed up by the breadth of our experiences—tells us what something may feel like. The two senses—sight and touch—are working together to communicate to the brain what a surface's tactile qualities are, the same way that smell complements taste. Physiologists might refer to this as a type of "sensory symbiosis": one sense complementing another.

Interestingly, sometimes the senses can be fooled. In Winslow Homer's *Breezing Up* (Fig. 6–59), we sense the softness of the sails, the coarseness of the boat, and the crispness of the water. Yet the surface

▶ Figure 6-57   Vincent Van Gogh, *Houses at Auvers*
(Courtesy, Museum of Fine Arts, Boston, Bequest of John T. Spaulding)

▶ Figure 6-58   John Singer Sargent, *The Daughters of Edward D. Boit*
(Gift of Mary Louise Boit, Florence D. Boit, Jane Hubbard Boit, and Julia Overing Boit, in memory of their father, Edward Darley Boit, Courtesy, Museum of Fine Arts, Boston, © 1992, All Rights Reserved)

▶ Figure 6-59   Winslow Homer, *Breezing Up (A Fair Wind)*
(National Gallery of Art, Washington, Gift of the W. L. and May T. Mellon Foundation)

▶ Figure 6-60   Textures Affected by Light

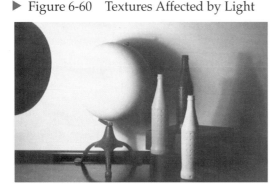

▶ Figure 6-61

of the painting itself is relatively even. What is happening is our eyes are reminding us of tactile impressions based on our recollections of actual textures: surfaces that can be perceived through the sense of touch. In Homer's painting, we are responding to the *illusion* of actual textures.

We observe, therefore, that the definition of texture has two parts.

1. Actual tactile quality—how a surface feels; or
2. Implied tactile quality—how a surface looks like it would feel.

In the absence of light, texture cannot be optically perceived; thus, our visual perception of a texture is highly dependent upon how a light source reveals the qualities of the surface. The optically perceived texture of a surface depends on

1. The quality of the light source,
2. The nature of the surface reflecting the light,
3. The distance from the light source, and
4. The orientation of the surface to the light source (Figs. 6–60–6–63).

▶ TWO- AND THREE-DIMENSIONAL CONCERNS OF TEXTURE

> Texture and medium are inextricably related to tool, technique, and ground.

We previously discussed Seurat's portrait, *Seated Woman* (see Fig. 3–12). Done in charcoal, this image was produced on rough paper using the side of the charcoal with varying degrees of pressure to produce the light-and-dark effects. The effect is of an atmospheric softness, a form lacking hard, tangible contours and massive, bulky proportions. Imagine this form done on smooth paper or painted in oils. Would the textural effects be the same?

A single medium may yield a variety of textural effects, depending on the technique by which it is applied to a ground.

Pablo Picasso exploited pencil lead in his drawing of *Le Vieux Musicien* (see Fig. 6–11). He used the tip of the pencil to create hard, crisp shapes and the side of the pencil to create softer areas. Vincent van Gogh loaded his brush with paint and exploited the oozy, juicy, fluid texture of oil paints in his painting entitled *A Cornfield, with Cypresses* (Fig. 6–64). In contrast, Joseph Turner smoothed out all of his paint to create a shimmering illusion of translucent and reflected light in his *Keelmen Heaving in Coals by Moonlight* (Fig. 6–65). Rembrandt applied his paints very heavily to the ground, building up surfaces that frequently were both optically and texturally rich. In his *Self-Portrait* (Fig. 6–66, 1658), Rembrandt's lively use of the textural quality of the paint medium can be seen in the collar of the coat and hand of the artist. *Man with the Golden Helmet* (Fig. 6–67), attributed to the school of Rembrandt, also exhibits a heavy application of paint in the helmet, enough so as to cast actual shadows on the painting, itself. This *impasto* technique is not a violation of the integrity of the medium; rather, it demonstrates another characteristic of the oil paint medium. Also, these two oil paintings, in addition to the Turner and Van Gogh, illustrate different effects of *paint quality*—the inherent characteristic(s) of the medium.

In the hands of capable artists, the textural range of a medium can be exploited for a variety of effects without necessarily violating the integrity of the medium.

▶ Figure 6-62

▶ Figure 6-63

▶ Figure 6-64   Vincent Van Gogh, *A Cornfield, with Cypresses* (The National Gallery)

▶ Figure 6-65   Joseph Mallord William Turner, *Keelman Heaving in Coals by Moonlight*
(National Gallery of Art, Washington, Eidener Collection)

▶ Figure 6-66   Rembrandt, *Self-Portrait*
(Copyrighted by The Frick Collection, 1937, photographed in 1949)

▶ Figure 6-67   School of Rembrandt, *Man with Golden Helmet*
(Berlin (West), Bildarchiv Foto Marburg/Art Resource, NY)

Traditionally, media used by sculptors can also have a variety of textural effects. Michelangelo's *The Prisoner* (Fig. 6–68) exhibits areas that have been smoothly polished in comparison to other areas left rough or "unfinished." The contrast between rough and smooth is significant: The smooth next to rough looks smoother, whereas the rough next to smooth looks rougher. By placing contrasting characteristics of visual components side by side, the extreme and opposite effects of those components are emphasized. Rodin observed this effect of *simultaneous contrast* in the unfinished Michelangelos and purposely contrasted textured areas in his own sculptures to heighten their visual effectiveness (Fig. 6–69).

▶ Figure 6-68   Michelangelo, *The Prisoner*
(Alinari/Art Resource, NY)

▶ Figure 6-69   Auguste Rodin, *The Thinker*
(The Rodin Museum, Gift of Jules E. Mastbaum)

▶ ACTUAL TEXTURES IN TWO-DIMENSIONAL ART

Artists may choose to apply different actual textures right on their ground or mix them in their paints. Paint quality can be enhanced by the addition of materials to the paint, such as sand, oyster shell chips, or even plaster. This enhances not only the visual effect of an image, but the actual texture of the painted surface, as well. Additionally, the paint can achieve a unique distinctiveness depending on how an artist manipulates a brush or builds up paint on a ground. Paint quality, therefore, is affected by tool, technique, medium, and ground, and by mixing for-

eign materials into it. The medium takes on a character all its own rather than being used for imitative purposes.

Instead of painting pictures of newspapers, Juan Gris, Picasso, and other artists cut or tore and applied newspaper fragments and other printed materials directly to their paintings. The use of paper on the canvas not only provided visual interest, but enhanced actual textural variety. Any paper-type, from tissue to construction papers and from paper bags to poster boards—not excluding photographs or paper cups—may be used to enhance the textural and visual integrity of an image. This art form involving the application of various papers to a ground is termed papier collé. The paper relationships may stand alone or they may be drawn and painted on, too.

Other materials in addition to paper may be added to enhance the textural and optical effects of an image. A variety of actual textures from found objects—such as buttons, cloth, and leather—when combined with painted or drawn textural effects on a two-dimensional ground, make up an art form known as *collage*. A collage may or may not take the form of a representational image. Max Ernst introduced the collage to France in the early twentieth century (Fig. 6–70).

Collage and papier collé are very different. Papier collé utilizes paper, only, on the ground. This is the style frequently used by teenagers to make posters and room decorations. Only when additional

nonpaper items are added does the art form become a bona fide collage.

An artist may choose not to use a prepared, flat ground on which to arrange found objects. Frequently, the objects and their varied textures are arranged in boxes, a type of *assemblage* (Fig. 6–71). This gives the objects a sense of sanctity and enhances their textural qualities by surrounding the objects with the "neutral" texture of the box and isolating them from other textures.

Pattern and Texture

In drawings, the use of hatched and cross-hatched lines, in addition to stippling—while not simulations of actual textures—do imply tactile qualities (Pieter Bruegel the Elder, Fig. 6–72). Similarly, the

▶ Figure 6-70   Max Ernst, *Two Children Are Threatened by a Nightingale*
(1924, oil on wood with wood construction, 27½ × 22½ × 4½", The Museum of Modern Art, New York, purchase, © Jan. 11, 1994)

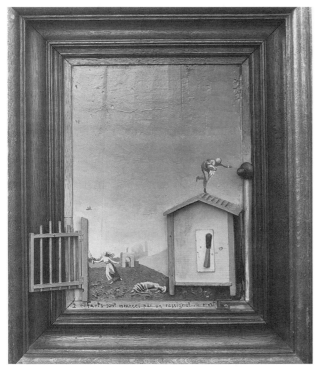

▶ Figure 6-71   Joseph Cornell, *Hotel Goldene Sonne*
(Hirshhorn Museum and Sculpture Garden, Smithsonian Institution, Gift of Joseph H. Hirshhorn, 1966)

dabs of paint in Sisley's *Meadow* (Fig. 6–73) evoke a quality of softness.

The conspicuous repetition of a visual motif on a surface which creates a sense of visual harmony is termed *pattern*. For example, the crosshatching in the previous examples created patterns from the crisscrossing lines and shapes. When the repetition of a motif is on a small scale, such as the crosshatched lines, it may evoke a tactile effect or textural quality known as *invented texture*. The repetition of a texture may create a pattern, and the repetition of a pattern may create an invented or actual texture.

▶ Figure 6-72   Pieter the Elder, Bruegel, *Landscape with the Penitence of Saint Jerome*
(National Gallery of Art, Washington, Ailsa Mellon Bruce Collection)

▶ Figure 6-73   Alfred Sisley, *Meadow*
(National Gallery of Art, Washington, Ailsa Mellon Bruce Collection)

▶ WHAT TEXTURE CAN DO ...

As an Objective Device

Why do visual artists use or concern themselves with texture? What does texture do in an artwork? The primary functions of texture in art are to (1) describe and (2) define the surface qualities of subject matter.

Many artists try to copy subject matter as accurately as possible to make their images appear lifelike and plausible. Previously, we introduced the imitating of textures—*simulated textures*—in an art style known as *Trompe l'oeil*. This style of art requires accurate depictions of local textures—those textures which are optically perceived to be "natural" to a particular subject.

Other art forms, such as genre—images depicting scenes from everyday life—require similar attention to depicting textures as they appear to the eye. In Greuze's *Broken Eggs* (Fig. 6–74), we observe a domestic interior which gave Greuze an opportunity to depict a full range of textural qualities: rough wooden beams, crisp linens, soft flesh, and slimy broken eggs. The convincing depiction of the textures contributes to the plausibility of the setting and the telling of a moral lesson about "fleeting innocence."

Is it any wonder that set and costume designers for the theater study paintings, especially genre art, to get an accurate image of life at different times in history? The review of genre art is a most helpful aid in determining building materials, the textures and prints of fabrics, and the

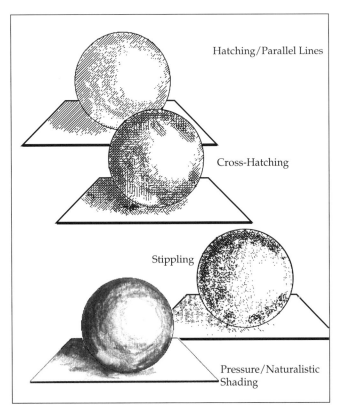

Hatching/Parallel Lines

Cross-Hatching

Stippling

Pressure/Naturalistic Shading

▶ Illustration 6-15   Graphic Processes

▶ Figure 6-74   Jean Baptiste Greuze, *Broken Eggs*
(The Metropolitan Museum of Art, Bequest of William K. Vanderbilt, 1920 [20.155.8])

styles of dress, architecture, and furnishings from various times in history.

As a Subjective Device

Bellini does more than describe and define the textures he simulated in his painting, *Christ Carrying the Cross*, which we previously reviewed (see Fig. 6–50). We have no problem "feeling" the crispness of the linen garment, the softness of the flesh and flowing hair, and the hard density of the cross. What Bellini has done to emphasize these qualities is to put them against a background that is void of textures. The dark areas behind the cross act as neutrals against which we can determine how rough or how smooth a given surface is. Additionally, the uncluttered white garment also acts as somewhat of a neutral. Thus, the lights and darks establish areas of neutral values to contrast and compare the relative softness of the organic face. Then, by placing this face against the hard, geometric form of the massive cross, we feel the face to be soft and vulnerable, again through simultaneous contrast. By having areas of greater and lesser textural interest, the artist is directing visual attention by selective enrichment of the visual field. Also, the diagonal placement of the cross and the resulting diagonal negative shapes deny stability, thus enhancing the drama of the image.

Understanding that an objective function of texture is to describe surface qualities, you now understand that subjective functions of texture include

1. Providing contrast, as in *Christ Carrying the Cross*, and
2. Embellishing areas of the picture plane, whether the composition is representational—as seen in Leonardo's *Ginevra de' Benci* (Fig. 6–75) or highly abstracted—as in Morris Graves's *Little-Known Bird of the Inner Eye* (Fig. 6–76).

▶ Figure 6-75   Leonardo de Vinci, *Ginevra de'Benci (obverse)*
(National Gallery of Art, Washington, Ailsa Mellon Bruce Fund)

▶ Figure 6-76   Morris Graves, *Little-Known Bird of the Inner Eye*
(1941, tempera on tracing paper 20¾ × 36⅝", The Museum of Modern Art, New York, purchase,
Photograph © 1994 by The Museum of Modern Art, NY)

Paul Klee's image entitled *Death and Fire* incorporates unsophisticated (child-like?) shapes on an unsophisticated ground—burlap (Fig. 6–77). The harsh burlap texture shows through the thin paint. The jarring shapes and colors, along with the conspicuously abrasive textural quality of the burlap, yield a foreboding and discomforting image of menacing doom and gloom. Texture, therefore, is a significant component in contributing to the content of a work. Textural materials may be added to the surface of a painting, such as in a collage; texture may be simulated, such as in the works of the Trompe l'oeil artists; or it may even come from the medium and ground, as demonstrated in the Van Gogh and Klee paintings. Sculptors exploit textural qualities of a medium, also, to enhance the content and visual interest of their works.

It is imperative that students of art understand how texture contributes to meaning in visual communication, in addition to observing how texture describes and defines visual forms.

▶ Figure 6-77   Paul Klee, *Death and Fire*
(Kunstmuseum Bern-Paul Klee-Suttung)

▶ **SECTION GLOSSARY**

Actual Textures   Surface qualities which can be experienced through the sense of touch; three-dimensional.

Art from Found Materials   Art made from found, junk, or scrap materials; sometimes involving new materials, but materials that are not traditionally associated with art.

Artificial Textures   Manufactured actual textures.

Assemblage   A form of sculpture noted by similar or dissimilar materials joined together incorporating constructive techniques. (Sometimes a synonym for FOUND/SCRAP/JUNK ART.)

Collage   An art form involving the attaching of a variety of actual textures from found objects, combined with painted or drawn effects, to a ground.

Found/Scrap/Junk Art   A misnomer. Art may be made from found junk or scrap materials, but the result should not be junk or scrap art! A more appropriate label is ART FROM FOUND MATERIALS or ASSEMBLAGE.

Genre Art   Images depicting everyday scenes of the middle class.

Haptic   Something that relates to the physical sense of touch.

Implied Textures   Surfaces which appear to have tactile qualities. See SIMULATED TEXTURES.

Invented Textures   The repetition of a motif on a small scale which evokes a tactile quality; two-dimensional.

Local Textures   Those qualities which are optically perceived to be inherent to a particular surface.

Natural Textures   The surfaces of natural forms which are naturally produced.

Paint Quality   The inherent characteristic(s) of a medium as exploited by the artist.

Papier Collé   An art form involving the application of various papers, combined with painted or drawn effects, to a ground.

Pattern   The conspicuous repetition of a visual motif on a surface, which creates a sense of visual harmony.

Sensory Symbiosis   One sense working with and complementing another.

Simulated Textures   Imitated surface qualities.

Simultaneous Contrast   The principle that any visual component can vary in appearance depending on the nature of the visual component placed next to it.

Texture   The actual or implied tactile quality of a surface.

SECTION PROJECTS: TEXTURE

1. EXPERIENCE AND ASSOCIATION

   Construct an object or object surface that looks like it would feel one way, but actually feels quite differently, thus contradicting "sensory symbiosis."

2. TOOL, TECHNIQUE, MEDIUM, GROUND

   a) Using either pencil or charcoal, draw a still-life composition on smooth paper; and draw the same composition on rough (watercolor, charcoal, or other heavy-toothed) paper. Do not suppress the differences; rather, allow the differences between the two papers to be evident and conspicuous.

   [Mount both on a single page.]

   b) On a page that might be referred to as a "sampler," design a display of a variety of graphic techniques with a single medium to illustrate that medium's range of textural effects.

   [Any medium.]

   c) Paint or draw a well-designed image of your liking on an atypical ground possessing significant actual texture. Consider carpeting, fur, tree bark, bricks, rocks, and the like as your ground. Allow the texture of the ground to complement the image. Don't try to suppress that texture, exploit it!

3. PAPIER COLLÉ

   Create a papier collé presentation exploiting the expressive potential of one medium on a variety of paper types which depict a wide range of tooth, value, color, and texture.

4. PAINT QUALITY

   Exploit the expressive textural effects of acrylic paint by creating a composition which incorporates its range of paint quality. Other media may be added.

5. COLLAGE

   a) Create a collage that incorporates objects or materials that exploit at least three textural qualities that can be incorporated into a unified composition.

   b) Trail or draw one or more distinctive media across a variety of nonpaper grounds in a manner which reveals the various textural effects of the same media on those different grounds.

6. GRAPHIC TECHNIQUES

   In drawing a still life, exploit stippling, cross-hatching, and the use of parallel lines to de-pict the range of textures present. Use no more than three or four objects in your design in order to keep your relationships clear. Consider a great enlargement of the subject matter within the picture frame. Keep contour to a minimum.

   [Any media.]

7. INVENTED TEXTURE

   Areas of neutral textural qualities make contrasting textural effects stand out (simultaneous contrast).

   a) Design a composition of figures in a landscape or in an interior where the surfaces are areas of flat color and invented texture. Since the surface treatments are abstractions of the natural surface effects, it is logical to present abstractions of the figures, too.

   [Any media.]

   b) Take three letters or numbers of any typeface, enlarging them in a dynamic composition that involves the use of invented texture on the surface or background of the forms. Keep some areas visually neutral to enhance the contrasting effects of the textures.

   [Any media.]

8. ACTUAL TEXTURE

   Three-dimensional media may be involved in the creation of actual textures. The variety of actual textures capable of being produced in clay are almost limitless. Paying attention to the textures in one medium and simulating them in another develops observation and technical skills.

   Using clay as your medium, copy one of your tennis shoes as carefully as possible in terms of *size* and *shape*, and simulate the textures as faithfully as possible.

9. INDEPENDENT PROJECT

   You may want to pursue some other ideas you may have had regarding ways that texture can be depicted. For example, compositions involving invented texture may be created on a typewriter or computer by repeating a common character and varying its size and degree of boldness.

VALUE AND COLOR

▶ USAGE

Throughout our discussions of the visual components of art, we have come to realize how interrelated all of the components are. You recall, for example, that lines can make up shapes and textures, and textured areas can be shape areas. Line and dot were studied together because of line's dependence on dot. Now, it is again necessary to combine two of the visual components, value and color, under a single unit because they are inherently dependent upon common principles of light and vision. In this text, however, we will look more closely at the principles of value first and then the principles of color.

Listing value as one of the visual components of art causes some people a little difficulty because they perceive value to mean the worth of the art object. Since many students and other individuals are preoccupied with how much a work of art may sell for when it is finished, they infer that the component, value, relates to an image's selling price. Additionally, value may imply the importance or respect an artwork is worthy of claiming, or an art object's usefulness. These interpretations of value, however, do not relate to the visual components of art or the response of vision to visual stimuli. Rather, they have social and economic implications. Studying the visual components of art, one needs to orient one's thinking of value to visual characteristics.

Having seen that almost all art contains line, shape, and texture, we observe

▶ Figure 6-78

that art is also made up of light and dark areas and light and dark forms.

> This relationship of light to dark in visual art is termed value.

Color, on the other hand, is a concept that most people have little problem with in regard to art. It appears that the majority of the population feels that color is what art *is* or should be all about.

> It is unfortunate that too many people feel the successful use of color in a painting is determined by how well the colors may match a living room carpet or den sofa.

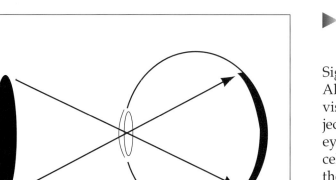

▶ Illustration 6-16   Eye Diagram

▶ Illustration 6-17   Light Sources

▶ OUR PERCEPTIONS OF VALUE AND COLOR

Sight is only possible where there is light. All objects and their colors and values are visible because light is reflected from object surfaces. The reflected light enters the eye and stimulates the photosensitive cells in the retina of the eyeball. Although the ancient Greeks understood the structure of the eye and were even capable of performing surgery on the eye, it wasn't until the seventeenth Century—fairly recently in the history of humankind—that Christoph Scheiner discovered light enters the eye and carries images with it. Prior to this time, various theories held that the eye emitted energy to pick up what was around it; that the eye was a transmitter of energy rather than a receiver.

The eye is really a light catching device. The source of light may be projected from or reflected off of something. Either way, light usually is perceived as traveling in straight lines, carrying with it an image as determined by the arrangement of reflected light rays. As an image is cast on the retina, the photosensitive nerve endings there are stimulated. The degree and nature of the stimulation is passed from the retina along the optic nerve to the brain where the image is formed in your mind's eye. Sight, therefore, occurs in the eye and in the brain. As a result, we perceive value and color, in addition to a variety of other visual stimuli. In fact, it has been estimated that one-third of the human brain is devoted to vision and visual memory!

WHAT VALUE AND COLOR ARE

All light is not created equally.

You have observed this when buying clothes, for example. A shirt or blouse may appear to be one color in a store under artificial lighting and another color outside. That is why some people carry a garment to a window or out on the sidewalk to look at it under natural light—to see what the "true" colors really are—before buying it. Colors in photographs that are shot outdoors may look very nice, yet when photographs are made indoors under incandescent lighting, using "outdoor" film, the images may look yellowish. What is it that accounts for these variations in our perception of color? And what makes one color look lighter or darker than another *shade* or *tint* of the same color?

The amount of light striking the specialized photosensitive cells in the retina of the eye determines how light or dark something appears. The greater the amount of light received, the lighter or brighter something appears; the less light received by the retina, the darker the image appears. Photographic film that is sensitive to the amount of light it receives is used for black-and-white photography.

The amount of light received by either the retina of the eye or photographic film determines our impression of the visual relationships of light to dark: value.

A discussion of our perception of light necessarily involves much more than just our response to the quantity of light.

In 1666 Isaac Newton, at the age of twenty-three, observed that white (natural) light, when passed through a prism, broke down into bands of color known as the *spectrum*. Newton also observed that the colored bands of the spectrum could be regrouped into a white beam of light when passed through a second prism, thus definitively proving that color comes from white light.

The white light that was passed through a prism was broken down into bands of colored light in accordance with the length of their waves, or wavelengths, as seen on an oscilloscope. Each color of the spectrum has an identifiable wavelength, red having the longest wavelength and violet having the shortest (Illus. 6–18). The major wavelengths of the visible spectrum are identified as red, orange, yellow, green, blue, indigo, and violet—easily remembered in the proper order by

▶ Illustration 6-18   Wavelength Diagram

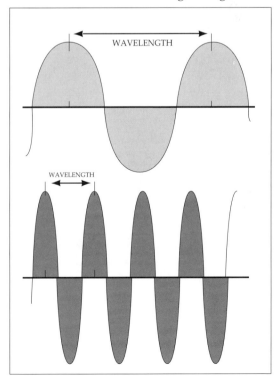

▶ Figure 6-79 Local Value

the first initial of each color, spelling the name ROY G. BIV.

> Color, therefore, is defined as the response of vision to the quality of a wavelength.

The amount of light reflected from a surface determines how light or dark that surface appears. All objects reflect a certain amount of light: Writing paper reflects just about all of the light it receives, whereas ink reflects very little; grass and apples reflect about the same amount of light. The quantity of light an object inherently reflects under "normal" daylight conditions is referred to as its *local value* (see Fig. 6–79). Similarly, the quality of wavelengths that are reflected by an object under "normal" daylight conditions reveals that object's *local color* (see Fig. 6–80).

The retina of the human eye is structured to pick up the difference between quantity and quality of wavelengths. Photosensitive cells in the retina are specialized: Photosensitive rods are stimulated by light and respond to the amount of light they receive, whereas photosensitive cones respond to the qualities of wavelengths. They work in harmony to communicate to the brain not only the perceived color, but also how light or dark that color may be—the value of the color. From dissections and comparisons with other mammals, the presence or absence of rods and cones in eyeballs is one indicator that some animals do not see in color.

▶ PRINCIPLES OF VALUE

Understanding that color comes from white light and that value is determined by a quantity of reflected light, we realize that if no light strikes the retina there will be no vision—in the absence of light there is no color and there are no value relationships. Value and/or color contrasts are necessary to see forms, any forms. In the presence of light, the optically perceived amount of light reflected from a surface depends on

1. The nature of the light source (natural, fluorescent, incandescent),
2. The nature of the surface reflecting the light (rough, smooth, light, dark),
3. The distance of the surface from the light source (intensity) , and
4. The position of the surface relative to the light source (angle of reflected light) (Fig. 6–81a–d).

(You may recall that these variables affecting the way we perceive value are the same as the variables affecting the way we see texture.)

 ## VALUE SCHEMES: OBJECTIVE

You have observed that when light falls on a surface that has a gradual curve to it, such as a sphere, there is a gradual and even gradation of value change from light to dark. However, when light falls on surfaces that have abrupt changes of planes, such as a cube, there are abrupt changes of value. Because there are no abrupt changes of surface directions on a sphere, there are no abrupt changes of value. This overall relationship of lights and darks on a form or in a composition is known as a *value scheme* (Fig. 6–82).

You should be sensitive to some primary optical characterisitcs regarding the effects of light falling on a sphere and the resulting value scheme. First of all, to perceive the sphere, you must have a light source. The *highlight* is the part of the surface of the sphere—or any other form—which catches and reflects most of the transmitted light from the light source to the observer. The highlight appears to be the form's surface closest to the light source. The side away from the light receives less light than the directly illuminated side. Little or no direct light strikes the form behind the widest part of that form, thus putting the "back" half in the shade of the "front" half. The darkest part of the shade is known as the *umbra*, and the lighter part is termed the *penumbra* (Illus. 6–19).

Additionally, little or no light strikes that area of the plane behind the form because the form comes between the plane and the light source. The unilluminated

▶ Figure 6-81

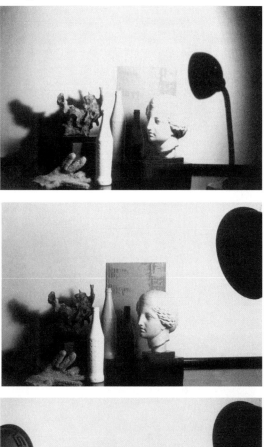

▶ Figure 6-82   Effects of Light on a Cube and Sphere

▶ Illustration 6-19   Value Scheme

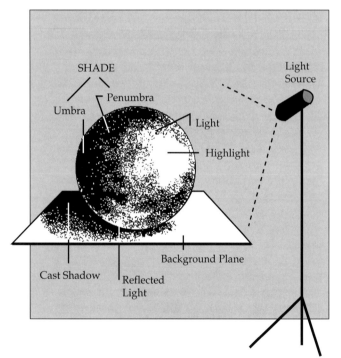

relationship of the form to the direction of the plane receiving the shadow. Also, not all shadows have clean, hard contours. When you look very closely at cast shadows, you observe that when a light source is far away from a form casting a shadow, that shadow will have fuzzy edges, in contrast to the light source which is very close to a form casting sharp-edged shadows (Fig. 6–83).

Only part of the background plane in Illustration 6–19 is in shadow. Some light is reflected from the illuminated areas of the background plane onto the darkest part of the shaded area of the form. When light from the light source bounces off a surface onto a form, that surface becomes an indirect, or secondary light source casting *reflected light* onto the form.

If you were able to peel off a narrow strip from the surface of the sphere with the value scheme imprinted on it, you would see a gradual change of value from white at one end to black at the other, as in Illustration 6–20. Then, if you divided the strip into fairly even blocks, you would see that there are about seven distinct stages of value changes between white and black, yielding a nine-stage *value scale*. A painting which accurately depicts the effects of light falling on a curved form is Ingres's *La Source* (Fig. 6–84). Do you see the same even gradation of values across the curved surfaces of the form?

As previously described, when a light source reveals the three-dimensionality of a form, the value scheme has distinctive characteristics known as a *representational value scheme*. The resulting representational value scheme which evokes a three-dimensional appearance of light and dark relationships is termed *chiaroscuro*, and is evident on the flesh, fabric, and furnishings in Fig. 6–85.

The light source which illuminates the subject matter in a two-dimensional

area on the plane which is shielded from the light by the form is termed a *cast shadow*. Be alert to occasions when the cast shadow may not be an accurate indicator of the true nature of the form casting the shadow. The cast shadow may not have the same characteristics as the form casting the shadow due to variables in the nature of the light source and in the

▶ Figure 6-83   Quality of Shadows

▶ Illustration 6-20   Value Scale from a Sphere

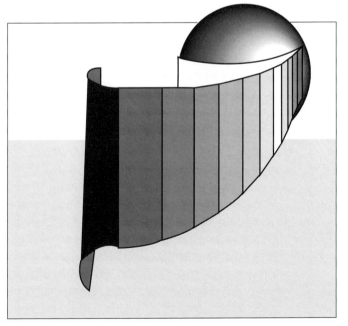

▶ Figure 6-84   Ingres, *La Source*
(*Musée du Louvre,* © Photo R.M.N.)

image may be located inside or outside of a picture frame. In Leonardo da Vinci's *Last Supper* (see Fig. 5–6), which we have looked at before, you can easily see that the light source appears to be coming from the front-left, outside of the border.

The figures in the composition are all uniformly illuminated from the left and the shaded areas of their bodies are on the right. Also, the architecture on the right side of the composition is illuminated from the left, whereas the architecture on

▶ Figure 6-86   Georges de la Tour, *St. Joseph the Carpenter and the Young Christ*
(Musée du Louvre, © Photo R.M.N.)

▶ Figure 6-85   Ivan Le Lorraine Albright (American, 1897–1983), *Into the World There Came a Soul Called Ida*
(Oil on canvas, 1929/30, 142.9 × 119.2 cm., Gift of Ivan Albright, 1977.34, photograph © 1994, The Art Institute of Chicago; All Rights Reserved)

> Value contrasts are an effective means of directing viewer attention in a composition, even if the focal point is conspicuously off-center, as in this case.

the left is in shadow. This yields a representational value scheme, a natural relationship of values which accommodates physical laws, thus representationally revealing the three-dimensionality of the forms.

Nowhere in Leonardo's painting, however, is there a light source evident within the frame of the composition, as there is in Georges de la Tour's *Saint Joseph the Carpenter and the Young Christ* (Fig. 6–86). The candle in La Tour's painting provides

1. The source of light and
2. The focal point of the composition, as the forms closest to the candle are most brightly illuminated.

Since the forms turn away from the strong candlelight, the unilluminated parts of the forms blend into the darkness of the negative spaces surrounding the forms. The sensitive modeling of the forms through light and dark contrasts (chiaroscuro) is seen in the lines of age on Saint Joseph's face and the delicacy of the silhouetted cord around his neck. Can you see where La Tour has also used delicate value contrasts to reveal the smoke above the candle, catching the light as though caught in a high-speed photograph?

The *Saint Joseph* painting also illustrates another important facet of value and shading:

> When a colored surface turns away from a light source, the color becomes a darker value of that same color—it does not turn black.

This is seen on the head of Saint Joseph and the chest of the young Christ. Additionally, shadows are not inherently black or some other neutral value; rather, shadows are darker values of the surface receiving the shadow.

> The colors in shade and shadow are darker because they are receiving less light. There is a diminished quantity of light, but the quality remains the same.

In contrast to the effects of illumination observed in La Tour's painting, objects illuminated by a strong, direct light source tend to have little variation in lights and darks—everything looks pretty much "bleached out." There is so much light coming from the light source and bouncing off of all the surfaces receiving light that there is no subtlety of tonal transition. The surfaces of the forms are flooded with direct and reflected light, and everything appears flattened since the expected, or "normal" three-dimensional value schemes have been altered by an unnaturally strong or unusually close light source.

Representational value schemes are also significantly altered when there is more than one light source. We usually experience the outside world illuminated from a single light source—the sun. However, if multiple light sources cast multiple shadows, this may alter traditional light-and-dark relationships that we know, thus abstracting our perception of the subject matter (but not necessarily to a major degree).

Does the street corner in Edward Hopper's *Night Hawks* (Fig. 6–87), illuminated by street lights and window displays, appear almost unnatural and uninviting due to the severity of the value contrasts in addition to the harshness of the multiple paths of light?

The model in Philip Pearlstein's *Female Nude on Platform Rocker* (Fig. 6–88) may appear somewhat dehumanized in a dehumanized setting due to multiple and exaggerated shadows. The shadows on the wall look potentially menacing and the shading on the torso and legs is not flattering, nor is it on the rest of the figure. With the nude, Pearlstein has taken traditional art subject matter and contradicted the expected imagery of a sensuous figure. Has this been accomplished by means of atypical value relationships, placement, and cropping? Is the resulting image almost surrealistic in effect?

▶ Figure 6-87   Edward Hopper (American, 1882–1967). *Nighthawks*
(Oil on canvas, 1942, 76.2 × 144 cm.; Friends of American Art Collection, 1942.51, photograph © 1994, The Art Institute of Chicago, All Rights Reserved)

▶ Figure 6-88   Philip Pearlstein, *Female Model on Platform Rocker*
(The Brooklyn Museum, 79.17, John B. Woodward Memorial Fund, A. Augustus Healy Fund B., Dick S. Ramsay Fund, and Other Restricted Income Funds)

▶ Figure 6-89   Michelangelo da Caravaggio, *The Conversion of St. Paul* (Alinari/Art Resource, NY)

▶ VALUE SCHEMES: SUBJECTIVE

Inventive and exaggerated uses of value can apply to both representational and abstract art. Exaggerated value patterns can run the gamut from objective to nonobjective works of art. In addition to recording natural, physical properties of light, light can be used in a composition as a device to

1. Heighten visual effects and
2. Convey drama and emotion.

Theater and film directors are certainly aware of the dramatic effects of altered lighting, as are restaurant managers and theme park developers. It is logical, therefore, that visual artists, too, would push the limits of the natural, physical laws of light and dark for the sake of heightened visual effects, plus emotion and mood, producing more severe value relationships.

A presentation of value that is similar to chiaroscuro, but exaggerated and more dramatic, is *Tenebrism*. Tenebrism was a style characteristic of the Baroque period (seventeenth century) in Europe. One of the leading Tenebrists of the period was the rogue, Michelangelo Caravaggio, who painted the scene of the *Conversion of Saint Paul* (Fig. 6–89). Strong light enters from above, flooding a limited part of the composition, focusing on the primary subjects. This produces strong and dynamic dark shadows, making the lights look lighter because of the contrast. The drama of light and dark is complemented by the exaggerated gesture of the fallen Paul against the passive positions of the horse and attendant. Can you imagine how effective this painting was when originally placed in a darkened part of a church?

This exaggeration of values can also be observed in the sculptures of Gianlorenzo Bernini, another Baroque artist. In the *Ecstasy of Saint Theresa* (Fig. 6–90), Bernini designed the light to come from directly above his sculpture. Accordingly, he employed dramatic undercuts in the sculpture to produce great contrasts of value, especially in the half-open eyes and mouth of the rapturous saint. These dark cavities evoke an aura of dramatic mystery.

Shapes are usually shaded in response to the direction a light is falling on them, yet artists have no obligations to record traditional lighting effects. Juan Gris painted light and dark relationships in harmony with his own needs of pictorial arrangement. In his *Portrait of Picasso* (Fig. 6–91), some of the shapes are shaded on the left, some the top, some the bottom, and others on the right. There is no consistent side that the shadows fall on, either. Interestingly, even though the blending of values appears to be contained on individual two-dimensional shapes that are placed on a variety of angles relative to the picture plane, the shading does not provide a consistent or clear indication of three-dimensional solidity since it does not abide by any consistent light source. Physical laws of light and shadow have been totally ignored, emphasizing a *nonrepresentational value scheme*.

Gris's *Portrait of Picasso* is alive and active, full of interesting yet unnatural—or "incorrect"—shape and value relationships. But to be "good" art, is it necessary that the light-and-dark relationships accommodate natural laws? Only if "good" art is dependent upon slavishly rendered representational images. (Is it?)

In Daumier's *Rue Transnonain, le 15 Avril* (Fig. 6–92), the values are not restricted to particular shapes; rather they accommodate the sense of a beam of light coming in an open window, unselectively illuminating everything it falls on. This is characteristic of an *open value scheme*.

▶ Figure 6-90   Gian Lorenzo Bernini, *The Ecstasy of St. Theresa*
(Alinari/Art Resource, NY)

Aside from being visually stimulating, the open value scheme also unifies everything that shares a common value: The father and his child killed in their sleep in the illuminated bed are one area of focus, and the child's grandparents—on the periphery of the light value—are of another phase of the narrative (probably killed while running in to see what was happening to the father and his child). The harsh, unnatural, bleaching quality of the light on the bed emphasizes the unyielding brutality of the murder of innocents. A *closed value scheme*, as seen in Figure 6–93, might also appear to repeat a flatter and less complementary light quality. The value relationships are clearly contained within primary shapes, thus isolating them from other components of the composition. As abstractions of representa-

▶ Figure 6-91   Juan Gris (José Victoriano
Gonzalez, Spanish, 1887–1927), *Portrait of
Pablo Picasso*
(Oil on canvas, 1912, 74.1 × 93 cm.; Gift of Leigh B. Block,
1958.525, photograph © 1994, The Art Institute of
Chicago; All Rights Reserved)

▶ Figure 6-93   An Example of a
Closed Value Scheme

▶ Figure 6-92   Honore Daumier, *Rue Transnonain, le
15 Avril*
(Babcock Bequest, Courtesy, Museum of Fine Arts; Boston © 1994,
All Rights Reserved)

tional value schemes, do you see how
open and closed value schemes can significantly contribute to the content of a
work?

Sometimes it is not understood how
an image like *Rue Transnonain* or similar
ones can be "art" since the subject matter
is not "pretty" or satisfying to look upon.
Is this a valid concern? Perhaps some justification can be found by looking at other
arts, such as poetry: Vile or ugly events
can be made beautiful and meaningful
when sensitively handled by the approach and devices a writer uses to make
a respected or admired piece. Similarly,

> The definition of art, "a visual form of
> meaningful expression," does not require
> beauty but does require significance and a
> form of presentation that makes an image
> visually rewarding and emotionally or
> intellectually stimulating.

In addition to representational, non-representational, open, and closed value schemes, there is a fifth value scheme: even. *Even value schemes* are characterized by shapes that have no individual shading from light to dark within their primary contours at all. Each shape in the composition is an even shade of one value of a neutral—there are no gradations of value within any single shape. An example of an even value pattern you find in your everyday world would be the checkerboard pattern of a black-and-white tile floor or chessboard: Each square is two-dimensional and occupied by a single, even value. Additionally, since each value is contained—or closed—in a specific shape area by its contour, this example is also referred to as a *closed value scheme*.

▶ TECHNIQUES OF PRESENTING VALUE GRADATIONS

You will recall from the previous section that light reveals texture.

> In most graphic works it is through value contrasts that texture is communicated.

Crosshatching and other graphic shading processes, such as hatching and stippling, are also used for depicting a full range of texture *and* value transitions, as in Elisabetta Sirani's seventeenth-century etching (Fig. 6–94). This image exploits shading techniques producing rich contrasts of value and texture.

As in the previous examples, many artists also find it helpful to shade the surface of a form in the direction the form's

▶ Figure 6-94   Elisabetta Sirani, *The Holy Family with St. Elizabeth and St. John the Baptist*
(The National Museum of Women in the Arts, Washington, D.C., Gift of Wallace and Wilhelmina Holladay)

surface appears to lie. The direction of the value-producing lines indicates the direction of the planes which make up the forms: curved lines for curved surfaces and straight lines for flat surfaces (Illus. 6–21).

If you were trying to simulate representational three-dimensional value schemes in a drawing, you would probably use the side of your pencil making very gradual changes in pressure, thus employing the graphic technique of naturalistic or pressure shading.

Of course, the same naturalistic effects of light and dark can be created in paintings, as well. In David's *Portrait of a*

▶ Illustration 6-21   Directional Shading

▶ Figure 6-95   Jacques-Louis David, *Portrait of a Young Woman in White*
(Chester Dale Collection, National Gallery of Art, Washington)

Young Woman in White (Fig. 6–95), you sense that the light source is in front of the figure and to her right—your left. The shapes closest to the light source are the brightest. They become darker as they get farther away from the source and as the planes of the shapes turn away from the light source.

The gradual gradation of value changes exhibited in this work by David is accomplished by the oil painting technique. (Oil painting was refined by Flemish panel painters of the early fifteenth century.) One of the advantages of painting with oils is that they dry slowly and thus permit the gradual blending of values and colors right on the canvas or other ground. After oils dry, translucent layers of toned oil paint (glazes) can be applied to further enhance value and color changes.

Both positive and negative shapes or space can be modeled with value. The background of the David portrait depicts a negative shape that is void of subject matter. The background plane has a relatively even value, except where there are cast shadows. The effect is of a flat background being close to the subject.

Negative backgrounds may have value gradations from top to bottom or right to left which imply that the space is advancing or receding. Because of the innumerable ways backgrounds and negative space can be shaded to imply three-dimensional space or depth, we observe that negative space is plastic. Illustration 6–22 depicts ways negative spaces, void of subject matter, can appear to advance and recede in space depending upon value relationships.

In an effort to make stone sculptures look more alive, more "real," Egyptian, Greek, and Gothic artists would frequently paint—polychrome—the sculptures that adorned their monuments, religious architecture, and tombs. In contrast, some cultures left their stone sculptures unpainted, without polychrome. To make these blank stones look more natural, small details would be carved or modeled—in the eyes, for example—to produce somewhat of a natural appearance of the shapes and colors of the pupil and iris. In the hands of the most competent of sculptors, this process of outlining the shapes or carving them in a manner to enhance natural value relationships produced surprisingly naturalistic effects of value. So similar to the lifelike appearances of the colors of the eye were these carving techniques that the technique has come to be known as *coloration*, as in the the head of Michelangelo's *David*.

In review of the techniques used to present value gradations, we see that value is an effective visual tool for providing visual clues about the three-dimensional and textural nature of a form or area.

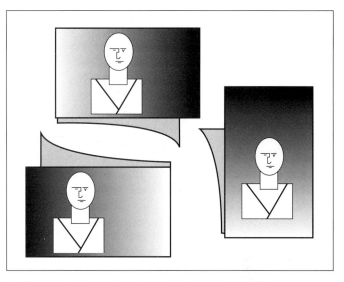

▶ Illustration 6-22　Modeling Space with Value

▶ CONCLUSIONS REGARDING VALUE

You have now observed that value involves more than simple shading. The more responsive you are to the many facets of value, the more potential you have for making significant images, both two- and three-dimensional. Value contrasts exist in your work as a result of your use of tool, technique, medium, and ground.

An overwhelming perception of value is that it involves a light source; but remember,

> Forms stand out from one another because of light and dark contrasts. Thus, the study of value does not always require the concept of projected and reflected light.

The successful use of value involves concepts related to either projected light or figure-ground value contrasts—no concept is more or less meritorious than the other; the validity of one depends on its successful integration in a composition.

Additionally, value relationships may contribute to the emotional content of the work, as we saw in the discussion of subjective value schemes. Further, the expressive use of value can be enhanced with expressive use of shape. As a result, realize that when you are working with value, you are not only establishing what something looks like or simply making a pleasing design, you are also establishing the mood of your image. But be careful not to oversimplify: Could you always use dark values to imply sadness and light ones to imply joy?

▶ PRINCIPLES OF COLOR

The relationship between value and color is inseparable. Both are dependent upon light, as you have seen. And since light is involved, you know that observed color will be dependent upon the quality and quantity of wavelengths reaching the rods and cones in the retina of the eye.

You also understand that white light is the source of color, but do you under-

▶ Figure 6-96   Pablo Picasso, *The Charnel House*
(1945, oil and charcoal on canvas, 78⅝ × 98½″, Collection, The Museum of Modern Art, New York, Mrs. Sam A. Lewisohn Bequest and Purchase)

▶ Figure 6-97   Lamar Dodd, *Pawley's Island at Night*

stand how the eye perceives the individual colors in clothing, paintings, rocks, and trees? White light falls on these objects, yet your eyes respond to something less than white light!

When one thinks of paintings, one usually thinks of colorful images—images that are *chromatic*: greens working dramatically with reds, or blues mildly contrasted against violets. However, it is not always necessary that a painting have a lot of color. In fact, some paintings are colorless, or *achromatic*—without color. These could be wash drawings or paintings done in India ink, or they may be oil paintings executed in varying values of gray—ranging from black to white—etchings, and so on (Lamar Dodd, Fig. 6–97).

Paintings may be colorless—achromatic, or colorful—*polychromatic*, possessing many colors. They also may consist of only one color. These are known as *monochromatic* paintings. Monochromatic images exhibit varying degrees of lights and darks—varying values—of a single color (Debbie Cline, Fig. 6–98). In the image of the water tower, the blue has been altered with black and white, but the blue is still blue—it is not green nor red because of the addition of black and white. Only the quantity of reflected light has changed by the addition of black and white, not the quality of the light itself. Black and white have had no effect on the color blue—they are neutral regarding their ability to change a color. Therefore,

> Since neither black nor white changes a color, they are referred to as neutrals instead of colors.

When a neutral makes a color lighter, it affects the color's *tint*, and when a neutral makes a color darker, it affects the color's shade. For example, white, when added to red, makes pink—a lighter tint of red—and black, when added to red, makes dark red—a darker shade of red.

▶ **PIGMENTS**

You remember that we said, "The amount of light reflected from a surface determines how light or dark that surface appears." All surfaces have varying capacities to reflect light according to the materials and pigments which make up those surfaces. The pigments are particles—either natural or synthetic—which have particular light-absorbing and light-reflecting characteristics. Dark pigments, such as black, absorb almost all of the light striking them; thus, an area that is filled with black pigments will reflect almost no light at all to the retina. As a result, your mind's eye sees that area as black, or dark. A white surface, on the other hand, absorbs almost none of the light which may strike it, reflecting all light to your eye, making that area appear very light, or white.

Recall Newton's discovery which unveiled the fact that white light carries different wavelengths, and that those wavelengths—when separated—indicated different colors to the human eye. *Color is the response of vision to the quality of a wavelength.* Surfaces that have colored pigments in them, as opposed to the aforementioned neutrals, reflect light in a somewhat different manner. When struck by white light—light which contains all of the colors of the spectrum, pigments absorb some wavelengths and reflect others. For example, the naturally occurring red pigments in an apple's skin absorb the orange, yellow, green, blue, indigo, and violet wavelengths, but reflect the red wavelength to the eye. This is why we see *red*, the local color of the apple. Thus, when white light falls on these objects, your eyes respond to something less than white light (Illus. 6–23).

> You may think of a pigment as a discriminating reflector of a particular wavelength, or you might say that it is a filter, absorbing some wavelengths and reflecting others.

Realizing that in order to see color, there must be reflected light, you can also say, "In the absence of light, there is no color." Just turn off the light in a room to "see" this.

▶ Figure 6-98   Debbie Cline, *Water Tower*

▶ **LIGHT SOURCES**

These principles associated with the reflected qualities of wavelengths have been based on light that is natural, or close to it: white light. But we know that not all light is white. We have discussed the fact that incandescent lighting yields yellowing effects and fluorescent lights yield bluish effects. Why?

Each type of light source has its own unique spectrum and only portions of spectrums are visible (Illus. 6–24). Some sources emit more of one wavelength than another, and some sources do not emit all of the traditional colors of the spectrum. For example, fluorescent lights emit more blue wavelengths whereas incandescent lights emit more yellow wavelengths. As a result, images and forms look more blue than "natural" under fluorescent light and more yellow under incandescent

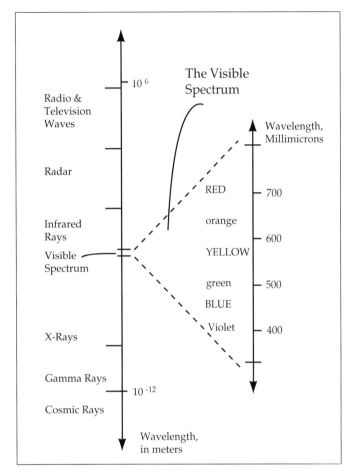

The Visible Spectrum

Radio & Television Waves

Radar

Infrared Rays

Visible Spectrum

X-Rays

Gamma Rays

Cosmic Rays

10^6

10^{-12}

Wavelength, in meters

Wavelength, Millimicrons

RED

orange

YELLOW

green

BLUE

Violet

700

600

500

400

▶ Illustration 6-24   Visible Spectrum

light. But why might a red apple appear black in blue light?

In order to understand why things look different under different lighting, review the previous paragraphs on the light-reflecting capabilities of *pigments:* Pigments will reflect and absorb specific wavelengths as determined by their individual characteristics. A red apple, for example, reflects red when the "red" pigments are struck by light possessing the red wavelengths; the same pigments absorb any nonred wavelengths. A light which only projects red light would strike the apple with red wavelengths and the apple would continue to reflect and ap-

pear red. But if a projected light were blue—one projecting only blue wavelengths—the red apple would absorb the blue and, since the apple receives no red from the light source to reflect, the apple would appear black.

▶ PIGMENT COLOR THEORY

As with any great discovery, there were those who were skeptical of Newton's new observations and there were those who enthusiastically embraced his breakthrough. Johann Wolfgang von Goethe, a German poet and philosopher, as well as a student of light and vision, spent many years bitterly denouncing the findings of Newton. Francois Voltaire, on the other hand, said that Newton was "the greatest man that ever lived." Yet what makes the discovery of the spectrum meaningful to artists?

The Color Wheel

In observing the similarity of the hues at each end of the spectum, Newton joined them together to form a circle which we now refer to as the *color wheel*—a circular arrangement of colors which perpetuates the order of the spectrum (Illus. 6–25).

What were the advantages in placing the ends of the spectrum together to form a circle? If the band were joined together just to break the monotony of a linear presentation, there would be no advantage. However, by bending the spectrum "strip" into a circle, many vibrant color relationships were revealed.

Most people are familiar with the common color wheel; the placement of the colors on this wheel has been observed by most students from the earliest levels of grade school. But the relationships depicted in the color wheel are not "common"; they are sophisticated and potentially very expressive relationships. The sensitive viewer of art realizes how the skilled artist's selection and use of color contributes to the excitement and content of an image.

> Color does much more than simply describe objective surface qualities.

Around the circle are located the colors of the spectrum. Since you are primarily dealing with pigments in a color wheel instead of light alone, you label the colors a bit differently. For example, "indigo" is blue-violet. Also, the term *color* is used interchangeably with the term *hue*. Traditionally, *hue* has been used to define a color's relative position in the spectrum, but through common usage, hue and color have become synonyms; this is evidenced by the fact that we refer to the color wheel as a *color* wheel, not a *hue* wheel.

Color Positions

The arrangement of colors on the wheel places the first color of the spectrum, red, at about the eight o'clock position. Why? Is this just a random place to start, or is there a conspicuous reason that red should be located at no other place on the wheel?

Look at the wheel again. Observe that by placing the red at eight o'clock, the other colors/hues are equally distributed around the circle. Going in a clockwise direction, yellow ends up at the top while violet ends up at the bottom. Now, if you recall that value and color are related, you observe that yellow is the lightest in value of all the colors of the spectrum and violet is the darkest in value. By arranging the

colors in the circular arrangement as described above,

1. The color of lightest value is placed at the top of the color wheel and the color of darkest value is placed at the lowest level; and
2. There is a general progression from dark to light of most colors from the bottom to the top of the color wheel (see Fig. 6–99, the black-and-white photo of the color wheel).

As a result of these placements, you have discovered and given order to two properties of color: hue and value.

Color Triads

There are twelve colors on the color wheel—a few more than the seven labeled in the spectrum. Where did the other colors come from?

Again, from your earliest grade-school experiences you know that you mixed colors to create new ones. On the color wheel you mixed red and yellow to make orange, yellow and blue to make green, and blue and red to make violet. But where did you get red, yellow, and blue? To say "from a bottle or tube" might

▶ Figure 6-99   Color Wheel
(Photo by Carol Hopchak)

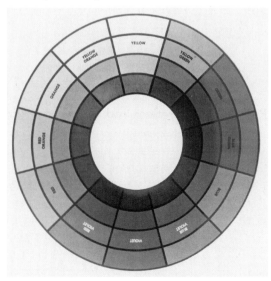

appear sarcastic or flippant, but in reality this is true, for you cannot mix any two colors to create red, yellow, or blue. As a result, they are termed *primary colors.* Interestingly, they fall equally spaced on the color wheel and, when connected with lines (see Illus. 6–26), form an equilateral triangle known as the *primary triad.*

Mixed primary colors create new colors, orange, green, and violet. These *secondary colors* (to have a primary you must have a secondary, and vice versa)—when connected by line—also form an equilateral triangle, not surprisingly known as the *secondary triad* (see Illus. 6–27). Combined, the overlapping primary and secondary triads create the form of the Star of David.

The labels of the spectrum are the primary and secondary colors of the color wheel plus indigo, or blue-violet. Blue-violet is created by mixing blue and violet together, as red-violet is created by mixing red and violet together. As you go around the color wheel, you can continue to mix primary and secondary colors to create *tertiary colors*, of which there are six. This forms the tertiary triads (Illus. 6–28), of which there are two. Be alert to the fact that

> When you identify a tertiary color by name, you describe it with the primary color's name first, followed by the secondary color's name, as in "yellow-green."

The twelve colors of the color wheel are now in place. However, this does not mean there is nothing more to learn from the wheel, nor that there are no additional colors. Countless other colors can be made by mixing tertiaries and secondaries, and these new colors can be mixed with each other, and so on and so on (similar to dividing one by a half by a half by a half). You could go on forever, but that would be unnecessary for the purpose of depicting the basic principles of color.

▶ COLOR RELATIONSHIPS

The color wheel not only places the extreme value contrasts at opposite ends, it also establishes how many value levels there are for color between the neutrals, black and white. There are seven levels, or strata, on the color wheel: Violet—being very dark—is on the ground, or first level, and yellow—being very light—is at the top, or seventh level (Illus. 6–29). Recall the *value scales* from the previous discussions of value: It was said that there are seven levels of gray between black and white, as observed in the transition of light across a spherical or similarly curved form (see Illus. 6–20).

You see from the value levels of the colors that the transition on the left side of the color wheel is smoother than on the right side. Also, you can see that the hues on the left side are a little bit lighter than their corresponding hues on the right. Do you also see how blue is lighter in value than the other hues at or near its level? It is apparent from these observations that there are subtle irregularities in the relationship between value and color.

The individual value levels of both neutrals and colors can be labeled. As both colors and neutrals approach black or white at the ends of the scale, the middle value at the middle level is termed *medium.* Hues and values above medium are in the light range (remember the sphere!) and those below medium are in the dark range, as further defined in Illustration 6–29.

The circular arrangement of the color wheel places colors side by side in an arrangement that depicts still another interesting feature: Colors that are beside each other on the color wheel share a common hue. They are termed *analogous.* Additionally, colors that are directly opposite each other are termed *complementary.*

When lines are drawn to connect all of the complementary colors, a structure similar to the spokes of a wheel emerges, with brown being the hub. Thus, this arrangement of colors is known as the color *wheel* as opposed to the color *circle*.

If you were to recall the discussion of Newton's theory of light and wavelengths, you remember that he directed the colors of the spectrum back through a prism, thus recreating white light. But when you mix all of the pigments of the color wheel together, you do not get white; rather, you get brown.

Colors are at their purest quality of wavelength (highest saturation of pure hue) when located in their traditional position on the outer band of the wheel. As such, they are referred to as being at their highest spectrum *intensity*.

> Intensity can only be altered by mixing a color with its complement—by mixing across the color wheel. This has the effect of visually neutralizing the color.

▶ COLOR SYSTEMS

Value, hue, and intensity are characteristics of color dependent upon the relationship between pigments and light.

> Due to the ability of a pigment to absorb or subtract wavelengths from a light source, we refer to the color systems associated with the absorbent and reflective nature of pigments as subtractive systems.

Artists, scientists, and people in industry have always been fascinated with the various ways the three physical properties of color—hue, value, and intensity—could be best presented to serve their own needs. On the traditional color wheel, value is observed on the vertical scale, hue is observed around the wheel, and variations in intensity are observed across the spokes of the wheel. However, the color wheel does not suit everyone's needs.

Early in the twentieth century, Albert Munsell, himself an artist, designed a color system different from the color wheel which was later to be standardized and adopted as an industrial model for naming, or at least identifying, the tints and shades of five basic hues: red, yellow, green, blue, and purple. The addition of five resulting secondary colors yielded ten basic hues of the Munsell system. Illustrated on a three-dimensional model, value is located on the ascending scale of each arm and the spectrum intensity of the hue is located at the outermost position of each level. The various hues are located on each arm of the model. Each color's position—each location—on the model is given a numerical and letter coefficient according to its location. This makes it possible for other people with similar models to easily identify the same value or intensity of a particular hue when given its coefficient.

The concept of establishing a standard nomenclature for colors was relatively new for the early 1900s, yet today we can think of countless industries that standardize their own individual color systems. For example, you have bought paint by identifying the color you wanted by a particular name, then observed a salesperson referring to a book—the company's color standard—to find the appropriate proportions of various pigments and base to use in mixing your color selection. Graphic artists use Pantone® colors as a nationwide standard of papers and inks. Additionally, textile manufacturers, along with countless other manufacturers of colored items, employ their own color systems which best suit their needs.

Standards are necessary for identifying specific physical properties of color because many variables affect the way a color can look. For example:

1. The nature of the ground influences the visual effects of color. Consider, for example, what a color looks like printed on a light or dark paper.
2. Illumination under varying light sources affects color.
3. The number of coats of colors applied to a ground will also affect that color's opacity and value.

Munsell endeavored to reduce these variables by systematizing the physical properties of color into a single industrial standard that would be utilized by most manufacturers across the nation. But today there are too many industries and technologies to make a single standard applicable to all situations.

In this text's approach to the study of color, the traditional color wheel as it has been introduced will be used as a standard. The color wheel gives us an indication as to how different colors may look in a composition according to their placement on the wheel.

> Remember, the color wheel is a guide as to how colors relate to one another. By no means should it be construed as a color "formula" for making successful art.

Understanding the wheel's color relationships will guide you in exploiting the potential of color, but this alone will not guarantee your making "art." The color wheel is a *tool*, and like any tool, the misuse or ignorance of it can ruin your work. So, to make the most of this new tool, study, observe, and experiment with the principles that have been outlined thus far.

▶ THE ARTIST'S USE OF COLOR

Color Scheme

We have observed that the primary objective use of color is to describe the surface appearance of forms—to depict the local color of subject matter. This may involve quite an elaborate arrangement of colors on the canvas, frequently referred to as the color scheme. The full spectrum of colors may be employed by an artist in a color scheme. The color scheme involves the arrangement and selection of colors used in a particular work of art, be it a painting or a sculpture.

Palette

The selection of colors, the actual colors used by the artist, refers to the artist's *palette*. You know that a palette is also the term for the board or surface used by an artist upon which paints are mixed. A palette is seen in the hand of the nineteenth-century artist, Henri Fantin-Latour, working on a canvas in *A Studio at Batignolles*. Fantin-Latour is surrounded by his friends who include Renoir and Monet (Fig. 6–100).

Gustave Courbet, in his 1863 painting *Magnolias* (Fig. 6–101), used colors representing the entire range of the color wheel. In a less naturalistic manner, Marc Chagall painted the fanciful *I and the Village* (Fig. 6–102), again incorporating a palette that utilized all of the colors of the spectrum. On the other hand, Matisse's *Venus* (see Fig. 6–51), is monochromatic and Malevich's *White on White* (see Fig. 5–28) is achromatic; thus, monochromatic and achromatic palettes have been used. What could be the expressive purpose behind these artists' selection of color? Is the function more than just narrative, and if so, what is being accomplished via color?

In Pablo Picasso's 1923 painting, *The Lovers* (Fig. 6–103), we observe two interesting features regarding the use of color. First, Picasso has given us a lesson in color theory: he has (1) used all the colors of the color wheel and (2) actually incorporated and inverted the progression of colors in the color wheel, placing yellow and yellow-orange at the bottom, then moving in a clockwise direction through greens, blues, violets, and reds. Most interestingly, at the center of Picasso's composition are white forms. Remember, color comes from white light, and the colors of the spectrum can be redirected through a prism producing white light when "remixed." However, you know that when the pigments of the color wheel are mixed, they form brown, so Picasso painted brown hair somewhat near the center of the composition. Secondly, these colors represent moods—a universal characteristic of color. The variety of human emotions and moods surrounds the young lovers, as illustrated by the full range of colors. Picasso's color scheme is both visually delightful and meaningful.

It appears that Andy Warhol also wanted to do a composition based on the order of the color wheel in his 1980 composition entitled *George Gershwin* (Fig. 6–104), a portrait of a great American composer. Interestingly, each of the four quadrants of the picture plane is treated differently—all but one is filled with dynamic color relationships. By looking at the painting, we feel that Gershwin's body and spirit were consumed with energy, as depicted by the color relationships, but that his vision and forward-thinking mental activity appear clear, as

▶ Figure 6-100   Henri Fantin-Latour, *A Studio at Batignolles*
(Orsay Musée, © Photo R.M.N.)

the quadrant that corresponds with his forehead and eyes is uncluttered. All of this content is communicated through the color scheme of the color wheel.

> Remember, it is the artist who determines the content of a work; no artificial formula can, in itself, assure artistic success. Both Picasso and Warhol incorporated similar color schemes, but each artist's image yields a conspicuously different effect.

In the paintings by Courbet, Chagall, Picasso, and Warhol, it appears that they used a somewhat unlimited palette in terms of the selection of colors; whereas in the paintings by Matisse and Malevich the palette appears severely limited, incorporating very few, if any, colors.

A limited versus an unlimited palette: There seems to be the implication that one would have more opportunity for significant artistic expression if one employed an unlimited palette. Why would one limit oneself to just a few colors and values when the whole rainbow is out there?

An artist has selective vision; this is the blessing that distinguishes the eye and mind of the artist from the lens and film of a camera. An artist creates, choosing to include any color, line, shape, value, or texture desired. Also, an artist may exclude anything that does not help the composition and content of the resulting image. By employing a discriminating, selective eye, the artist focuses our vision on a particular objective—streamlining the means of communication.

Earlier in this text you observed that the fifteenth-century Italian architect Leon Battista Alberti stated that classical beauty implied perfect visual harmony. For Alberti, harmony was dependent upon the judicious selection of components to include and exclude in one's art; successful selection meant that nothing could be added to or taken away from an image or form without disastrous aesthetic consequences. Accordingly, an artist may choose to "limit" the palette if it is believed that it will help to communicate more clearly. Or, an artist may choose to employ an unlimited palette. The palette that is best is the one the artist chooses to help communicate most effectively. Following are some features of color that influence what type of palette an artist may choose, and why.

Color Associations

Color is frequently regarded as one of the most universally understood components of art. Associations related to color are often determined by the common experi-ences of humankind. For example, almost all people of all cultures associate heat or warmth with the color red. This comes from experiences with stoves, fires, and the sun. The emotional connotations, therefore, that are associated with red—and even yellow or orange—are often danger, excitement, and energy, just to name a few. Red is also thought of as the color of the heart, so the passion of the heart—love—is also related to red (see Illus. 6–30).

Another color that has significance beyond the color wheel is green: a color representing nature, freshness, and growth. As a result, to many people green implies a sense of calm and serenity. To others, such as bankers, green implies money and growth; thus, green is often seen as a dominant color in bank advertising and marketing.

How many of you have not experienced "the blues," or listened to "the blues"? Blue has traditionally been referred to as a color of sadness or calm, of mysterious foreboding, perhaps because still, deep water is a deep blue, or the emptiness of space looks dark, dark blue. Violet is also a color associated with some of these feelings, and since there is some red in violet, there is more energy associated with violet than with blue.

An example of a cool palette of blues is Picasso's *The Tragedy* (Fig. 6–105). The figures appear self-conscious as they reach out to no one, except for the child who reaches to his father; their heads are bowed and their feet are bare: They are vulnerable. The background environment evokes calm through the emphasis of horizontal lines, and there is no harsh lighting. The overwhelming blue color scheme evokes more than just calm; there is an apparent sadness emphasized by the downward cast of the people's gestures and the dominance of blue, which has also been neutralized in some areas by its complement, orange. There is the impression that the individuals want to maintain their privacy, as the figures acknowledge only each other; the mother turns her back on those of us who look at her in sympathy. Picasso's use of shape and color, together, evoke this overwhelming sensation of sadness and withdrawal.

The neutrals also share some of the emotional connotations of color. White is often selected by designers to imply order and harmony, as in domestic interiors, for example. It is unspoiled and pure, a symbolic neutral also used in a great deal of religious imagery. Black—like blue—is often perceived as morbid due to cultural associations, but is also used to represent "class," as seen in tuxedos and limousines.

Because of experiences equating colors such as red, orange, and yellow with heat, these colors—and their associated tertiary colors—are referred to as warm or hot. On the other hand, colors such as violet, blue, and green—and their associated tertiary colors—are often thought of as being cool due to their association with water and cool depths. If you looked at the color wheel, you would find that you could draw a line somewhere between yellow and yellow-green downward, somewhere between red-violet and red (see Illus. 6–30). This line establishes two sides of the color wheel: a warm side and a cool side. It is a practical reference point for artists when determining their palettes.

▶ **OPTICAL EFFECTS OF COLOR**

Simultaneous Contrast

The quality that enables one component to simultaneously emphasize contrasting features of another component, thus emphasizing the differences between them, you recall, is termed *simultaneous contrast*. When this principle was applied to line for example, it was observed that a straight line placed next to a curved line made the curved line look very curved and the straight line appear very straight (Illus. 6–31). This principle is equally applied to value, shape, and texture. Regarding color, we observe some fascinating effects of simultaneous contrast.

Instead of placing a straight line next to a curved one or a rough texture next to a smooth texture, place a warm color next to a cool one. Immediately you will notice how much cooler the cool color appears, while at the same time the warm color looks warmer (Illus. 6–32). Try working with complements: Take yellow, for example, and place it beside violet—again, you will get simultaneous contrasting effects of color. But in addition to emphasizing contrasts of hue, in this particular example you also get a significant simultaneous contrast of value (Illus. 6–33): The yellow looks lighter and the violet looks darker.

Further drama can be achieved by surrounding one hue or neutral with a contrasting hue or neutral. Continue to contrast yellow and violet: Observe in Illustration 6–33 how the yellow square, when surrounded by violet, looks to be a more vivid yellow. It looks more vividly yellow for two reasons: First, the yellow is surrounded by its complementary hue, thus making the yellow stand out in contrast; and secondly, the yellow is so much lighter in value than violet that it also stands out due to the contrast in value.

Compare the effects of yellow surrounded by black and of yellow surrounded by white. You observe when the value contrasts are reduced, the simultaneous contrast of colors is reduced. Inter-

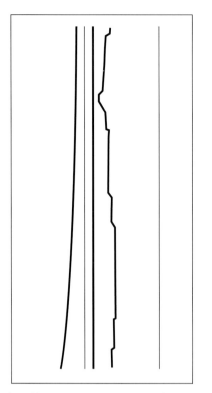

▶ Illustration 6-31   Simultaneous Contrast: Lines

that simultaneous contrast is affected by hue and value *and* the vertical intervals between them.

There is an exception to every rule, and the principle of simultaneous contrast is no exception to that! Simultaneous contrast, while emphasizing opposite effects, may—on occasion—emphasize similarities. For example, in the case of analogous colors, you may place one color next to its analogous color and the common hue will be emphasized. Similarly, if you surround a color with an analogous hue, the common hue between the two will also be emphasized (Illus. 6-36). We should, as a result of our investigation, refine our definition of the principle of simultaneous contrast to read:

> **Any visual component can vary in appearance, depending on the nature of the visual component placed next to it.**

Optical Mixing of Colors

The principle of simultaneous contrast has been exploited by artists of varying cultures for many, many centuries. Perhaps the best known artist to have systematically established a "scientific" basis to the theory of simultaneous contrast was the late nineteenth-century artist, George Seurat, whom we discussed when the component dot was introduced. Art critic John Canaday refers to Seurat as "the most systematic painter who ever lived." Working in the technique known as *pointillism*—small dots of color collectively forming an image—Seurat juxtaposed dots of warm and cool colors so that there would be an *optical mix of the colors in the eye of the viewer*, rather than on the canvas. Pointillism yielded a more intense blend of colors due to the principle of simultaneous contrast. Twentieth-

estingly, when the high-light yellow is surrounded by the neutral white, it makes the yellow appear somewhat darker due to simultaneous contrast, yet when the same high-light yellow is surrounded by the very low-dark black, the high-light yellow looks even lighter (Illus. 6–34).

In the preceding paragraph it is written "when the value contrasts are reduced, the simultaneous contrast of colors is reduced." You can observe this again, by looking at the color wheel—note that green is on a level two steps higher than its complement, red. When you place red and green side by side or surround one with the other, there is some simultaneous contrast (see Illus. 6-35), but not as much as you saw in the yellow-violet contrast. Therefore, relative to color, we observe

century artist John Clarke perpetuated this technique in his painting entitled *Seurat* (Fig. 6–106), painted in 1968. The detail shows how

1. The colors do mix in the eye of the viewer, and
2. The cool tones next to the warm tones make the warms appear warmer and the cools look cooler.

Numerous artists have employed in their palettes varying color schemes involving simultaneous contrast to effect a more stimulating image. In Claude Monet's *Rouen Cathedral*, 1894 (Fig. 6–107), you observe how he has painted the cathedral in blues and violets. And for contrast, the sunlit portion of the portal doorway is painted yellow and the shaded part of the same door violet. The yellow not only makes the cool violet look like a very cool shadow, it also—in contrast to all of the blue and violet in the composition—adds energy, a "punch," to the overall visual effect.

The principles of simultaneous contrast are not limited to painting. In staging Franco Rubartelli's photograph (Fig. 6–108), the effort was made to carefully simulate the value, color, and texture of rocks on the head of the model in the center of the picture plane. In order to keep the overall effect visually vibrant, an orange stone was placed near the head to draw your attention to it. The orange stone was surrounded by blue stones, thus emphasizing the coolness of the image (a deathlike quality?). As a result, the orange stone enhances content and provides variety and focus through simultaneous contrast; the inclusion of the small orange stone adds energy to the image.

The sixth-century church of San Vitale is located in Ravenna, Italy. On the half-domed ceiling above the altar is the image of *Christ Enthroned Between Angels*

▶ Figure 6-106   John Clem Clarke, *Seurat*
(Collection of Sydney and Francis Lewis)

and Saints. As you observe in Figure 6–109, the blues and violets of Christ's robes and the angels' wings stand out in significant contrast against the golden background. You see, therefore, that the principle of simultaneous contrast is not a discovery made by "modern" artists, nor is it limited to "modern" art.

In addition to examples in art, simultaneous contrast is a principle unwittingly adopted by many people in their clothing. For example, men may choose to wear yellow or orange ties with their blue suits; red-headed men and women will often wear green in order to make their hair look more vibrant. However, a mistake of many adolescents with a bad complexion is to wear green, for the green emphasizes its complementary color in skin tones.

Many more examples of art exist which demonstrate the use of complementary colors. Another type of palette involves *split complements*: a color and the two colors on each side of its complement, such as green, red-violet and red-orange. The visual energy is not diminished, and the variety of colors is enhanced.

Afterimages

Two optical effects related to color have already been mentioned. They are

▶ Figure 6-108　Franco Rubartelli, *Veruska*
(Reproduced by special permission of *Playboy* magazine, copyright © 1970 by *Playboy*, photo by Franco Rubartelli)

▶ Figure 6-109　*Christ Enthroned Between Angels and Saint*
(©Art Resource)

1. Simultaneous contrast and
2. The optical mixing or colors.

A third optical effect is the *afterimage*. Sometimes the photosensitive cells which line the back of the retina become overstimulated by extremely strong stimuli or by an extremely long look at particular stimuli. In such cases, the light-stimulated cells continue sending messages to the brain after the stimuli are gone or a stronger one is received. If you have had your picture taken with a flash-camera and "seen" a white dot long after the photo was taken, or stared at something for a long time and continued to "see" that something in your mind's eye long after you looked away, you have experienced the effects of overstimulated photosensitive cells producing afterimages.

Photosensitive cells respond to both the quantity and quality of wavelengths. Usually, it takes a fairly long exposure to a stimulus for color to remain "fixed" in your mind's eye after the source of the stimulus has departed. Bright light, on the other hand, takes less time of exposure to "fix" an image. The duration and strength of an afterimage, therefore, is directly related to the strength and quality of the image and the duration of exposure to the stimulus.

Red and blue, being of the same relative value, will produce similar afterimaging effects. However, the afterimage effect of yellow is much greater due to the brilliance of yellow's natural or local value. Since the stimulus—yellow—is greater, the effect is more rapid and lasts longer.

▶ COLOR AND BALANCE

You now have a feeling for the strong visual effects of the lighter-value colors as opposed to the darker ones. The lighter colors impact on the mind's eye more vividly. You need to be aware of this when designing with color. Some compositions are predominantly yellow or orange. Others have a dominance of blue or violet. If you were trying to establish a visual equilibrium of color, you would need to be able to control the way the various colors impact on the mind's eye, and the different proportions required.

Illustration 6–37 depicts visually balanced relationships between the complements yellow and violet, green and red, and blue and orange. In each example you feel a satisfactory resolution of proportions in each hue, although the "amounts" of color vary. In a similar manner, Monet was able to keep his image of Rouen Cathedral chromatically balanced (see Fig. 6–109).

▶ COLOR SCHEMES

In our earlier discussion of *value*, the principles of open, closed, representational, nonrepresentational, and even value schemes were discussed. The same principles apply to color. Therefore, substitute *color* for *value* in each of the preceding examples to discover ways beyond naturalistic representation that color can be used.

A few illustrations of various color schemes include Piet Mondrian's *Broadway Boogie-Woogie* (Fig. 6–110) and *Composition in White, Black, and Red* (see Fig. 5–10). These are examples of even color schemes. Each rectilinear shape is two-dimensional and occupied by a single, even value of a color or neutral. And (like the value scheme) since each color or neutral is contained—or closed—in a specific shape area by its contour, these examples are called closed color schemes.

Closed color schemes were also utilized in designs by Mary Cassatt (Fig. 6–111). The broad and flat areas of color and value are contained by the primary contours of the shapes. Her images—

which incorporate large, flat areas of color and value—were strongly influenced by the woodcuts of Japanese artists, like so many other images by nineteenth-century artists.

Fernand Léger combines both *even* and *representational* color schemes in his painting, *The City* (Fig. 6–112). The telephone pole near the center of the composition, along with the figurative forms near the bottom and the semicircular forms at top-center, all incorporate naturalistic gradations of value and color. This produces a representational color scheme. However, there is a dominant use of the even color scheme in the areas of flat color restricted by contours. *The City* is a huge

▶ Figure 6-111 Mary Cassat, *The Bath*
(The National Museum of Women in the Arts, gift of Wallace and Wilhelmina Holladay)

painting, measuring about 8 feet by 10 feet. Léger places the recognizable form of the telephone pole near the center to draw us into the painting, and we almost believe it is real. But through the contradictory means of the various color schemes and abstracted shape and color relationships, Léger creates the illusion of a surrealistic city—to scale—that jars us and challenges our experiences and definitions as to what a city really is.

Color and Abstraction

Paolo Uccello was clearly a misguided artist, as you observe in his painting, *The Rout* (Fig. 6–113), from the larger painting, *The Battle of San Romano*. Can you imagine any self-respecting Renaissance artist painting purple and violet horses during an age that celebrated objective, rational discoveries made in optics, anatomy, and spatial relationships! This image is, indeed, a contradiction to the times in which it was painted. But if you look closely, you will see that the figures in the background landscape are conspicuously out of proportion to their surroundings, too. In the foreground, the "land" on which the soldiers fight looks more like a stage floor (and the background a stage backdrop). Quite neatly, the spears mostly fall parallel to one another. Additionally, the horses have been simplified to basic, geometric shapes. In the end, what you observe is a composition where most of the visual information has been abstracted to one degree or another, and the abstraction of the horses really doesn't look too bad. In fact, in light of all of the other liberties taken by Uccello, the horses would probably have looked awkward if their colors were more natural.

So, Paolo Uccello was not misguided. In fact, he had a very clear understanding as to how to make his forms more visually dynamic; more than just narrative subject matter. It might even be said that Uccello was ahead of his time in his understanding and application of abstraction.

In the end, you observe that

> There is nothing wrong with changing, rearranging, or altering color for the individual needs of artistic expression.

But be careful, if you consider abstracting one visual component in a composition, you should consider abstracting others—as Uccello did—so that no single component will stand out too conspicuously. (On the other hand, if you want a single component to really stand out, now you know how to do it!)

▶ COLOR AND THE THREE-DIMENSIONAL ARTS

Think of the great stone sculptures which adorn the classical buildings of Greece. Visualize the bleached white surfaces of monolithic Egyptian stone sculptures (Fig. 6–114) or the monumental carvings on the Gothic cathedrals of Europe. The pale or colored stones, in their overall tonal simplicity, evoke an "otherworldly" quality, a sense of presence unequaled by many, more recent sculptures.

These sculptures, however, were not always *achromatic*. Through the passage of time, their surfaces have succumbed to the ravages of their environments. Blowing sand, rain, snow, humidity, and other natural elements have caused the original *polychromed* surfaces of the sculptures to wear away, leaving behind the appearance of the natural stone.

Figure 6-80 *Local Color*

Illustration 6-23

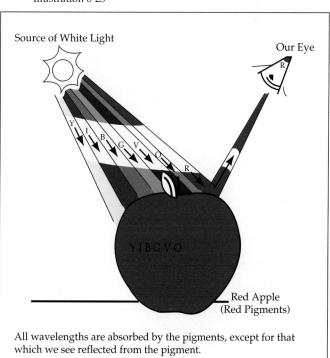

Source of White Light

Our Eye

Red Apple
(Red Pigments)

All wavelengths are absorbed by the pigments, except for that
which we see reflected from the pigment.

Reflective Characteristics of Pigment

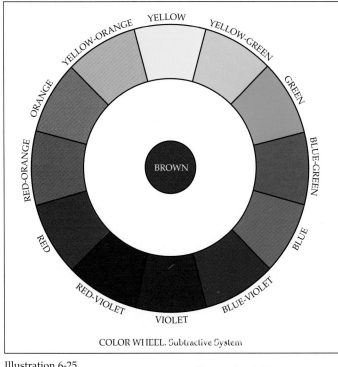

COLOR WHEEL. Subtractive System

Illustration 6-25

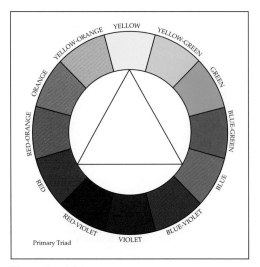

Primary Triad

Illustration 6-26

Illustration 6-30

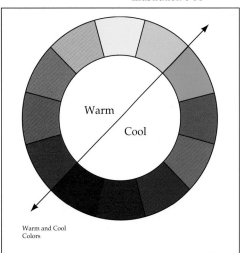

Warm and Cool Colors

Illustration 6-29

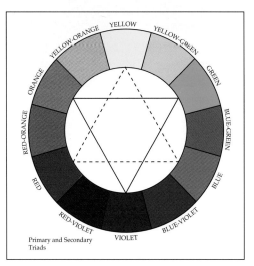

Primary and Secondary Triads

Illustration 6-27

Illustration 6-28

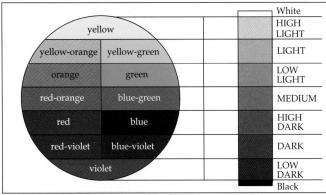

Color and Value

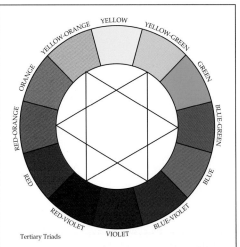

Tertiary Triads

Figure 6-101 Gustave Courbet, *Magnolias*
(Kunsthalle Bremen, © 1863 Öl auf Leinwand, 73 x 109 cm)

Figure 6-102 Marc Chagall, *I and the Village*
(Oil on canvas, 6'3 5/8" x 59 5/8", Collection of the Museum
of Modern Art, New York, Mrs. Simon Guggenheim Fund)

Figure 6-103 Pablo Picasso, *The Lovers*
(Chester Dale Collection, © 1993 National Gallery of Art,
Washington, 1923, oil on linen, 51 1/4" x 38 1/4")

Figure 6-104 Andy Warhol, *Ten Portraits of Jews of the Twentieth Century (George Gershwin)* 1980
One from portfolio of 10 screenprints on Lenox Museum Board, 40 x 32 in.(© 1995 The Andy Warhol Foundation, Inc.)

Figure 6-105 Pablo Picasso, *The Tragedy* (Chester Dale Collection, © 1993 National Gallery of Art, Washington, 1903, wood, 41 1/2″ x 27 1/8″)

Illustration 6-32

Simultaneous Contrast: Warm/Cool

Illustration 6-33

Simultaneous Contrast:

Color and Value Relationships

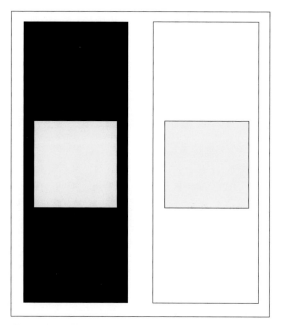

Illustration 6-34

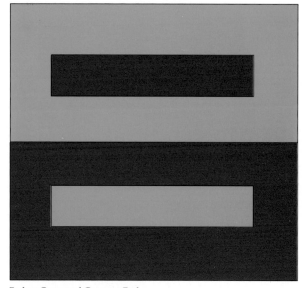

Red on Green and Green on Red

Illustration 6-35

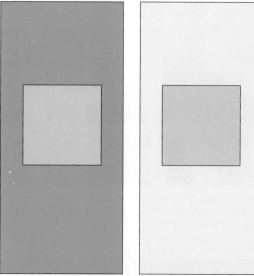

Yellow-Green on Green   Yellow-Green on Yellow

Illustration 6-36

Figure 6-107 Claude Monet, *Rouen Cathedral: The Portal (in Sun)*
(The Metropolitan Museum of Art, Bequest of Theodore M. Davis, 1915. Theodore M. Davis Collection. Oil on canvas. 25 7/8" x 39 1/4")

COLOR AND BALANCE:

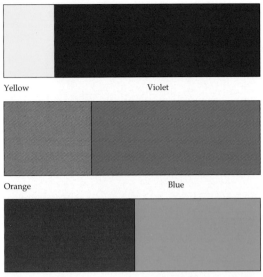

Yellow   Violet

Orange   Blue

Red   Green

Illustration 6-37

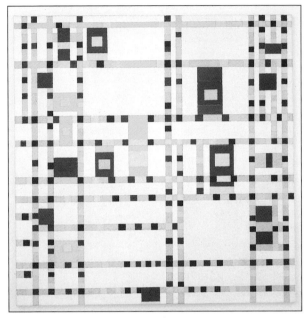

Figure 6-110 Piet Mondrian, *Broadway Boogie-Woogie*
(Oil on canvas, 5" x 50", Collection of the Museum of
Modern Art, given anonymously)

Figure 6-112 Ferdnand Leger, *The City*
(Oil on canvas, 91" x 177 1/2", Philadelphia Museum of Art:
A.E. Gallatin Collection)

Figure 6-113 Paolo Uccello, *Niccolo Mauruzi da Tolentino at the
Battle of San Romano (The Rout)*
(Reproduced by courtesy of the Trustees, The National Gallery,
London)

Figure 6-114   Abu-Simbel, *Exterior*
(Photo by Virginia I. Davis)

Figure 6-115 Pre-Columbian, Maya, *A Ruler Dressed as Chac-Xib-Chac and the Holmul Dancer*, © 600-800
Ceramic with traces of paint, 9 3/8 in. h.
Photograph by Michael Bodycomb

Figure 6-116 Alexander Calder, *Untitled*
(Gift of the Collectors Committee, © 1994 Board of Trustees, National Gallery of Art, Washington, 1976, aluminum and steel, 358 1/2" x 912")
Photo by Philip A. Charles

Illustration 6-39

Figure 6-118 George Segal, *Blue Girl on a Black Bed*
(© 1994 George Segal/VAGA, New York; Virginia Museum of Fine Arts, Richmond, Gift of Sydney and Frances Lewis)

Illustration 6-40

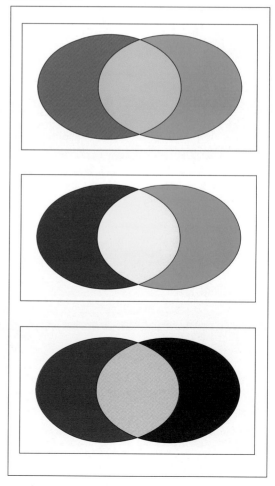

PROJECTED COLORED LIGHT: Shadow Effects

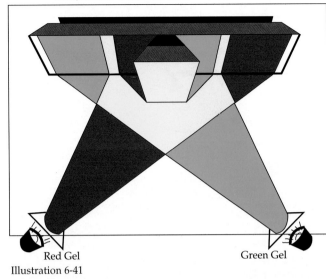

Red Gel   Green Gel
Illustration 6-41

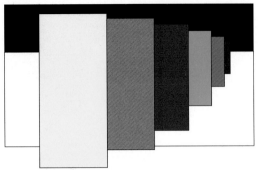

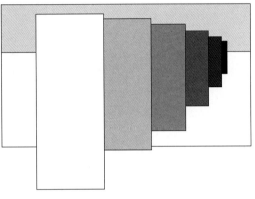

Illustration 7-13

Figure 7-14 Thomas Cole, *American Lake Scene* © 1846
(Mint Museum of Art, Charlotte, North Carolina, Gift of Mr. and
Mrs. William S. Lowndes)

Figure 7-17 Paul Cezanne, *Still Life with Ginger Jar and
Eggplants*
(The Metropolitan Museum of Art, Bequest of Stephen C.
Clark, 1960. Oil on canvas, 36" x 28 1/2")

Figure 7-20 *Atmospheric Perspective*
(Photograph by Thomas Morgan)

Many of the antique stone sculptures we observe today were originally painted to make them look more lifelike. Historian Sir Eric Thompson referred to the "quickening color" given sculpted forms by pre-Columbian Mayans. The image of a god, for example, became more compelling, more lifelike, more "real" when it was polychromed in a manner that simulated natural appearances (Fig. 6–115).

> In three-dimensional art forms, there may be two sources of color: the inherent color of the medium or an applied color.

An artist is frequently drawn to a medium due to its alluring color qualities, such as those found in wood, clay, stone, or polished steel. A sculptor may want to design a form that works with a medium's natural color.

> The color of the material a sculpture is made of may contribute to that form's significance.

For many artists, concealing the nature of the medium—its natural texture or color—with paint or other media would be a violation of the integrity of the medium.

> In the 1930s there arose a philosophy in art that taught "truth to materials." This attitude emphasized the necessary and desirable relationship between form and medium.

David Smith, for example, sought to enhance the stainless steel surfaces of his sculptures by polishing them in a manner that would absorb and reflect light in a diffused way. These sculptures were meant to be seen out-of-doors, in nature. He painted other sculptures so they could exist equally well in an interior or exterior environment (see Fig. 2–21, p. 20). Do they?

Sculptors may choose to use applied color as a means to further define shape, draw attention to, or simply stimulate surface and form, a concept revitilized from the ancients by artists including Alexander Calder (Fig. 6–116).

Consider the effects of color on two related sculptures by George Segal (Figs. 6–117 and 6–118). Originally, he produced sculptures out of white plaster which yielded conspicuous emotional qualities, such as fragility, vulnerability, and blandness. Later, due to the fragile nature of plaster, Segal had his forms cast in bronze but tinted white, thus retaining most of the connotations associated with the plaster forms. More recently, Segal started adding color to the bronzes, purposely trying to effect a mood and content different from that established by the white forms.

As you have seen from these examples, color is a very strong component when used on three-dimensional forms. It may overwhelm subtle value gradations which define shapes; it may obscure textural qualities; or color may visually dominate the form entirely. These are things color can do *to* sculpture, but if the artist has a particular objective, these might also be things color can do *for* sculpture.

> Color is not inherently bad when used on sculpture, this you have seen; rather, color—like all of the other components—must be used for a purpose which enhances the aesthetic merit and supports the content of the work.

▶ Figure 6-117   George Segal, *Bus Riders*
(Hirshhorn Museum and Sculpture Garden, Smithsonian Institution, Gift of Joseph H. Hirshhorn, 1966, George Segal/VAGA, New York)

▶ LIGHT COLOR THEORY

At the beginning of this discussion on color, you learned that the source of color is white light, and color depends upon (1) the nature of the light source and (2) reflective properties of a surface. A surface has varying capacities to reflect light, you will recall, depending on the material makeup of the surface, in addition to its pigmentation. The nature of the light source you saw as a variable since light can come from different kinds of light, such as the sun or an incandescent or fluorescent bulb, to name a few.

You also saw the effect of red light projected on an apple as opposed to natural light, or even blue light. This emphasized the fact that

> A pigment cannot reflect a particular wavelength if it does not receive that wavelength.

For example, project light through a blue filter onto an apple from a light source that possesses all the colors of the spectrum. The blue filter will filter out all of the other colors of the spectrum: red, orange, yellow, green, indigo, and violet (thus the term filters, or *gels*). Gels—colored sheets of thin, translucent plastic—remove specific wavelengths from projected light.

An interesting demonstration of the light-filtering capabilities of gels is to individually project light through a colored gel onto a color wheel. The projected hue along with the same hue on the color wheel will look nearly the same. The related analogous hues on the color wheel will also appear fairly close to their "natural" appearance. The other colors of the wheel, however, are not as easy to identify since they are not receiving the necessary range of wavelengths. When projecting blue light, for example, onto an apple, the red pigments in the skin of the apple are absorbing all of the wavelengths but cannot reflect "red" since it is only receiving "blue." Repeat this experiment with other hues. You will note that yellow comes the closest of all the projected beams to possessing the full range of the natural spectrum, as it is closest in color to white light.

Imagine placing two gels in front of a light source, first red then green (Illus. 6–38). When the light source is turned on, all of the white light wavelengths would strike the red gel and only red wavelengths would pass through (the others have been held by the gel). Now, add a green gel behind the red: All of the wavelengths striking the green filter (only red ones) will be absorbed by the green gel, and the green wavelengths—of which there are none—cannot be allowed to pass because they never got there. As a result, no light at all will pass through the two gels.

Gels absorb wavelengths; in other words, gels absorb light. Light is energy. Thus, when gels absorb light they are also absorbing energy in the form of heat. You may have noticed heat waves coming from the top of theater lights due to the absorption of heat energy. In the case of the red and green gels, so much energy is being absorbed by the gels that they can quickly become damaged and even ignite.

If you take all the gels away from the projecting light source and observe the illuminated colors of the color wheel, then take that same color wheel outside, the colors on the wheel may look a bit different. This is due to the nature of the projection bulb. Bulb manufacturers often try to make bulbs simulate natural white light, but an exact duplication is not possible. Specific data and diagrams regarding the spectrums of different bulbs are often available from manufacturers, should you need to know the nature of the spectrum you are using to illuminate your work.

The Additive System

In order to mix colors of projected light one does not mix filters in the manner one mixes pigments. When using projected light, colors are mixed by "stacking," or adding one projected color on top of another. Thus, we refer to light color theory as an *additive system*.

In a subtractive color wheel, when red, blue, and green pigments are mixed they produce brown. However, in the additive system, when red, blue, and green light are projected, you get white since the colors of the spectrum are mixing in terms of wavelength (Illus. 6–39). As a result, red, blue, and green are the primary colors of the additive system. Note that

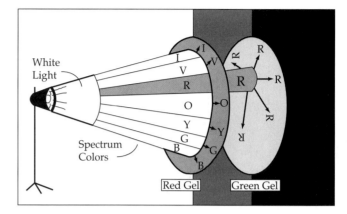

▶ Illustration 6-38   Light-Absorbing Nature of Gels

when you mix pairs of these primaries, you do not get the secondary colors that you might expect. For example, overlapped green and red (subtractive complements!) yield yellow in the additive process. Perhaps the closest "expected" result is the mix of red and blue projections yielding something of a red-violet, magenta (Illus. 6–40).

The properties of shade and shadow are different under colored light as opposed to white light, as you would expect by now, and this is especially true when two or more light sources are involved. Practice with multiple colored light sources to observe the dramatic effects of chromatic shade and shadow.

Remind yourself that a shadow is a darker value of the form receiving the shadow since that area of the form is not receiving any light—light has been blocked by the form casting the shadow. A shadow on a white surface might look a neutral gray or black, for example. A shadow on a red surface might look to be very dark red, or dark green on a green surface.

Study Illustration 6–41 to observe the following characteristics of shadow from multiple colored light sources: at a 45 degree angle from one side, project a red light onto a form which has a white background plane behind it. The plane behind the form will receive red light in all areas except the shadow, which will be dark gray. Now, from the opposite side project a green light onto the object and overlap the red area on the background plane. When you have done this, you will observe that the previously described gray shadow is now reflecting green since that area is only illuminated by green—no red light reaches that area. There is a corresponding red shadow for the same reason. Stage designers have to be particularly sensitive to this, as they could inadvertently create multicolored shadows that might prove inappropriate to (and maybe more interesting than) the drama!

Stage, lighting, and window designers are just a few of the artists who work with the principles of the additive and subtractive color theories at the same time. Their challenge is great, for they have to work with pigmented materials that will work in a prescribed manner under one or more colored light sources.

▶ CONCLUSIONS REGARDING COLOR

The rainbow of colors is available to artists to use as a tool. No artist is obliged to use certain color relationships nor all colors of the color wheel in any given composition. While certain relationships and palettes have been observed to be effective for visual communication, there can be no certainty in saying all relationships and principles have been discovered or applied, and certainly no one other than yourself can establish what will be most effective for your work.

As with sculpture, all art forms must incorporate color in a manner that enhances the image and supports the content of the particular work of which it is a part. It is your job as an artist to make color work for you.

▶ SECTION GLOSSARY

Achromatic   Without color.

Additive System   Associated with the stacking or adding of one color of projected light on top of another. See LIGHT COLOR THEORY.

Afterimage   The photosensitive cells which line the back of the retina become overstimulated by extremely strong stimuli or by an extremely long look at particular stimuli and continue sending messages to the brain (1) after the stimuli are gone, or (2) until a stronger stimulus overrides the first.

Analogous Colors   Colors that are beside each other on the color wheel which share a common hue.

Cast Shadow   The unilluminated area on a background plane or surface which is shielded from light by a form coming between it and the light source.

Chiaroscuro   The simulating of representational value schemes with media which evokes the naturalistic appearance of lights and darks on a form.

Chromatic   Of or relating to color.

Closed Value Scheme   Relationships of light to dark are restricted or limited to particular shapes and areas; selective illumination.

Color   The response of vision to the quality of a wavelength. Syn.: HUE.

Coloration   Value relationships produced by carving in stone which create naturalistic value and color effects.

Color Scheme   The selection *and* arrangement of colors on a ground: open, closed, even, representational, and nonrepresentational color schemes. See VALUE.

Color Wheel   A circular arrangement of colors which perpetuates the order of the spectrum.

Complementary Colors   Colors which are opposite each other on the color wheel.

Even Value Scheme   Shapes that have no individual shading from light-to-dark within their primary contours; each shape in the composition is an even shade of one value of a neutral.

Gels   Colored sheets of thin, translucent plastic film that filter specific wavelengths from projected light. Syn.: FILTERS.

Highlight   The part of the surface of the sphere—or any other form—which catches and reflects most of the transmitted light to the observer. The highlight appears to be the form's surface closest to the light source.

Hue   Traditionally regarded as the name for the quality of wavelength as determined by its position in the spectrum. Syn.: COLOR.

Intensity   Colors at their purest quality of wavelength as depicted on the outer band of the wheel.

Light   That part of a surface which receives direct light from a light source.

Light Color Theory   An additive system incorporating the overlapping of projected beams of colored, primary light (red, blue, and green) to produce secondary colors; primaries of red, blue, and green—when mixed—produce white.

Light Source   The point of origin of illumination; for example, sun or light bulbs.

Local Color   The quality of wavelengths that are reflected by an object under "normal" daylight conditions.

Local Value   The quantity of light an object inherently reflects under "normal" daylight conditions.

Monochromatic   Of or relating to one color and its varying values.

Neutrals   Pigments of no hue, which when added to a color do not change the color but only its tint (lighter) or shade (darker).

Newton, Isaac   At the age of twenty-three in 1666, he observed that white (natural) light, when passed through a prism, broke down into bands of color known as the SPECTRUM.

Nonrepresentational Value Scheme   Light and dark gradations within shapes without a sense of a consistent light source.

Open Value Scheme   Relationships of light to dark are not restricted or limited to particular shapes and areas; unselective illumination.

Palette   The surface on which an artist arranges and mixes colors for painting; the actual colors used by an artist.

Penumbra   The lightest part of the shade.

Photosensitive Cells   Specialized cells known as rods and cones in the retina of the eye which chemically respond to quantities and qualities of light.

Pigment   Particles—either natural or synthetic—which have particular light absorbing and light reflecting characteristics.

Pigment Color Theory   A subtractive system, as in the COLOR WHEEL; primaries of red, yellow, and blue—when mixed—produce brown.

Polychromatic   Of or relating to many colors.

Polychrome   Paint color, usually on a sculpture or architectural form.

Polychromed   Painted sculpture or architectural form.

Primary Colors   Fundamental pigments of which others are comprised.

Reflected Light   Illumination bounced onto a form from a surface; a secondary light source providing indirect light.

Representational Value Scheme   A natural relationship of values which accommodates physical laws, thus representationally revealing the three-dimensionality of the forms.

Scheiner, Christoph   In the seventeenth century, he discovered light enters the eye and carries images with it.

Secondary Colors   Pigments which are the result of the mix of two primary colors.

Shade   (1) The part of a form which does not receive direct illumination; comprised of the umbra and penumbra. (2) The darkening of a color with a neutral.

Shadow   That part of a form which is denied direct lighting by another form.

Simultaneous Contrast   The principle that any visual component can vary in appearance, depending on the nature of the visual component placed next to it.

Spectrum   White light, when passed through a prism, is broken down into bands of colored light according to their wavelengths. The visible bands of light are identified as red, orange, yellow, green, blue, indigo, and violet. The measure of the various wavelengths is visible on an oscilloscope.

Split Complement   A color and the two colors on each side of its complement.

Subtractive System   Associated with the absorbent and reflective nature of pigments. See PIGMENT COLOR THEORY.

Tenebrism   Exaggerated CHIAROSCURO for dramatic effects.

Tertiary Colors   Pigments which are the result of the mix of a primary and a secondary color.

Tint   The lightening of a color with a neutral.

Triad   A relationship of three colors equidistant from one another on the color wheel. A connecting line between the three creates an equilateral triangle.

Umbra   The darkest part of the SHADE.

Value   The relationship of light to dark

Value Scale   Stages of value changes between and including white and black.

Value Scheme   The overall relationship of lights and darks on a form or in a composition. Syn.: VALUE PATTERN.

Wavelength   The measure from peak to peak or any other corresponding phases of consecutive cycles, as seen on an oscilloscope.

White Light   The source of color; light that contains the visible spectrum. (In its purest form, it is sunlight. It may be artificial, but variations in the spectrum are usually noticeable.)

SECTION PROJECTS: VALUE AND COLOR

▶ VALUE

Notes:

1. Value is a component that is conspicuously dependent upon light; however, light is a factor that can vary according to the time of day or the nature of the light source. Many assumptions are made when approaching a drawing, such as that it be done in good light and that the light source will be appropriate. While this is often true, such assumptions may limit your art. You need to challenge yourself to pursue lighting or no-light situations which challenge the "norm."

2. When a project calls for a particular light source, be careful to exclude other indirect sources of light, such as windows or general room lighting.

3. A "group of objects" should consist of forms that have interesting positive and negative shape relationships, vary in size, and so forth. In placing objects, consider putting them on different levels and varying the degree of overlap among them. It may be helpful to place objects on mats or pieces of fabric, partially concealing the base plane, to add further variety. Background planes may be close-up to catch shadows, or they may be removed, thus minimizing the effects of shadow.

Projects:

1. LIGHT SOURCES
    a) Do a drawing of a landscape at night that is illuminated only by the moon. Position yourself outside; do not look through a window.
    [Litho or conte crayon, or charcoal.]
    b) Set up a simple set of objects that have interesting positive and negative shape relationships.
        (1) Illuminate this arrangement using a single candle and do a drawing of it.
        (2) Illuminate this arrangement using an electric lamp and do a drawing of it.
    Pay particular attention to the amount of light, shade, and reflected light in each drawing. Exclude light from other sources.
    [Any graphic media; mount both on a single page.]

2. SHADOW
    a) Place your hand just slightly above a piece of paper and—as carefully as you can—draw what that shadow looks like.
    b) Now, lift your hand considerably above another piece of paper and draw the character of that shadow.
    Note the differences in edge quality and value density. Also, be sure to translate your observations into valid designs.
    [Any graphic media; mount both on a single page.]

3. FIGURE-GROUND
    a) Strongly illuminate a single object so that it casts a heavy shadow on a wall or other surface. Design a composition so that the shadow is a significant part of the overall image.
    [Any monochromatic media, including photograph or video image.]
    b) Observe a group of bicycles, pieces of furniture, drawing tables, desks, or any other large, complex objects. Find a vantage point that reveals the objects' negative shapes in an interesting manner.
    Lightly draw the primary contours of these forms. The negative shapes can be made more visually rewarding if they are filled with value—value of any type or technique. Fill these negative shapes with one or more value applications to arrive at a pleasing value pattern. Erase all drawn contours. All positive shapes will be white.
    [Any achromatic media.]

4. BALANCE OF VALUES
    A single medium has the potential for creating a great range of values. This range is possible even when the technique of applying the medium is varied. Ranges of value are observed in value scales, with black being at one end and white at the other, with seven

stages of value progressions in between.

Using a single medium, design a composition that exhibits the value range of four graphic techniques.

[Any medium.]

5. VALUE SCHEMES

   a) Even Value Scheme: No value gradations within the contours of individual shapes. Depicted values are uniform (flat) within a set of contours.

      Draw a series of objects using primary contours. Now, on this drawing, draw secondary contours only where value changes occur. Fill in these shapes with flat, even values, leaving some shapes white. Involve the negative shapes in your composition.

      [Any paint media.]

   b) Nonrepresentational Value Scheme: Value gradations within individual shapes; no sense of a consistent light source.

      Draw another series of objects using primary contours and, again, draw secondary contours only where the value changes occur. Now, extend some of the primary or secondary contours into the negative or other positive shapes, breaking them up, creating new shapes. Shade these according to nonrepresentational value scheme criteria. This will yield an *open value scheme* and may be related to *simultaneous perspective* and the Cubists.

      [Any graphic media.]

   c) Representational Value Scheme: The distinctive relationships of light to dark on a form which reveal that form's representational three-dimensionality. Usually, gradual value gradations exist from shape to shape, according to the orientation to the light source.

      (1) Selecting yet another set of objects, illuminate them directly from one side, observing the pattern of lights and darks that results. Carefully simulate this effect.

      (2) Repeat (1), above, but use two distinct light sources.
      Note: Observational skills are important when you make drawings from subject matter that is illuminated from

conspicuous light sources. A lot of introductory drawing and design students will frequently draw what they think they know about shade and shadow, not drawing what they see, often omitting any reference to the reflected light.

6. LOCAL VALUES:

   Local values are determined by the reflective quality of a surface and the source(s) of light. Careful attention to and faithful reproduction of the observed effects will yield a visually convincing image of the subject matter.

   Take a black-and-white photograph and trim the border from it. Then, draw an imaginary surrealistic extension of the subject/image from the photo, keeping the values of the extensions as consistent with the photo as possible such that the drawing could almost be mistaken for an actual photograph when the combined images are completed. The photograph should occupy no more than 50 percent of the final image.

   [Use drawing paper, rubber cement, and drawing pencils.]

7. INDEPENDENT PROJECT

   Write the instruction and provide the objectives for a project that is related to this chapter but not addressed in the aforementioned projects. Complete the project.

   [Any media.]

▶ COLOR

Notes:

1. Liquid tempera or tube gouaches work best on Bristol board for flat, even tones and easy mixing.

2. Bristol board resists warping more than most lightweight paper-based grounds.

3. Mix your colors in polystyrene egg cartons or other sectional trays for convenience.

4. When mixing colors, add "dark to light" instead of "light to dark," as the darker pigments of colors and neutrals are more intense. For example, when making gray tones, add small amounts of black to much

greater quantities of white; when making green, start off by adding a small amount of blue to yellow.

Projects:

1. MIXING COLORS:

   Take two primary colors and make a secondary color from them which yields a hue in which you cannot see a discernable trace (unmixed streaks) of either primary color—no fudging! Mix these yourself, don't paint from the bottle.

   From a 10 inch by 10 inch sample of your secondary color (on a paper ground), construct a three-dimensional shape. Interesting compositional additions can be made by strategically placing on your form subordinate indications of your primary colors.

   The objective is to develop facility in the mixing of even tones of color and to introduce color to an original three-dimensional form.

2. COLOR SYSTEM:

   There are many systems used to present the three physical properties of color: hue, value, and intensity. The Munsel system was good for industry at one time, and the color wheel appears to be fairly good for artists of all times (at least since 1666.) Unfortunately, the presentation of the color wheel, while functional, is not very moving visually; rather, it looks mechanical, reinforcing the concept of its being a "tool."

   Design a more visually meaningful presentation of the color wheel which incorporates color's three physical properties. You may wish to paint true hues on another sheet of paper, trim them accordingly, and mount them onto the design you estabish. Be sure to include an intensity scale, neutral value scale, and color value scale.

3. LOCAL VALUE AND LOCAL COLOR:

   Each color has its own local value dependent upon that color's level on the color wheel.

   a) Design a composition based on observed subject matter and carefully simulate the apparent *local values*.

   b) Repeat the same design, but fill in the shapes with their appropriate *local colors and values*.

[Draw or paint these on separate pieces of paper or Bristol board; mount on a single page.]

If done successfully, in a black-and-white photograph or photocopy, parts (a) and (b) should look very much alike in terms of value.

4. LIGHT SOURCE:

   a) Set up some oranges, apples, or other fruit on a shelf or table top, strongly illuminating them from a single side using a single light source.

      Use color media to copy the fruit as you observe it. Respond to the Tenebristic effects as they appear both in light and shade.

   b) The quality of light as determined by a light source directly affects the way a color appears to the human eye.

      Design a simple line composition in a rectangular format that can be repeated three times on a single paper.

      (1) In the first rectangle, paint the composition under natural light with a variety of colors.

      (2) In the second frame, paint at night—under fluorescent lighting (tubes)—simulating the colors as they appear in the first painting. Simulate the colors as carefully as you can; the colors that you see, not the colors that you think you ought to see. You will probably have to do considerable mixing—probably by adding blue—to get just the right, subtle tones.

      (3) In the final rectangle, paint at night—under incandescent lighting (regular round bulbs)—simulating the colors of the first rectangle.

   When all of the paints have dried, observe them under natural light, again. If you have avoided other light from filtering in while you painted under the varying light sources, you should observe discernable differences. This gives you an indication of how important it is for artists to (1) work under "good" light and (2) have their works displayed under comparable "good" light. Many disastrous visual effects have resulted when an artist paints under a light source that is not compatible with most exhibition facilities, or when an artist paints a commission for a client's home or business that has one light source and the artist's studio has another.

5. COLOR SCHEME:

a) Artists usually select and distribute their values, colors, and neutrals in a purposeful manner to facilitate movement, focus, balance, and the like. By systematically analyzing a painting, one can discern an artist's palette objectives.

Select a color print of a painting that includes objective subject matter (landscape, still-life, or the like) on which you can freely mark. Across the horizontal and vertical edges, make marks every one-quarter inch. Connect these diagonally, making a graph of diamond shapes. Label the left margin by letters per space, starting with "A," and label the top margin with numbers, starting with "1."

(1) On a piece of paper, reproduce the same grid. Observing your original print, determine a single, *dominant local value* in a given labeled diamond and paint that particular value in its corresponding location on your paper. (Each diamond will be one value, only.)

(2) On a second piece of paper, reproduce the original grid. Observing your print, determine a single *dominant color* in a given labeled diamond and paint that particular color in its corresponding location on your paper. (Each diamond will be one color, only.)

b) Color dramatically affects the way three-dimensional forms appear. Curved and flat surfaces of a single hue or value reflect light differently. Light also reflects from angular plane changes differently than from even plane changes.

Get four to seven empty drink cans—any size—and design a composition that will be used on each one; it may be objective—such as a new logo for a drink—or it may be nonobjective—just nice shapes. When you draw the contours onto the can (not on a separate piece of paper and then attached to the can), do not limit a shape to the existing planes of the can. Wrap a value or color over the edge of the top or bottom to carry your vision. You may also want to put a dent or two in the can to add variety to the form—if you do, repeat it as consistently as possible on all the cans. You may also choose to leave one or two ends open on the cans, thus making cylinders.

When you have applied the same contour line drawing of your composition to each of the four cans,

(1) Paint the first one with *achromatic values*;

(2) Paint the second can with *analogous colors*;

(3) Paint the third can with a *monochromatic palette*;

(4) Paint the fourth can with a *complementary palette*.

If you have the time and inclination, it would be helpful to paint and include three more cans (bent the same way, if at all) in a range of values: one white, one black, and one a neutral gray.

Present these cans glued (epoxy) to a base or to each other in a manner that will allow all of the cans to be easily viewed. Perhaps create a mobile or other kinetic sculpture!

c) In an original composition, incorporate the color scheme of the color wheel.

d) Looking in a mirror placed very close to your face, closely observe the range of colors (not shades and shadows) that are present in the flesh. Create a "bar graph" of these colors which indicates each color and its relative amount. For variety, you might want to present each bar radiating out from a central point, or in some other composition.

6. INDEPENDENT PROJECT

Write the instruction and provide the objectives for a project that is related to this chapter but not addressed in the aforementioned projects. Complete the project.

[Any media.]

SEVEN

Space

The following figures/illustration appear in the color insert: Figures 7–14, 7–17, 7–20; Illustration 7–13.

▶ USAGE

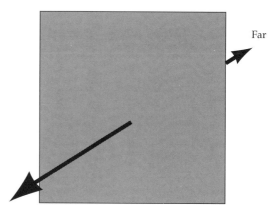

When one thinks of space, wonderful and delightful images may come to mind, such as the Starship *Enterprise* drifting through the universe, or the *Nautilus* with Captain Nemo exploring the unknown depths of the oceans. The essence of these two perceptions of space is unlimited vistas expanding in all directions—a feeling of emptiness. Interestingly, some dimwitted people are sometimes referred to as "spaced." Here, too, the connotation of emptiness—empty-headedness—is being portrayed.

▶ Illustration 7-1   Near to Far Relationship

▶ Illustration 7-2   Three Axes of Space

Space does not have to indicate infinite vistas or areas; rather, it can be used to define finite areas between two things, such as the space between telephone poles or subatomic particles. Therefore, we see that space has both very broad and very narrow applications.

▶ OUR PERCEPTIONS OF SPACE

Traditionally, space has been used to describe near-to-far relationships, a sense of an area or forms advancing and/or receding within a field of vision. Usually artists are involved with establishing space within the confines of a picture frame—a picture frame of any format: oval, square, or free-form. Robert Pirsig wrote in his book, *Zen and the Art of Motorcycle Maintenance*, that most of our experiences are perceived through a framing device. This may include eyeglasses, automobile windshields, window frames, and television sets. Pirsig celebrates motorcycle riding as allowing visual perception and experience without the traditional limitation of

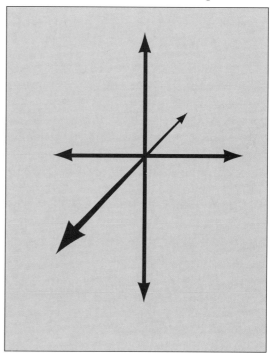

seeing things separated from us by a frame. Thus, space is perceived as surrounding us as opposed to being removed from us and observed.

Added to these near-to-far perceptions must be the sense of up-and-down relationships. The feeling of space is not

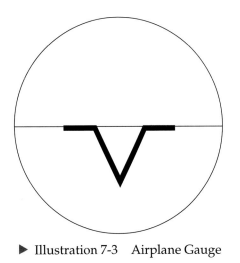

▶ Illustration 7-3   Airplane Gauge

▶ WHAT SPACE IS

Space is all around you, but you can't touch it. Space is a nonphysical entity, yet you will learn how it can be controlled and shaped. You will see that space, like the other visual components of art, is plastic. It is flexible and subject to the design objectives of the artist. It is not limited to depicting the world as we observe it; instead, artists can redefine space according to their own particular needs.

Therefore, in order to allow space to be defined in a manner which encompasses all of its subtleties and potential, you understand that

> Space is a limited or unlimited two- or three-dimensional area appearing to advance, recede, or extend in all directions, depending upon the visual clues provided by the artist.

When the depiction of space is bordered by a picture frame or other visual component, *space* may be referred to as *shape*, as in positive and negative shapes.

▶ TWO- AND THREE-DIMENSIONAL DETERMINERS OF SPACE

Objective Considerations

A lot of two-dimensional art appears to evoke the sensation of looking out of or in through a window frame at the image, the window frame being the image's picture frame. This does not mean, however, that all images must look like the outside world. This does mean that by looking through a picture frame, the connotation of looking through a window frame is often a natural one.

just from here to there in terms of a line going toward or away from the *horizon line*. Space necessarily implies perceptions of areas extending in all directions. One of the dramas of flight, of space travel, or of parachute jumping, for example, is the removal of something tangible from underneath of you, the removal of a common space-limiting device, such as the ground below your feet.

In previous chapters we observed that our responses to most visual components and their relationships are determined by our experiences. The same is true with space. Most perceptions of space will automatically imply a sense of the earth, sky, and a line where they meet—the horizon line. In perceptions of space from near to far, we have a natural inclination to interpret a dominant horizontal line as a horizon line. The horizon line is a dominant feature in many airplane gauges, for example, because the horizon line serves as a reference point to establish the plane's attitude in the air relative to the earth. The horizon line in art helps to establish the viewer's position relative to the image.

▶ Figure 7-1   Pablo Picasso, *Seated Woman*
(Paris 1927, oil on wood, 51⅛ × 38¼", The Museum of Modern Art, New York, Gift of James Thrail Soby, © Jan 11, 1994)

▶ Figure 7-2   Graetz, *Composition in Stainless Steel*
(Donald M. Kendall Sculpture Garden at PepsiCo)

Effects of advancing and receding space can be observed in relatively low, or shallow, relief sculptures, including those found on coins. In Donatello's *Feast of Herod* (Fig. 4–5) there are incorporated elements of low and high relief. High reliefs enhance illusions of greater three-dimensionality because undercuttings cast dark shadows. The effect of these shadows closely simulates the impression of deep space.

Sculpture that is fully three-dimensional exists in space. Thus, making illusions of space is usually not a concern. The challenge to the sculptor is to make a form that is aesthetically valid all the way around—from all viewpoints, also from above. It is absolutely proper for one or more sides of a sculpture to be dominant in comparison to other sides, just as it is often appropriate for various areas of a painting to be more dominant than others. Ultimately, though, each view of a three-dimensional form must provide a visually rewarding experience and contribute to its overall aesthetics.

Regarding sculpture, viewing experiences are sometimes most rewarding when one side of a form anticipates the next—when the sculpture draws the viewer around the piece, as in the sculpture of Graetz (Fig. 7-2). The successful sculpture has dynamic spatial relationships: Its proportions of height, width, and depth function to articulate the space it occupies, thereby giving space a sense of energy—energy of varying degrees.

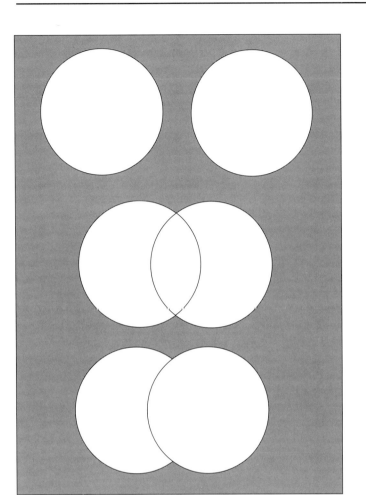

▶ Illustration 7-4   Overlapping and Space

▶ CONSTANTS OF PERCEPTION

An artist does not work with space in the same way that a visual component, such as line or shape, is manipulated. Space is not a visual component. Rather, space is created by the interaction of the visual and organizational components.

There are many clues that an artist can use to determine where in space a form is located. Clearly, not all images within a picture frame appear to be the same distance from us. If you are going to control the impression of near-to-far in

your art, you need to observe how spatial-modifying or -defining devices work in nature and how artists have responded to them in creating original art. Most of these space-defining devices are in harmony with experience.

Overlapping

The device which is, perhaps, the most dominant one in determining spatial relationships, aside from experience, is *overlapping.* When two forms of relatively the same size are placed side by side, it is difficult to distinguish whether or not one might be slightly in front or back of the other. However, if one form is to overlap the other, even slightly, there is absolutely no problem deciding which form is closer to you (Illus. 7–4). The only time this is not true is when the forms appear to be transparent, thus canceling, neutralizing, or contradicting expected placement; contradicting experience. This contradiction of any traditional or expected spatial effect is termed *spatial equivocation.* Transparency allows for the visual penetration of forms, thus reducing the impression of or denying a form's clear spatial location.

Relative Scale

From our experiences, we know that things closer to us appear larger than things that are far away. This is another of the constants of perception. This principle of *relative scale* applies equally to objective and nonobjective images. Even in the absence of a horizon line, smaller visual components still appear farther away; there is consistent diminishing scale of forms going from near to far. About the only thing that can cause something large to look farther away than something small is when another spatial determiner is involved, especially overlapping. Overlapping is so dominant that it can dominate just about any other spatial effect (Illus. 7–5).

Position

Another spatial device that works with relative scale is *position*. You have observed that those forms which are closer to you also appear to have their bases lower in the picture, and their tops will frequently rise higher in the picture plane. Forms that are far away will have both their bases and tops closer to the middle—the actual or implied horizon line; they look smaller. If all forms are lined up along the same base line, the shorter ones will often appear farther away, especially if their width has also been proportionally diminished (Illus. 7–6). Short forms placed higher in the composition often have the effect of being farther away from the viewer. Thus, the vertical placement of the top, bottom, or top and bottom of the forms affects your perception of spatial location.

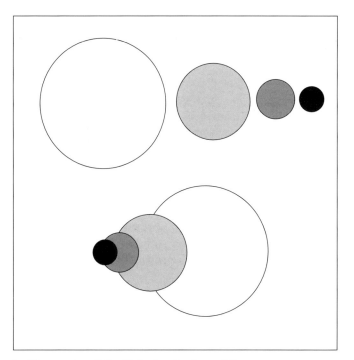

▶ Illustration 7-5   Relative Scale and Space

Convergence

In addition to leading the eye to the focal point of a work, as discussed earlier in the text, *convergence* describes spatial relationships. The traditional illustration used to describe relative scale and position is the image of a railroad track and some accompanying telephone poles converging and fading into the distance (Fig. 7–3). Although we know that things do not actually get smaller as they recede toward an implied or actual horizon line, we observe them to appear smaller. The distant ends of railroad tracks and highways, for example, appear smaller than the closer ends. The area defined by the telephone poles also converges and narrows toward the horizon line.

▶ Figure 7-3

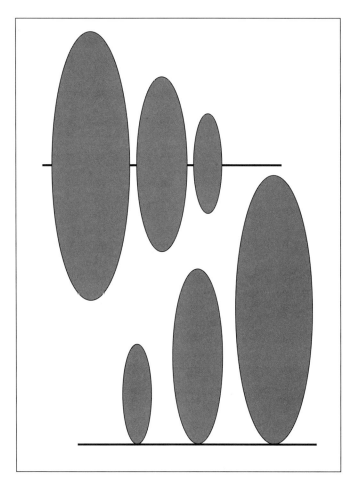

▶ Figure 7-5   Albrecht Dürer, *Demonstration of Perspective: Draftsman Drawing a Lute* (Kupferstichkabinett, Staatliche Museen zu Berlin, PreuBischer Kulturbesitz, photo by Jörg P. Anders)

▶ Figure 7-4   George Inness, *The Lackawanna Valley* (National Gallery of Art, Washington, Gift of Mrs. Huttleston Rogers)

Converging lines or shapes do not have to appear parallel. They may be wavy and curvy, as in a winding path or curvy road; yet, even as they creep toward the horizon line, the contour lines defining the edge of the road will appear to come closer together (Fig. 7–4).

Linear/scientific perspective. It appears that as forms get farther away they diminish in scale in a proportional manner. Yet it wasn't until the Renaissance that artists and scientists were able to make a mathematical/mechanical equivocation for the optical effects of convergence. They developed techniques of drawing in perspective that included horizon lines and vanishing points. This *linear perspective* made the effects of convergence and diminishing scale uniform and commensurate with experience (Fig. 7–5). The chief accomplishment of this revelation was that all forms in space could be systematically drawn in proportion to one another as they appeared to recede toward the horizon line (Illus. 7–7).

Mastering the technique of drawing in perspective is a meaningful and helpful way of giving order to space. However, being able to draw in perspective is not a guarantee that one will be able to make art—design and content are still at the core. If one is trying to make a landscape or cityscape look "right," then utilizing the techniques of drawing in linear perspective may be a means toward that end. Conversely, if one wants to make a landscape or interior look unusual, or "different," then contradicting the principles of linear perspective may be helpful, too (Escher, Fig. 7–6).

Using perspective as a means to an end gives artists the opportunity to plausibly describe space and depict other proportional relationships. Canaletto, in his paintings of St. Mark's (Fig. 7–7), uses perspective to define the plaza. Then he goes about emphasizing some of the motif relationships and the play of lights and darks for compositional considerations. Perspective helps Canaletto describe the three-dimensional space in a believable manner, but formal design considerations are paramount: His painting is not about perspective.

People of the Western world have grown accustomed to viewing the convergence of perspective lines receding to a common point—the vanishing point—on the horizon line. The lines going to the vanishing point accommodate the sides of forms that appear to advance and recede in space. There may be multiple vanishing points on the horizon , and there may also be a vanishing point above or below the horizon to accommodate vertical lines (Illus. 7–7). Thus, perspective may include more than one vanishing point.

Eastern societies have not always seen things the way Westerners have. In a

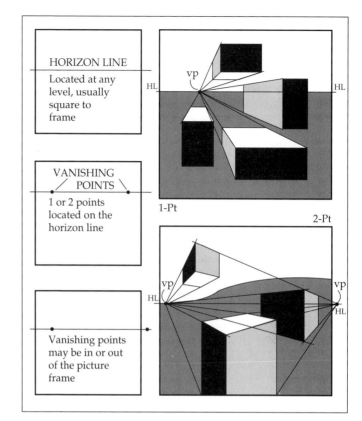

Start with the near FACE in one-point perspective, the near CORNER in two-point perspective.

▶ Illustration 7-7   Perspective of Horizon Line

▶ Figure 7-6   M.C. Escher, *Relativity*
(© M.C. Escher/Cordon Art Baarn-Holland)

▶ Figure 7-7   Canaletto, *Piazza San Marco in Venice*
(Fundacion Coleccion Thyssen-Bornemisza)

▶ Figure 7-8   Emperor Huizong, *Court Ladies Preparing Newly Woven Silk*
(China, Northern Song Dynasty, Early 12th Century, Chinese and Japanese Special Fund, Courtesy Museum of Fine Arts, Boston)

detail of the Song dynasty painting by Emperor Huizong, *Sewing* (Fig. 7–8), you observe that the rug broadens as it moves upward and back toward the horizon line. In a Japanese painting from the Kamakura Period (Fig. 7–9), you see the rooftops expanding as they appear to recede. This is the opposite of what most of us of our time in history would expect. Due to the vast exchange of knowledge and information made possible by way of telecommunications and print media, the concept of reverse perspective is less widely used today than in the past.

Vantage Points

When you observe forms in the landscape, you may do so from a variety of vantage points: from up high, down low, or straight on. These vantage points are not limited to linear perspective, but are frequently introduced in relation to perspective because the differences between the vantage points are readily illustrated.

If you were trying to depict the view of one looking down on something, as if from a mountaintop or airplane, you would show the tops of forms, and perhaps the sides, too. This is referred to as a bird's-eye view. Conversely, if you were lying down on the ground, looking up at forms, you would only see the sides, and no tops. Additionally, from the very lowest of vantage points you would see the bottoms of forms. This is called a worm's-eye view. Lastly, looking straight at a form, you would see the sides, and they would overlap the horizon line. This person's-eye view is different from the previous two views in that it crosses over the horizon line and the other two do not; they are seen either above or below the horizon line (Illus. 7–7).

Levels of Space

When you studied value, you learned that there are numerous stages, or levels between light and dark, whether you were discussing the value range of a color or neutral. In discussing space, you will also see that there are various levels between those forms which appear close up and those which appear far away.

Remember the association between the picture frame and a window frame: Those forms closest to the frame—either on the inside or the outside—are relatively near to you; thus we label this area as near space. Images on the "outside" appear to recede, thus occupying *receding space,* and those forms which appear to be advancing toward you are in *advancing space.* (See "Getting Started.")

Those forms which neither advance nor recede, you will recall, appear to lie flat on the picture plane in what is referred to as *decorative space.* Forms in decorative space have neither connotations of depth nor of advancing or receding—the only spatial effects lie across and/or up and down on the picture plane. In decorative space, there are no visual effects of anything being in front of or behind the picture plane. Forms in decorative space look flat. Any and all other spatial references occur in three-dimensional space. ("Decorative" space is not to be confused with popular associations of "decoration.")

Art historians suggest that the construction of the Eiffel Tower in Paris, France, heightened artists' sensitivities to images more representative of two-dimensional space than three. The elevated heights of the observatory in the tower allow an individual to look down onto the top of the landscape instead of out and across it. As a result, the horizon line rose higher and higher in one's vision and

▶ Figure 7-9   Japanese Painting, Kamakura Period, c. 1300 Kumano Mandala
(The Cleveland Museum of Art, John L. Severance Fund)

▶ Illustration 7-8   Advancing/Receding Space

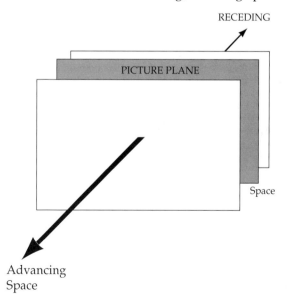

artistic compositions, finally moving up and out of the composition to where the view of the earth was seen as extending in width and height more than depth. The viewer of a landscape became more of an observer than a participant.

Camille Pissarro's *Places du Théâtre Français* (Fig. 7–10), a street scene viewed from above, emphasizes the patterns on the ground as interesting positive and negative shape relationships; the people appear as decorative elements, too, emphasizing their pattern as opposed to their identities. The dynamics of this new urban life are seen as the new patterns of city life. Pedestrian and vehicular movement are given form in a composition which emphasizes visual movements across and up-and-down the picture plane, but not through the plane. Some of the paintings by twentieth-century American artist Larry Poons, such as *Sicilian Chance* (Fig. 7–11), seem to be further adaptations of this idea of the movement of decorative elements around the picture plane, but not through it, thus defining decorative space. (Also see Mondrian's *Broadway Boogie-Woogie*, Fig. 6–110.)

In our discussion of value and color, you will recall that eastern art influenced nineteenth-century French art, art that depicted flat, unchanging values and colors within the contours of a shape. The background of Manet's *Dead Toreador* (Fig. 7–12) appears to be a flat shade of green above the figure and a tint of green below it, yet the change of values is not in harmony with an actual or implied horizon line. And since there is little chiaroscuro on the form and even less shadow, the image appears to exist in somewhat of a contrived space that is not wholly decorative nor three-dimensional.

Another factor which contributes to making the image of the dead toreador look a bit awkward is the angle it lies on

▶ Figure 7-10   Camille Pissarro, *Place du Théâtre Français*
(Los Angeles County Museum of Art, Mr. and Mrs. George Gard de Sylva Collection, © 1993 Museum Associates, All Rights Reserved)

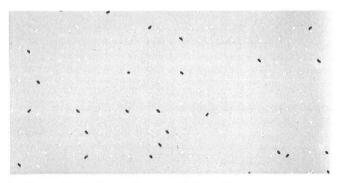

▶ Figure 7-11   Larry Poons, *Sicilian Chance*
(Hirshhorn Museum and Sculpture Garden, Smithsonian Institution, Gift of Joseph H. Hirshhorn, 1966, © 1994 Larry Poons/VAGA, New York)

▶ Figure 7-12   Edouard Manet, *The Dead Toreador*
(National Gallery of Art, Washington, Eidener Collection)

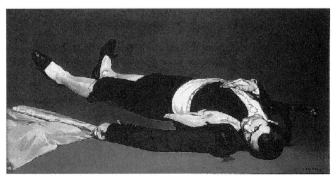

the ground plane: advancing slightly toward the foreground. As a result of this position, the upper part of the torso looks largest and overlaps parts of the lower torso, thus diminishing the sense of the actual length of the figure.

A Renaissance artist named Mantegna also dealt with this concept of the form appearing to overlap itself as it advances or recedes in space—*foreshortening*—in his image of the *Dead Christ* (Fig. 7–13). Accurately depicting a foreshortened form is difficult, at best, and even when wellhandled can yield spatial perceptions which may feel awkard and unnatural. Notice how Mantegna took "artistic license" by overemphasizing the size of the head and diminishing the size of the feet so that the feet would not be dominant in the work.

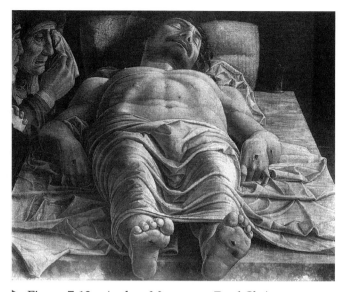

▶ Figure 7-13   Andrea Mantegna, *Dead Christ*
(Alinari/Art Resource, NY)

▶ RECEDING SPACE

Receding space is frequently subdivided into three different zones: the foreground, middle ground, and background (Illus. 7–9). The background may or may not be limited. When unlimited, the background dissolves in the distance with no limit to the receding space being perceptible. This unlimited background is termed *infinite space*. Infinite space, like the foreground and middle ground, may also extend up and across—vertically and horizontally— and not just recede.

American artists used to clearly organize their compositions into vistas exploiting these three different levels. They would provide visual clues for each level, such as tree stumps, rocks, lakes, and mountains. These clues served to

1. Draw you into the composition, and
2. Give order to space where no architectural landmarks or systematic set of converging lines were sufficient in themselves (Fig. 7–14).

▶ Illustration 7-9   Levels of Space

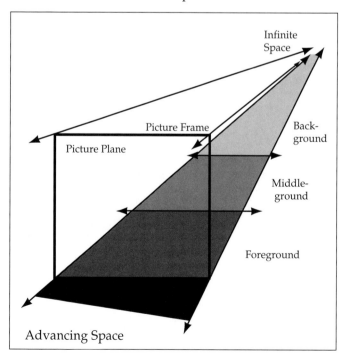

▶ Figure 7-15   David, *Le Servent des Horaces*
(Musée du Louvre, © Photo R.M.N)

RECEDING SPACE LIMITED BY BACKGROUND PLANES

▶ Illustration 7-10   Figure and Forms Occupying Different Levels of Space

Sometimes the receding space may be interrupted by an object or form that stops your visual progression back and through the picture plane. Receding space may be limited by background planes, buildings, or other visual devices (David, *Le Servent des Horaces*, Fig. 7–15; Illus. 7–10).

▶ ADVANCING SPACE

While it is not very difficult to depict the illusion of forms receding in space, it is conspicuously more difficult to allude to forms advancing in space. Many artists will have part of the image overlap the picture frame, advancing from the implied background to the actual foreground, in order to make something appear to intrude into your space. Artists at Versailles used this type of illusion in the War Drawing Room, painting horses in ceiling frescoes then continuing a horse leg, for example, into a three-dimensional sculpture as it overlapped the room's cornice. In the Cyclorama in Georgia, Civil War figures and cannons exist both in combined two-dimensional images and three-dimensional extensions as they "advance" from the outer wall to the floor.

Pearlstein's image of *Dr. William Quillian* appears too large to fit inside of its frame (see Fig. 7–16); a characteristic of Michelangelo's sibyls and prophets in the Sistine Chapel ceiling frescoes is that they, too, appear to overflow their space. The Pearlstein and Michelangelo figures, as a result, appear to advance in space, out of the confines of their actual or implied frames. This alludes to a sense of importance, prominence, or power associated with the subjects.

▶ SPATIAL PROPERTIES OF THE VISUAL COMPONENTS

Each visual component—when placed inside of the picture plane—inherently evokes a spatial orientation, and these spatial effects are conspicuously determined by experience. The spatial effects are compounded when two or more components interact within the picture frame. As soon as you place anything on the picture plane, it relates to the size and the proportions of the plane. And, depending upon where you place it, the component will yield some spatial effect, whether intentional or not. The relative scale and position of that component—as it relates to the plane and frame—will give the effect of that component existing in some level of space: advancing or receding. The degree of contrast between the component and the ground will yield a spatial effect, also.

Line and Shape

The measures of line and shape contribute significantly to the location of those components in space: Large, bold, visual components appear to advance in near space, whereas smaller, more delicate depictions of the components appear farther away in receding space. These impressions are complemented by their position relative to the actual or implied horizon line.

By the direction a diagonal line takes, it may "aim" toward the horizon line or toward the picture frame, thus directing your eye "in" or "out" of a composition. If a single line is conspicuously horizontal or vertical, its directional pull will be across the picture plane as opposed to through it, and the perceived depth of a composition may be reduced, depending on the line's length.

▶ Figure 7-16   Philip Pearlstein, *Portrait of Dr. William F. Quillian*
(Frumkin/Adams Gallery, Photo by Eric Pollitzer)

Shape, you know, refers to a plane, solid, or volume. As with line, if some of the contours of a rectilinear shape are not square with the frame—if they are placed on diagonals within the visual field—the shape appears to advance or recede according to the direction of the converging sides.

Curvilinear planar and volumetric shapes appear to advance or recede if there is an impression of convergence which may be complemented by placement and value relationships (Illus. 7–11).

Value

Previously, you saw how value can be used to model the three-dimensionality of a form—chiaroscuro. This establishes the three-dimensionality of a form in three-dimensional space. And, you recall, the area a form occupies—the space—can also be modeled with value, emphasizing that space is plastic.

Sometimes a flat area of dark or light against a contrasting background may appear to recede, as though it were a hole. And in other cases—due to its boldness—a dark or light shape or area may appear to advance (Illus. 7–12). These examples depict figure-ground reversals which have advancing and receding spatial effects.

Color

Color has many connotations and qualities: objective and subjective, warm and cool, and, most notably, mood. Another significant quality of color is spatial:

▶ Illustration 7-11

▶ Figure 7-18   Josef Albers, *Homage to the Square: Apparition*
(Solomon R. Guggenheim Museum, New York, Photo, Robert E. Mates
© The Solomon R. Guggenheim Foundation, New York, FN61.1590)

▶ Illustration 7-12   Spatial Qualities: Value

> Colors often seem to advance or recede in varying progressions according to how warm or cool they appear (Illus. 7–13).

Many artists choose to model their forms with warm and cool colors instead of varying values of colors to keep a form visually vibrant. For example, the shading on an apple might move from yellow in the highlight to red in the light, through varying hues of red-violet to violet in the umbra, that is *warm colors advance and cool ones recede*. Cezanne exploited the spatial characteristics of color in his still-life paintings (Fig. 7–17). The modeling of a form with colors refers to the plastic nature or use of color.

Of course, spatial qualities may apply to nonobjective works. The colored shapes in the works of Josef Albers (Fig. 7–18) and Alexander Calder, for example, appear to "move" back and forth. The movement of these colors and values is complemented by relative scale, position, and simultaneous contrast.

Texture

Boldness and degrees of contrast are features which impact on all of the visual components' spatial effects. Accordingly,

▶ Figure 7-19   Richard Anuskiewicz, *Iridescence*
(Albright-Knox Art Gallery, Buffalo, NY, Gift of Seymour H. Knox)

the bolder and more apparent a texture appears, the closer it seems to be, as in the leaves of a nearby tree. Conversely, the more void of surface texture a form appears, the farther away from the picture plane it may appear.

Dot

By the lack of dimension associated with dot (or point), it is usually evaluated in relationship to other spatial devices, unless dots are grouped to produce line, shape, value, color, or textural areas. A single dot is so small that, when seen alone, it may look like a distant star or advancing point, depending on other clues provided within the picture plane.

 ## UNINTENTIONAL SPATIAL EFFECTS

Avoiding any sense of advancing or receding space is very difficult in a composition, due, in part, to what we said about the role of experience and any visual component's having inherent spatial qualities when seen against a ground. Therefore, when working with line, shape, value, color, texture, and dot, be sensitive to the fact that there may be spatial effects on your picture plane which you had not expected or cannot totally control. Be responsive to this and understand how the "unexpected" may help your compositions stay "alive."

Is it important that we be able to define the exact spatial location of each component in Anuskiewicz's *Iridescence* (Fig. 7–19), that we know exactly where each component lies relative to the picture plane? Or, do we understand that unexpected and fluctuating spatial effects may be visually exciting and unpredictable?

ATMOSPHERIC PERSPECTIVE

Atmospheric perspective is frequently used as a synonym for *aerial perspective*. However, "atmospheric" is better since the atmosphere directly affects your perception of space. You know, for example, that a star appears to twinkle because of the effects of moving air between you and the star—the atmosphere has a direct effect on your perception of that star.

> As you observe forms ranging in location from near to far, the effects of the air between you and the forms contribute to your impression of how far or near they appear.

You have heard of the Blue Ridge and Smoky mountains, and of "purple mountain majesties." Yet these descriptions are not in harmony with what you know about mountains: The mountains are green due to trees, brown due to season, or gray due to rock formations. Mountains are really the color of what lies on their surfaces. They appear to be different, however, because

> Colors appear to become neutralized over great distances, that is, the visual impressions of distant mountains are affected by the qualities of atmosphere between your eyes and the mountains (Fig. 7–20).

In addition to color, the shapes of the distant trees on the mountains become less well-defined. A tree close to you, for example, is clear and distinctive; all of its individual parts are discernable. However, a tree far away loses its clarity. Individual branches and leaves become shape clusters and many individual trees are seen collectively as tree clusters. Shape distinctions are lost over great distances; shape contrasts are neutralized, along with color contrasts. Also, as the trees recede in space, the apparent textures of their leaves and bark diminish in proportion to their distance away—in proportion to the neutralizing of shape and color. In this example, you have also observed that the clarity of shape edge—*contour* or *line*—is neutralized.

In conclusion, you see from the previous example that all of the visual components are neutralized as they appeared to recede in space.

> There is a consistent and equal diminishing of contrast in line, shape, value, color, and texture in atmospheric perspective.

SUBJECTIVE DETERMINERS OF SPACE

When an artist maintains a crispness of all visual components from near to far—when there is no neutralizing of effects, this *spatial equivocation* contradicts what you feel should occur. As a result, the spatial effects are reduced and the space does not feel as deep—the composition appears flatter, more abstract. Often, when an artist chooses to abstract one element of space, one or more visual components may be abstracted, as well. For example, shapes may be made transparent and/or simplified throughout a composition; colors may be flattened—subtle modeling of forms may be ignored; local colors may be varied. None of this is wrong, it is artistic

▶ Figure 7-21   Robert Gwathmey, *Portrait of a Smile*
(NAA-Gift of Mr. & Mrs. Thomas Woods, Sr., Sheldon Memorial Art Gallery, University of Nebraska-Lincoln,
1954.N-81; © 1994 Estate of Robert Gwathmey/VAGA, New York)

selection intended to enhance spatial effects, the content of the work, and its visual uniqueness.

Certainly many compositions, such as the Gottlieb and Albers we looked at earlier, have no intentional references to the experienced world—the spatial references rebut or contradict what most of us know to be the way things are. In these and other examples, the placement of abstract and nonobjective forms in contrived space can be delightfully and visually rewarding (Fig. 7–21).

▶ **CONCLUSION**

Space is around us and in front of us; it exists as an illusion and as a reality. Forms may displace space or represent it.

Space need not necessarily recede nor advance; it can be penetrated, shaped, and modeled.

Space is not used in a composition, spatial effects are created. They are a result of your manipulation of the visual and organizational components, the way you relate line, shape, value, color, and texture. You determine the spatial effects; you determine what is appropriate for your imagery. Be careful to control space, to create it purposely and intentionally, to complement the content of your artwork.

► **SECTION GLOSSARY**

Aerial Perspective See ATMOSPHERIC PER-SPECTIVE.

Atmospheric Perspective The neutralizing of the visual components as they appear to recede in space. Syn.: AERIAL PERSPECTIVE.

Foreshortening The apparent diminished axis of a form created by a form's overlapping itself as it advances or recedes in space.

High Relief Sculpture A form of relief sculpture that has significant projections beyond the surface of the background plane; usually involves significant undercuttings.

Horizon The location where the lower edge of the sky meets the upper limit of the earth's surface.

Horizon Line A drawn line noting the location of the horizon, which helps to establish the viewer's position relative to the image.

Infinite Space Unlimited extensions in any or all directions.

Linear Perspective A mathematical/mechanical equivocation for the optical effects of convergence involving techniques of drawing that incorporate horizon lines and vanishing points.

Low Relief Sculpture A form of relief sculpture that has a very limited projection off of the surface of the background plane.

Relief Sculpture A form of three dimensional art that is attached to a background plane; primarily frontal.

Space A limited or unlimited two- or three-dimensional area appearing to advance, recede, or extend in all directions, depending upon the visual clues provided by the artist.

Spatial Equivocation A contradiction of any traditional or expected spatial effect.

Undercuttings Recessed areas behind a forward-facing plane in a relief sculpture.

Vanishing Point An implied location on the horizon line where receding forms that lie parallel to the surface of the earth would, if extended to infinity, appear to diminish into a single dot.

Vantage Point Location from which something is viewed; bird's-eye, person's-eye, and worm's-eye views.

View See VANTAGE POINT.

UNIT PROJECTS: SPACE

Note: If you use mechanical devices in creating the following images, be sure to remember that the drawing technique you use should complement the designs. For example, in perspective drawings, lines receding to the horizon line may or may not be complementary to the design.

1. PLASTIC SPACE

   a) Design two compositions using the same subject matter (objective or non-objective) in each, locating that subject matter

      (1) in unlimited—infinite—space, and
      (2) limited space, that is, the subject matter will remain the same, but the space it occupies will not.

      This may be achieved through a variety of means, including shading, background planes, and other spatial devices. Keep the size of your subject matter the same in each composition.

      [Any media; mount both on a single page.]

   b) Design two compositions using relatively the same subject matter (objective or nonobjective) in each, so that the subject matter

      (1) appears to recede, and
      (2) appears to advance.

      [Any media; mount both on a single page.]

2. SCULPTURE

   a) Sculpt a cameo relief in any plastic medium (for example, wax, clay) that alludes to qualities of infinite space, yet incorporates no undercuttings. This necessarily includes references to atmospheric perspective.

   b) Using wire as your medium, sculpt a form that fully exploits three-dimensional space and yields rewarding viewing experiences from all vantage points.

   c) Design a composition that is cropped by the picture frame, emphasizing a feeling that the image is advancing. Some part of the composition should actually—in three-dimensional form—overlap your frame.

   d) Construct an atectonic three-dimensional form incorporating voids (see *shape*). Place the completed form on a turntable or sculpture stand beside a camera on a tripod so that the form is directly in-line with or slightly below the camera's viewfinder. Take pictures of the form rotated at about thirty degree intervals yielding twelve photographs of the form, all taken with the camera in exactly the same position. (More photos would be advantageous.) Stack the processed photos in the order they were taken, stapling them together at one edge. Having thus created a "flip book," rapidly flip through the photos to see your sculpture "turn" in space.

3. SPATIAL EQUIVOCATION

   a) Create the image of a setting that appears to recede away from the picture plane. Place in that setting at different elevations subject matter that is—in actuality—all the same size, thus creating optical illusions and contradicting traditional spatial perceptions. The resulting effects will go against what one would expect or "know."

      For example, in a landscape, all the buildings from near to far—those placed at different levels on the picture plane—may be the same building reproduced several times and all have the same measurements. The same may be true of other variables, including people, trees, or simple geometric forms.

      [Any media.]

   b) From a magazine or other source, cut out a picture of a landscape. Mount this photo on one side of your page, and on the other side paint a modification of the composition giving the effect of nontraditional space. You may do this by giving all shapes hard contours (maybe outlined) and decorative color or values. The techniques you employ will be "anti-atmospheric perspective."

   c) A significant device used to flatten space is to make forms transparent. From a magazine or other source, cut out a picture of a setting that appears naturalistic. Mount this photo on one side of your page, and on the other side paint a modification of the composition giving the effect of nontraditional space using transparency and two-dimensional value schemes.

4. VANTAGE POINTS

Position yourself in an elevated location (in a tree, on a roof, or other significantly high place) and draw the view below the horizon line. The horizon line should be perceived as being well-above and outside of the picture frame. Alter the composition to a small degree, emphasizing decorative relationships. The image should appear more representational than not. Even value or color schemes may be employed.

5. DECORATIVE SPACE

Understanding that the visual components of art almost always yield a three-dimensional quality of space when placed on the picture plane, design a composition using just two components (shape and color, line and value, etc.) that appear as close to decorative space as possible. It may be helpful to paint the picture plane a color to get rid of the idea of images on paper, or it might be helpful to omit negative shapes altogether.

6. ATMOSPHERIC PERSPECTIVE

Using two- or three-point perspective, draw a series of geometric shapes in space incorporating atmospheric perspective. Include one or more human figures of any size at any location to enhance the effects.

7. SPACE AND COLOR

In a nonrectangular format, design a series of geometric forms in unlimited space that appear to advance and recede according to their color and size relationships.

8. INDEPENDENT PROJECT

Write the instructions and provide the objectives for a project that is related to this chapter but not addressed in the aforementioned projects. Complete the project.

[Any media.]

EIGHT

Presentation

Have you ever walked into a gallery and had trouble looking at some of the paintings because the frames were too dominant? Have you ever felt the frames were competing with the images for attention? Have you seen sculptures placed on bases which seemed inappropriate? Perhaps the wood finish of a base conflicted with the wood texture or grain of the sculpture on that base, or the bolts used to attach a form to a base were distracting.

Conversely, you have seen paintings that were in absolute harmony with their frames and sculptures that were well-matched to their bases. Can you identify the governing principles associated with a well presented work of art?

Presentation involves a visually unified, complete work which—in itself—is ready for viewing. The presentation of art is different from the display of art in that display is oriented to the particular environment in which the art is placed for viewing. Also, displays (like exhibitions) are considered temporary as compared to installations which are more permanent.

Devices used for the presentation of art, such as mats and frames for paintings or bases for sculpture, can serve a variety of similar purposes:

1. A presentation device should complement a work of art rather than stand as a work of art itself, independent of the image.

Interestingly, the Metropolitan Museum of Art in New York City hung a show, entitled "Italian Renaissance Frames," comprised of hand-carved and -decorated frames, most without paintings within their borders. These frames were presented as works of art in themselves,

▶ Figure 8-1   Framing Materials

▶ Figure 8-2   Constantin Brancusi, *Fish*
(1930, gray marble, 21 × 71 × 5½″ on a 3 part pedestal of marble 5⅛″
high, and 2 limestone cylinders 13″ and 11″ high × 32⅛″ diameter at
widest point, The Museum of Modern Art, New York, acquired through
the Lillie P. Bliss Bequest, © Jan. 11, 1994, The Museum of Modern Art)

which they are in terms of detail and craftsmanship. As an artist or museum curator, you can anticipate the challenge of filling such a frame with a painting that is complemented but not dominated by that frame.

Often, presentation devices are seen as a means of embellishment. Artists and curators, while seeking to enhance the significance of a work, can unintentionally detract from its merits by presenting it with unnecessary attention-getting devices. Care must be taken not to overwhelm either the image or the viewer.

2. Another consideration in the use of a presentation device is whether that device successfully separates the image or form from its environment, if that is required.

An exhibition coordinator might feel an elaborate frame is necessary to draw at-

tention to a particular work, but that frame might actually compromise the objectives of the work by dominating it. On the other hand, a frame or base can serve to define the visual limits of the work, clearly establishing its boundaries in a seemingly boundless environment.

3. Not all presentation devices are secondary to the works; some are seen as a part of the work.

For example, the wooden frames on a William Harnett painting and on Charles Willson Peale's *Staircase Group* are seen as actual parts of the visual designs. Brancusi's geometric base on his *Fish Form* (Fig. 8–2) emphasizes the organic quality of the sculpture, providing significant contrast and emphasizing its content, while at the same time separating it from its environment.

4. Presentation devices often serve practical functions.

A frame or mat provides a location to secure hanging devices, just as a base can provide a means of physically stabilizing a sculpture and hiding or disguising screws or other necessary mounting devices.

5. A frame or mat may function as a cropping device.

Artists are often amenable to matting or framing a work because of the cosmetic function of covering up erratic marks on the outer edges of the work. It is nice to have the option of cutting, cropping, and remounting a finished artwork—an advantage that is available to but not very practical for sculptors. Images often look considerably different when they are taken off the easel and subsequently framed and placed on the vastness of a wall. Thus, an artist may want to alter a work's exterior dimensions or include only a portion of a work in a final presentation. Renoir's *Girl with a Watering Can* and Manet's *Dead Toreador* (see Fig. 7–12) were both cropped by the artists from larger images.

THE PRESENTATION OF TWO-DIMENSIONAL ART

Numerous workshops are held all around the country to teach matting and framing practices. While these workshops are helpful in teaching framing techniques and craftsmanship, they do not offer any hard-and-fast rules about what always or never will work for a particular image. This is due to a variety of factors. For example, when you consider that all display spaces are different, how can it be assumed that any single presentation device can automatically be appropriate for any given image? Due to the variety of hanging environments, the simple metal frame has become the standard for many artists, especially if their works are traveling and a single display environment cannot be established. The metal frame is more generally suited to a wide range of exhibition environments and is usually noncompetitive with the work.

Professional framers will tell you that decisions regarding appropriate presentation devices are dependent upon

1. The nature of the image, and
2. The objectives of the owner.

The overriding principle governing what is or is not appropriate is common sense—*aesthetic* common sense. For example, different mats can be chosen to complement existing hues. The size and elaborateness of frames are also determined by the nature of the image, display requirements and environments.

The governing rule of thumb regarding matting is to leave a wider border of mat at the bottom than on the remaining three sides, which are usually equal in width. The reason for a wider bottom border is to help "lift" the image. Sometimes images will appear to sink into the frame when all four sides of the mat have the same width. Sometimes the bottom border will actually look thinner if it has the same width as the other three sides. Of course, mats are not always necessary to help "set-off" a work.

THE PRESENTATION OF THREE-DIMENSIONAL ART

A base under a sculpture is as much a part of the total presentation as is a frame around a painting. Too often, however, a base is regarded as an incidental element. In the designing of sculpture not intended to be self-supporting, the relationship of a base to a sculpture should be considered as early in the design process as possible. This is to help assure unity between the sculpture and its base.

Several factors need to be taken into consideration when working with a base.

1. The base must be safe. It should be structurally sound and remove any potential risk of the sculpture's harming a viewer.
2. If the work is intended to be exhibited outdoors, the base needs to be made of a weatherproof medium or weatherproofed and given provisions for securing it to the ground in case of extreme weather (or vandalism).
3. In both exterior and interior exhibitions, lighting can be built into the base if appropriate. Display lighting is usually supplied from a track, stand, or table, in addition to natural lighting.

4. As with a mat or frame, the color and texture of the base, in addition to its overall proportions, must be in harmony with the form. The base may be a dominant visual element of the work, thus requiring appropriate attention from the beginning of the design process.

▶ CONCLUSION

The presentation of an artwork can literally make or break that image. When care is taken to include the base, frame, or mat as a complementary design factor, the total work benefits. When the presentation device is seen as an accessory—an embellishment—and not adequately dealt with, the efforts of the artist and the expressive potential of an image can be compromised.

The decision of whether to use a presentation device or not is always an individual one. There are some instances in which a mat, frame, or base is not required. Some paintings are best presented as originally conceived and executed by the artist, without an added boundary to limit the viewer's experience. And by the same token, a sculptor may have intended that a work be free-standing, without evidence of physical support or presentation devices.

In the end, the success of a presentation is dependent on whether the means employed by the artist to present a work complement the image's content and enhances the viewing experience.

NINE

But Is It Art?

CRITICISM AND EVALUATION

TALENT AND ARTISTIC SUCCESS

The artistic success of an image is not dependent upon the level of natural, or "raw," talent an artist possesses, nor can one claim artistic success because one's parent was an artist. To be an artist, one needs to combine the lessons of art history with the lessons of life; the passions of emotions along with a passion for an artistic medium. One must be predisposed to artistic organization and expression, in addition to employing the full depth of one's intellect.

A Darwinian scholar noted that

> We are what we are because of our biology in conjunction with the environment.

However, bicyclist Michael Shermer wrote:

> Inheritability of talent does not mean inevitability of success.

Cartoonist Reggie Smythe wrote that his primary character, Andy Capp (Fig. 9–1), was

> . . . a lad who's been blessed with every gift, except the gift of shifting [himself] to use 'em.

Clearly, making art requires a combination of

1. Innate design sensitivities, and
2. Physical and intellectual work.

Additionally, working creatively necessarily involves imagination, originality, understanding, and emotional involvement.

DEGREES OF ART

Perhaps one of the greatest difficulties in looking at art is trying to determine how good something is. The underlying question that comes to the surface is "Good for what?" Yet this question distracts one from pursuing the ultimate validity of the art.

▶ Figure 9-1
(Reprinted with special permission of North American Syndicate)

Utilitarian objects of a high visual and technical caliber often are not referred to as art because they are "good for" something—they are utilitarian or decorative. This emphasis on the practicality of something is used by some to debase a form's status as "fine art."

The layperson frequently judges the success of art by admiring technical virtuosity, attention to detail, or overt naturalism of subject matter. Unfortunately, this perspective denies (1) the communication potential of design and (2) the power of direct experience with art.

Also, if justification for an art object is sought by acknowledging its manifestations of social, religious, or political ends, then the artwork is being judged by non-aesthetic criteria.

The degree of quality in an artwork is significantly oriented to its historical period. When two works are compared, each one's historical period must be considered. Attempting to determine the aesthetic worth of an image without broad historic and stylistic references is inadequate and inappropriate.

Another often repeated way to determine the degree of quality or worth of an art object is to observe the amount of money one is willing to spend for the art. Monetary value is frequently perceived as the most accurate indicator of an art object's aesthetic merit. If one were to concur with this, I would encourage the reading of Robert Hughes's article in *Time* magazine (April 13, 1987) upon the announcement of Van Gogh's *Sunflowers* selling at auction for $39.9 million. Hughes wrote:

> There is no rational price for a work of art. That price is solely an index of desire, and nothing is more manipulative than desire . . .

Desire can be based on

1. The availability of other works by that artist,
2. The availability of similar works by other artists,
3. "Fashionable" collecting of that artist's work, and
4. Status of ownership.

The desirability of a major work is too infrequently based on its aesthetic merits.

THE KNOWLEDGEABLE OBSERVER

The artistic success or credibility of an artwork is always going to be a relative consideration, a comparison. Unfortunately, many images are not understood when they are created. The significance of a work may not be perceived until some time has passed. Allowing people to compare it to "masterpieces" helps them to see how well it "holds up" and how much other artists may or may not be influenced by it.

This partially contributes to the reason some artists and their artworks are not appreciated until after the artist's death.

John Canaday, a former art critic of the *New York Times*, wrote:

> In the process of selection and evaluation [of art] a great deal of trash must be examined carefully before it is discarded.

This process takes time and reflection. There are no shortcuts in determining artistic quality. "Untested" images are regularly put on the walls of institutions of art. There, an uninformed public may be duped into believing that all it sees is art. Perish the thought! However, in that same environment inquisitive and thoughtful people can determine for themselves what the merits of unknown or untested images may be.

Those who have studied art and art history and are in touch with the dynamics of their society and the pursuits of human intellect are not held back by a singular criterion such as "the test of time" in determining artistic excellence. Individuals have chosen to take the time to study art because they know that the study will enrich and add meaning to their lives. These people come from all socioeconomic backgrounds. They have the confidence and skills to make educated and reflective judgments about art objects. In addition to being everyday citizens, these individuals include art educators and historians, artists and art critics.

Honoré Daumier's lithograph of *The Influential Critic* illustrates what can happen when the role of the art critic runs amuck. Here, the critic addresses his notepad with a pompous sanctimoniousness, and the public addresses him with respect, tipping their hats. The big problem is that nobody is addressing the art! The people look to the critic for the justification of the image, not to their own intellect. And the critic looks to the glory of his own writing, not the image, apparently seeking to make his words take the place of the image and thus achieve his own glory. Daumier observed the misdirection of the critic and the public in his day, as we may do in our day as well.

> In the production of artwork, the public—the viewer—needs to be considered, but the public should not be accommodated.

The objective of the artist is visual expression, and that requires a viewer, a public. From the first pages of your text and throughout its chapters, you have learned that *art is a visual form of meaningful expression*. While artists' imagery may be motivated by the state of their society—including the public—their imagery is a responsive statement, not just an echo. As a visual form of meaningful expression/communication, art is not a mindless regurgitation of the existing nature of things.

> It is important that evaluations of art be mindful—dependent upon thought and reflection, with principles to guide—not mindlessly overseen by feelings that restrict and attitudes that are static.

THE RECOGNITION OF MERIT

The vacuous statement so often heard in art galleries and studio classes, "I may not know art, but I know what I like," often means one likes what one knows and does not like that which is unfamiliar. Other catch phrases, "I don't care if no one else likes it, I do," and "I just like it, because," are equally inane disclaimers of value, yet universally embraced by art laypersons. "It's art to me" frequently says more about the speaker than the art, and that is not necessarily complimentary. Statements similar to "I don't like that because I don't know what it is supposed to be (do)" help to identify the intellectually inert who are not willing to accommodate the possibility that art is something more than narration. People do not take relatives, advertisements, or movies at face value; nor should they judge art simply on initial impressions.

In studio environments, it is the object of instructors to direct the teaching to help students understand what factors determine artistic merit. Design educator Hin Bredendieck, a student of the Bauhaus, wrote:

> It is precisely the aim of design education to impart to the student the means of achieving authority and command in order to gain ascendancy over the accidental.

This is not to negate room for the accidental as being a contributing factor in making art, no less than we acknowledge serendipity's place in the science laboratory. Rather, the purposeful command of all the visual components and their arrangement makes one's meaningful expression more authoritative.

By studying examples of art from various artists and time periods, artists learn what has been successful for others. By purposely making an effort to study what makes other works aesthetically meaningful, the observed principles and techniques become part of an artist's working vocabulary and mental resource file.

The process of determining the value of art, we now understand, is a comparative one involving an analysis of styles, techniques, societies, and artists. In the analytical process, we do not mean to imply that if an artwork does not rank at the highest level it is not art. Rather, art exists on a variety of levels. However, we have to be wary of those forms which appear meaningless, imitative, and void of content which many try to perpetuate as art.

THE CRITIQUE AND ART CRITICISM

Studio exercises have the potential to yield significant art, yet that is not necessarily their objective. Through design projects various principles are emphasized. The design projects' objectives are to explore and exploit particular concepts. When evaluating the merits of projects done for a design or other studio class, therefore, the primary concerns are to determine whether or not teaching objectives have been met and that students have been encouraged and given an opportunity to creatively respond to those objectives. Should studio work exist on a high plane of creative expression and transcend a project's aesthetic and/or compositional goals, so much the better.

▶ POPULAR CRITERIA

Determining the height of this "high plane of creative expression" can often be a bewildering process for the layperson and art student alike. Sometimes intuition, a "gut feeling," is a primary indicator as to a work's merit.

> The credibility of intuition is dependent upon one's artistic sensitivity and background, knowledge, and experience.

Another "analytical" process some place value in is the "goose bump factor": a viewing experience so significant that goose bumps are raised on one's arm. An alleged third indicator of artistic success may be whether or not one continues to "see" an image in one's mind's eye after having left the presence of a given image. Just as a musical tune can be carried around in one's head, the same may be true of visual images.

These evaluation criteria are not without their pitfalls, however. For example, a loud noise can raise goose bumps but may not be music; and a "smiley face" can linger in your visual memory for a long time, just as the effects of a green apple can linger in your stomach. A smiley face, however, is no more art than is a green apple a gourmet delight just because it stays with you. Therefore, we need a more reliable and, perhaps, less subjective process of evaluation.

▶ THE STUDIO EVALUATION PROCESS

The evaluation process is known as a *critique*. Its function is to observe and comment on the relative strengths and weaknesses of an art object. Additionally, when evaluating studio projects it is helpful to cite what it is that makes up the "strengths" and the "weaknesses." Furthermore, when weaknesses are cited, it is good to consider what could have been done to avoid the weaknesses, or how they could be reworked into strengths. It should be recognized that some errors cannot be remedied, but the observation

of design errors should serve as a lesson to both the student artist and the others in the class.

> The critique is a learning process for all involved.

This critique is art criticism. Criticism, by definition, is a process of making judgments based on evaluations—there is nothing implied which says that a critique is inherently negative. Unfortunately, however, connotations associated with criticism are negative. The words *criticism* and *critical* often make one think of fault-seeking adventures, and may cause one to take the defensive if one's work is being reviewed. Movie and book reviews, for example, are most often perceived as opportunities for critics to show how clever *they* can be when they want to cut something down. Rarely are these reviews—these critiques—seen as being meaningfully constructive and enlightening.

In reality, critics of creative endeavors do not always stand on the outside and look in from a detached and impersonal perspective. For example, American artist Ben Shahn wrote in his book, *The Shape of Content,*

> An artist at work upon a painting must be two people, not one. He must function and act as two people all the time and in several ways. On the one hand, the artist is the imaginer and the producer. But he is also the critic, and here is a critic of. . .inexorable standards.

Art educator and critic Edmund Feldman states:

> The chief goal of criticism is understanding. . . .

He goes on to say

> . . . we derive pleasure from understanding. . . .

Taking the time to slow down enough to really look at and study a work of art in order to truly understand it will yield satisfaction. New doors of insight will be opened and passages of new experiences will be explored.

During the studio critique process, the following questions should be addressed by both the students and the instructor:

1. Have the *objectives* been met as outlined in the project?
2. Does the work exhibit a *design consciousness* that enhances the project's objectives and overall image? If sculptural, did the image exploit three-dimensional space in a meaningful way?
3. Does the project depict a use of tools and materials—*craftsmanship*—that is appropriate to and in harmony with the objectives and apparent content of the work?
4. Is the concept presented in the image a suitable and *creative response* to the objectives of the project?
5. Is the image *presented* in a manner that complements the image; that is, was the choice and use of a framing or presentation device (line mat, frame, sculpture stand) a meaningful addition to the work? Are there any presentation factors (spiral edges, finger smudges) which detracted from the pleasure of the viewing experience, or were all visual presentation factors successful contributors to the content of the work?

If the critique reveals that the studio project has been successful in the five cited areas, a larger question needs to be asked. "How good is it, really? Is it art?"

Answering these questions involves asking more. Feldman suggests a procedural review of the work, of which the following is a modification:

1. What devices does the artist use for communication?

In addition to actually describing what you see in terms of *subject matter*, you should study the artist's use of *tool*, *technique, medium, and ground*, along with the relationship between the *visual* and *organizational components of art.*

2. Is there original communication taking place revealing a particular content, and what is the significance of that content? Does the work carry you to a different (1) emotional, (2) spiritual, or (3) intellectual level from the one you had been on?

Russian author Leo Tolstoy wrote

> The artist must do more than express his emotions; he must also communicate to others. Emotional infection is essential to art.

3. Is the work presented in such a way that all visual information supports the content; that is, is the content dependent upon the given means of presentation—form—for its success?
4. What can the work be compared to in order to demonstrate its relative merits, including other student work, other professional work, examples from the history of art, and so forth?

This four-stage review will indicate where the work may stand on a vertical scale of success. Remembering that the work in question was produced as a studio project aimed at exploiting certain design or other visual considerations, being compelled to entertain the previous four questions is a significant acknowledgement of the work's merit, especially at the student level.

Remind yourself that this review process does not guarantee authoritative art criticism; it is a guide intended to provide analytical direction and consistency of evaluation. There are still a lot of subjective issues left up to the sensitivities of the reviewer—again, sensitivities based on knowledge and experience. Key words and phrases used in this guide, such as . . . enhances; . . . in a meaningful way; . . . in harmony with; . . . suitable; . . . pleasure of the viewing experience; . . . successful; . . . the degree of; . . . and relative merit, call upon the viewer's discretionary judgment.

Beyond the classroom, similar questions can be asked of images that are put forward as art, no matter what their location—museums, galleries, or textbooks. Remember, what you see labeled by someone else as "art" may or may not be art.

Practice this review process with both familiar and unfamiliar works. You may be surprised to find that some "old favorites" can become more meaningful or a bit disappointing. Some new or unfamiliar works, which once seemed threatening or unimportant, may have a lot to offer, or—after closer scrutiny—indeed, may have nothing to say.

> You should feel confidence in your ability to approach unfamiliar works and make judgments based on your own knowledge and experience.

▶ **UNIT GLOSSARY**

Art Criticism A process of making judgments regarding art based on knowledgeable evaluations.

Critique The process of evaluation of an art form. Its function is to observe and comment on the relative strengths and weaknesses of the art form being observed.

Epilogue

You have learned in this text that there is no formula, no insurance package available which will guarantee your ability to make a successful and meaningful image. To demonstrate that there is no guarantee or formula for making good art, all you have to do is (1) look at the creative processes that many, many significant artists have gone through in order to resolve their final compositions and (2) observe how many varied forms of art there are. If there were strict rules and formulas for success in making art, then most aspiring artists would work inside those rules, perpetuating what is acceptable and offering little that is *innovative and insightful.*

The creative process is not easily defined and creative artists do not accommodate a universal, standardized creative formula. Rather, they modify their ideas, drafts, and designs according to their individual expressive needs. They approach each new creative project with the wealth of their knowledge and the individuality of their experiences. In the back of their minds is the history of art as they have come to know and use it.

An artist is aware of what artists from other generations and cultures may offer. However, an artist may choose to ignore or incorporate those lessons. (Gauguin, Fig. E–1). Today's artist is an informed maker of art as a result of color slides, libraries, and the print and video media. A portrait painter, for example, knows what Leonardo's *Mona Lisa* looks like and how it relates to other portraits by master painters. A sculptor may know the work of Bernini and keep those images of Bernini's forms—along with countless other works by other artists—stored away in the back of the subconscious for later reference.

▶ Figure E-1   Gauguin, *Self-Portrait* (Dated 1889)
(Image no. 1814, National Gallery of Art, Washington, Chester Dale Collection, 1962)

The object of this text has been to begin filling the back of your mind—your subconscious—with information about the tradition of image-making, and the reasons some of the images of that tradition are meaningful. It has also been the object of this text to help you find your place in that tradition. This text does not try to fill you with the passion necessary to make art; it cannot create the passion that you bring to your art nor can it define the passion that you want to express through your art. The passion is your passion—your expression. It is for you to develop and evolve. All of the components of visual expression lie dead and meaningless on the easel or workbench without your passion.

What makes one artist's or student's work stand out from another's is the individual passion that they bring to their work. These passions are demonstrated in the fascinating range of images that have been produced by people from Cro-Magnon to modern. You have observed the range of human creative expression and passions from the variety of examples provided in this text. You have become more comfortable and proficient in working with some media. You have discovered the expressive qualities of working with particular media-ground relationships. Most important, you have learned that the relationship between the tool, technique, medium, and ground cannot be taken for granted. You have seen that a single medium has a broad range of expressive applications. You have seen that a single subject matter can be treated with a wide range of interpretations—as wide and broad as there are different artists and personalities. Therefore, you have learned that there are several identifiable factors you must consider when making art. Be careful, however, not to get so concerned and preoccupied with the tangible components of art that you lose sight of the intangible: the passion.

Passions flow at different levels: You may wear them on your sleeve or keep them hidden deep inside of you. "Still waters run deep" is an expression often cited to denote the individual who feels strongly and thinks deeply, but is quiet and meditative on the surface; who keeps passions in check. Others sob openly or complain bitterly, having no objection to letting people know what they are feeling at any time. Neither type of person is necessarily better than the other, although some passions, expressions, images, and aesthetic ideas seem more socially appropriate in some situations than others.

Fortunately, there is no *universal* voice or social restriction stating what images can be put on a canvas or carved into stone. Instead, there exist in societies restrictions as to when and where images can be exhibited.

Accordingly, avoid too many preconceived ideas about what is and is not art. Greeting-card and album-cover designers do not necessarily hold the rule books for determining meaningful aesthetic quality. Endeavor to look at artworks with openness and objectivity. As we said earlier, be willing to go beyond the "safe" in making your own art and in responding to new and different art; take a new look at yourself and your world. Dig deep down inside yourself; put your hands on those feelings and make those feelings known. Be willing to take chances. Rodin broke the rules of sculpture by creating figures with irregular surfaces; Michelangelo elongated the human form beyond the constraints of physical reality; David Smith used structural steel instead of fine marble to make sculpture; and Robert Smithson plowed the earth with a bull-dozer instead of modeling clay with his thumb. As you look back it all seems so right and natural, yet as you look forward the future directions of art seem so uncertain—they are. The artistic future for these artists, too, was uncertain. But they boldly stepped forward into aesthetic unknowns, following their convictions; armed with their passions and a knowledge of and sensitivity for design. The artists you study are those who have been willing to challenge the popular concepts of what art is—they have been willing to redefine art. They have led the way in discovering new media, techniques and imagery, in confronting and overcoming that which was "safe" in art and in themselves.

Each of us has a dream about what our future and the future of art will be like. The reality of the future and our dreams will, in part, be determined by how passionately others pursue their dreams and expand known boundaries. Often, when we see one person pushing ahead strongly it gives us courage to push harder, too, and give substance to our own dreams. Lewis Carroll, in stating this interdependence of creative thinkers and doers, wrote:

> He was part of my dreams—but then I was part of his dream, too.

If what you are doing seems right for you and the world isn't following, that doesn't mean you are wrong. It means you must push yourself even harder to determine your commitment to the direction your passions are taking you. If you feel better and better about what you are doing, keep pushing. The world will catch up; the world will share your dreams; the world will share your vision.

Glossary

Aboriginal art The art native to or indigenous of a particular group of people.

Abstract/Abstraction A stylization, rearrangement, or simplification of form for the purpose of artistic expression. Abstract images are most often derivative of forms actually seen or experienced.

Accent Emphasis placed on an element in a composition by an artist to give that element particular visual significance. The relative visual prominence or dominance of a line as determined by its placement or location, attitude and direction, measure, and embellishment.

Achromatic Without color.

Actual Textures Surface qualities which can be experienced through the sense of touch; three-dimensional.

Additive Process The building up, modeling, or assembly of a medium.

Additive System Associated with the stacking or adding of one color of projected light on top of another. See LIGHT COLOR THEORY.

Advancing Space Pictorial area which appears to advance toward the viewer from the area closest to the picture plane.

Aerial Perspective See ATMOSPHERIC PERSPECTIVE.

Afterimage The photosensitive cells which line the back of the retina become overstimulated by extremely strong stimuli or by an extremely long look at particular stimuli and continue sending messages to the brain (1) after the stimuli are gone, or (2) until a stronger stimulus overrides the first.

Alberti, Leon Battista Renaissance architect; believed Classical beauty involved the perfect harmony of all visual part, that nothing could be taken away from or added to a beautiful form without detracting from the form.

Analogous Colors Colors that are beside each other on the color wheel which share a common hue.

Approximate Symmetry A minor variation of visual components from one side of a composition to the other while still maintaining a conspicuous similarity between the two sides.

Architecture The art and science of designing and erecting space-defining forms intended for human interaction.

Art A visual form of meaningful expression.

Art Criticism A process of making judgments regarding art based on knowledgeable evaluations.

Art From Found Materials Art made from found, junk, or scrap materials; sometimes involving new materials, but materials that are not traditionally associated with art. Also see ASSEMBLAGE.

Artificial Textures Manufactured actual textures.

Assemblage A form of sculpture noted by similar or dissimilar materials joined together incorporating constructive techniques. [Sometimes a synonym for FOUND/JUNK/SCRAP ART.]

Association Relationship.

Asymmetrical Balance A conspicuous, purposeful lack of sameness between the left and right sides of a composition that ultimately maintains a feeling of equilibrium. Syn.: OCCULT BALANCE.

Atectonic A three-dimensional form which has significant protrusions or extensions into negative space, deemphasizing mass and bulk, while extending the form's energy.

Atmospheric Perspective The neutralizing of the visual components as they appear to recede in space. Syn.: AERIAL PERSPECTIVE.

Attitude One form's physical orientation to another.

Axis A line (usually implied rather than actual) which runs through the length, height, or width of a form at that form's center. An axis may run through a volume, such as a rod through a rolling pin, or it may run across a surface, like a line across or down the middle of a page.

Balance The arrangement of visual forces yielding a felt equilibrium.

Binder An agent which holds pigment particles in suspension so that the pigment can be spread on in a film which will eventually harden to keep them permanently bound together and adhered to a surface. Syn.: VEHICLE.

Biomorphic Shapes See ORGANIC SHAPES.

Calligraphic Line A free-flowing line (curved or straight) which changes in length and width. Syn.: PLASTIC or MODELED LINE. See PLASTIC.

Chiaroscuro The simulating of representational value schemes with media which evokes the naturalistic three-dimensional appearance of lights and darks on a form.

Chromatic   Of or relating to color.

Closed Composition   The primary visual components within the picture frame fit easily inside of the limit of the picture frame and do not appear to extend beyond that limit. Opposite of *open composition*.

Closed Value Schemes   Relationships of light to dark are restricted or limited to particular shapes and areas; selective illumination.

Closure   The concept of an implied boundary which keeps the grouping of visual forms in the composition from visually running off the picture plane.

Collage   An art form involving the attaching of a variety of actual textures from found objects, combined with painted or drawn effects, to a ground.

Color   The response of vision to the quality of a wavelength. Syn: HUE.

Coloration   Value relationships produced by carving in stone that create naturalistic value and color effects.

Color Scheme   The selection *and* arrangement of colors on a ground.

Color Wheel   A circular arrangement of colors which perpetuates the order of the spectrum.

Complementary Colors   Colors which are opposite each other on the color wheel.

Constructive Technique   Related to the additive process, involves the joining of materials by mechanical means.

Content   The ultimate meaning or significance of a work of art.

Contour Line   A line which notes the edge of shape, color, texture, or value areas, and the change of direction of shape edges and surfaces.

Contrast   Differences which are evident through comparison.

Convergence   A technique using lines or clusters of forms which proportionally diminish in scale or taper toward a common point located in the composition; most frequently, as forms get farther away they diminish in size, proportionally coming together toward a common point on or near the horizon line.

Craftsmanship   The skill and technical virtuosity with which one handles tools and media.

Craftspeople   Those who handle their media and tools with expert skill producing objects primarily for utilitarian ends.

Critique   The process of evaluation of an art form. Its function is to observe and comment on the relative strengths and weaknesses of the art form being observed.

Cropping   Limiting the vastness of the field of view (limiting the subjects from their environment) by altering the shape and/or dimensions of the picture frame. Syn.: PICTURE FRAMING.

Cross-Contour   A line which traces the undulations of a surface between two points of a primary and/or secondary contour.

Curvilinear Shapes   Shapes made up of curved contour lines.

Decorative Space   Pictorial area which appears to lie on the surface of the picture plane, neither advancing nor receding. ("Decorative" space should not be confused with any connotation associated with "embellishment.")

Design   The arrangement of the visual components of art.

Dominance   Area or feature of a composition that is of primary visual importance thus commanding the attention of the viewer.

Dot   The smallest visual component on a ground, having only enough contrast against the ground as to be visible. Syn.: POINT.

Economy   The selective inclusion and exclusion of visual stimuli in a composition, usually involving a sense of thrift—nonessentials are avoided. Frequently yields the "essence" of a form.

Ethos   Dispassionate and objective response to circumstances.

Eurythmy   Proportional and other visual relationships in a composition that work well together and look "right." Syn.: UNITY.

Even Value Scheme   Shapes have no individual shading from light to dark within their primary contours; each shape in the composition is an even shade of one value of a neutral.

Fabrication   The process of producing a three-dimensional form, usually from sketches or models, by welding, building, sewing, or other such assembly techniques.

Figure-Ground Relationship   The shape relationship of subject matter against its background on the picture plane.

Focal Point/Focus   Location on the picture plane to which the artist has directed your vision via artistic devices which may include contrast, convergence, accent, or clarity of form.

Foreshortening   The apparent diminished axis of a form created by a form's overlapping itself as it advances or recedes in space.

Form   The visual result of the aesthetic decision making process; the interaction of subject matter, medium, tool and technique, ground, and the visual and organizational components of art, and their resulting visual effects.

Format   The shape of the overall surface on which an image is applied, including square, rectangular, round (tondo), free-form, or multi-panel (diptych, triptych, polyptych).

Found/Scrap/Junk Art   A misnomer. Art may be made from found, junk, or scrap materials, but the result should not be junk or scrap art! A more appropriate label is ART FROM FOUND MATERIALS or ASSEMBLAGE.

Gels   Colored sheets of thin, translucent plastic film that remove specific wavelengths from projected light. Syn.: FILTERS.

Genre Art   Images depicting everyday scenes of the middle class.

Geometric Shapes   Shapes which appear to have been mathematically constructed.

Gestalt   A psychological or symbolic sense of completeness and total resolution yielded from an incomplete or open-ended configuration of parts.

Golden Mean Rectangle   A mathematically constructed rectangle with sides having a ratio of about 5:8; considered by many cultures and individuals to have "ideal" proportions.

Ground   The term for any physical material on which a two-dimensional image is created. This is not usually a three-dimensional consideration since sculptural forms are created out of a medium, not onto a ground.

Haptic   Something that relates to the physical sense of touch.

Harmony   Agreement of visual parts.

Hieratic Scale   A form of presentation perceived to be an effective means of showing the relative importance of figures within a composition; used by societies or individuals to depict the religious, political, or physical importance of an individual.

Highlight   The part of the surface of the sphere—or any other form—which catches and reflects most of the transmitted light to the observer. The highlight appears to be the form's surface closest to the light source.

High Relief Sculpture   A form of relief sculpture that has significant projections beyond the surface of the background plane; usually involves significant undercuttings.

Horizon   The location where the lower edge of the sky meets the upper limit of the earth's surface.

Horizon Line   A drawn line noting the location of the horizon, which helps to establish the viewer's position relative to the image.

Hue   Traditionally regarded as the name for the quality of a wavelength as determined by its position in the spectrum. Syn.: COLOR.

Impasto   Paint applied thickly to a ground, creating a surface texture that is conspicuously built up.

Implied Textures   Surfaces which appear to have tactile qualities. See SIMULATED TEXTURES.

Infinite Space   Unlimited extensions in any or all directions.

Integrity of a Medium   The functional and aesthetic suitability of a material as applicable to a particular image.

Intensity   Colors at their purest quality of wavelength as depicted on the outer band of the wheel.

Invented Textures   The repetition of a motif on a small scale which evokes a tactile quality; two-dimensional.

Ism   Euphemism for a style of art; derived from art movements such as Romantic*ism*, Impression*ism*, and Real*ism*.

Kinetic Art   Art that physically moves by natural or artificial means (mechanical or nonmechanical).

Light   That part of a surface which receives direct light from a light source.

Light Color Theory   An additive system incorporating the overlapping of projected beams of colored, primary light (red, blue, and green) to produce secondary colors; primaries of red, blue, and green—when mixed—produce white.

Light Source   The point of origin of illumination; for example, sun or light bulbs.

Line   The visible path of a moving point.

Linear Perspective   A mathematical/mechanical equivocation for the optical effects of convergence involving techniques of drawing that incorporate horizon lines and vanishing points.

Local Color   The quality of wavelengths that are reflected by an object under "normal" daylight conditions.

Local Textures   Those qualities which are optically perceived to be inherent to a particular surface.

Local Value   The quantity of light an object inherently reflects under "normal" daylight conditions.

Low Relief Sculpture   A form of relief sculpture that has a very limited projection off of the surface of the background plane.

Manipulative Process   Sculptural technique involving the shaping of a plastic medium, such as clay.

Maquette   A small, three-dimensional preparatory study for a sculpture, French term meaning "model."

Mass   An area that appears to have bulk and density—a feeling of solidity.

Media   The plural form of MEDIUM. (The term *multimedia* is redundant. When more than one medium is used in a work of art, the work is referred to as MIXED MEDIA.)

Medium   The material of which an artwork is made, such as oil paint, charcoal, or marble. The plural form is MEDIA.

Mixed Media   The use of more than one medium in a work.

Mobile   Suspended sculpture that rotates according to air currents; invented by Alexander Calder.

Möbius Strip   A looped strip of material constructed to have only one surface or plane.

Model   Able to be shaped at will, usually regarding a plastic medium (see PLASTIC).

Monochromatic   Of or relating to one color and its varying values.

Monolith   A large, single piece of stone.

Monolithic   A quality of massiveness and monumentality, either actual or implied, usually associated with a single stone used in sculpture or architecture.

Monumental   Having the (1) visual impression or (2) attribute of great size.

Motif   A visual component conspicuously repeated in a composition; not necessarily involved in an individual pattern.

Movement   A path of visual direction that is determined by the artist's selective emphasis on and organization of various visual components.

Mural   An image painted directly on a wall or ceiling, frequently large in scale.

Naturalism   Objective recording of observed subject matter. (Naturalism is not a true "ism"; rather, it is an artistic device.)

Natural Textures   The surfaces of natural forms which are naturally produced.

Negative Shape   An area void of primary subject matter. Syn.: NEGATIVE SPACE. See VOID.

Neolithic   The "New Stone Age"; dates of practical usage vary somewhat, but usually begin around 8000 B.C., continuing to about 3000 B.C.

Neutrals   Pigments of no hue which when added to a color do not change the color but only its tint (lighter) or shade (darker). Black and White.

Newton, Isaac   At the age of twenty-three in 1666, he observed that white (natural) light, when passed through a prism, broke down into bands of color known as the SPECTRUM.

Nonobjective Art   Nonrepresentational art; imagery is not based on anything observed or experienced.

Nonrepresentational Value Scheme   Light and dark gradations within shapes without a sense of a consistent light source.

Objective   Standardization and adherence to observable, identifiable, quantifiable characteristics.

Occult Balance   See ASYMMETRICAL BALANCE.

Open Composition   The primary visual components within the picture frame appear to extend beyond the limit of the frame. Opposite of *closed composition*. See CROPPING.

Open Value Scheme   Relationships of light to dark are not restricted or limited to particular shapes and areas; unselective illumination.

Organic Shapes Shapes with undulating, free-flowing contours; frequently they resemble the shapes of living forms. Syn.: BIOMORPHIC SHAPE.

Organizational Components of Art Principles which govern the arrangement of the visual components of art, including dominance, proportion, balance, variety and harmony, repetition and movement, and economy.

Paint Quality The inherent characteristic(s) of a medium as exploited by the artist.

Paleolithic The "Old Stone Age"; dates of practical usage vary somewhat, but usually begin around 30,000 B.C., continuing to about 8000 B.C.

Palette The surface on which an artist arranges and mixes colors for painting; the actual colors used by an artist.

Papier Collé An art form involving the application of various papers, combined with painted or drawn effects, to a ground.

Paragone A Renaissance debate intended to determine the relative importance of the three different art forms: two-dimensional arts, three-dimensional arts, and architecture.

Pathos Personalized and sympathetic response to circumstances.

Pattern One of the visual components is used often and placed in relatively close proximity to more of the same visual component so that similar parts are read together as a unit; the conspicuous or systematic repetition of a visual motif on a surface, which creates a sense of visual harmony.

Penumbra The lightest part of the shade.

Photosensitive Cells Specialized cells known as rods and cones in the retina of the eye which chemically respond to qualities and quantities of light.

Picture Frame The boundary of a two-dimensional image, either implied or actual. Every visual entity within the picture frame is the responsibility of the artist.

Picture Framing See CROPPING.

Picture Plane An implied surface area spanning all of the points on the interior of the picture frame.

Pigment Particles—either natural or synthetic—which have particular light-absorbing and light-reflecting characteristics.

Pigment Color Theory A subtractive system, as in the COLOR WHEEL; primaries of red, yellow, and blue—when mixed—produce brown.

Planar Of or related to planes.

Plane An actual or implied, limited or unlimited two-dimensional surface that has no mass and which may exist in two- or three-dimensional space. Planes may be either curvilinear or rectilinear.

Plastic Sculpturally, a medium which retains its shape after being shaped and modeled, such as clay. Generally, an entity's ability to be willfully modeled or altered, such as space or line.

Plastic Shape See PLASTIC.

Pointillism The application of paint in small dabs or dots of color to a ground; the colors are intended to visually mix in the eye of the viewer as opposed to being physically mixed on the artist's palette.

Polychromatic Of or relating to many colors.

Polychrome Paint color, usually on a sculpture or architectural form.

Polychromed Painted sculpture or architectural form.

Positive Shape The area defining primary subject matter. Syn.: POSITIVE SPACE.

Primary Colors Fundamental pigments of which others are comprised.

Primary Contour A line which describes a form by tracing its outline. Syn.: OUTLINE.

Primitive A disparaging term, implying technological or cultural deprivation, that should not be used to describe a country or its art. (Not to be confused with ABORIGINAL ART.)

Proportion The visual agreement of relative parts.

Radial Balance The visual emphasis on the distribution of forms and forces around a central point.

Realism A style of art that depends on a high degree of representational imagery that yields an ultimate significance. This emphasis on ultimate significance, or "content," is what separates it most from "naturalism."

Receding Space Pictorial area which appears to recede away from or behind the area of the picture plane.

Rectilinear Shapes Shapes made up of straight lines.

Reflected Light   Illumination bounced onto a form from a surface; a secondary light source providing indirect light.

Relief Sculpture   A form of three-dimensional art that is attached to a background plane; primarily frontal.

Repetition   The recurrence of a visual component.

Representational   Images having a visual resemblance to tangible subject matter; ranges from objective to abstract imagery. (Not an ISM.)

Representational Value Scheme   A natural relationship of values which accommodates physical laws, thus representationally revealing the three-dimensionality of the forms.

Rhythm   The viewing pace and movement along visual paths.

Rules of Thumb   Generalities regarding perceived truths which are handed down over time; usually taken for granted and not investigated or challenged.

Sacred   Of or relating to a particular faith.

Scheiner, Christopher   In the seventeenth century, he discovered light enters the eye and carries images with it.

Secondary Colors   Pigments which are the result of the mix of two primary colors.

Secondary Contour   A line which describes changes of shape, color, texture, or value areas, and the change of direction of shape edges and surfaces which lie inside of the primary contour.

Secular   Conspicuously omitting any reference to a particular faith.

Sensory Symbiosis   One sense working with and complementing another.

Sgraffito   One medium scratched or scraped through to reveal a contrasting value or color beneath it.

Shade   The part of a form which does not receive direct illumination; comprised of the umbra and penumbra. The darkening of a color with a neutral.

Shadow   That part of a form which is denied direct lighting by another form.

Shape   A two- or three-dimensional area that has an actual or implied limit. The limit may be a drawn contour line or the edge of a physical form.

The limit may also be the location of a visual *contrast* from one value, color, or texture to another.

Silhouette   The area described by a primary contour which is filled in with an even, overall value or color; no secondary contours are evident.

Simulated Textures   Imitated surface qualities.

Simultaneous Contrast   The principle that any visual component can vary in appearance, depending on the nature of the visual component placed next to it.

Slip   A mix of water and powdered clay which results in a medium that has the consistency of tomato soup. It is used either for joining pieces of clay or casting clay forms.

Space   A limited or unlimited two- or three-dimensional area appearing to advance, recede, or extend in all directions, depending upon the visual clues provided by the artist.

Spatial Equivocation   A contradiction of any traditional or expected spatial effect.

Spectrum   White light, when passed through a prism, is broken down into visible bands of colored light according to their wavelengths. The visible bands of light are identified as red, orange, yellow, green, blue, indigo, and violet. The measure of the various wavelengths is visible on an oscilloscope.

Split Complement   A color and the two colors on each side of its complement.

Stippling   A graphic process using small dots of varying proximity to one another for the purpose of making value gradations.

Style   Identifiable and characteristic trends associated with group movements or individual directions.

Subjective   Qualitative, personalized, and nonconformist concepts.

Subject Matter   The point of departure or idea stimulating the artist's imagery; may or may not be identifiable or representational.

Substitutive Process   Sculptural technique involving the changing of the medium of a form from one material to another by way of molds and casting.

Subtractive Process   Sculptural technique involving traditional carving applications on stone, wood, or any other appropriate medium.

Subtractive System Associated with the absorbent and reflective nature of pigments. See PIGMENT COLOR THEORY.

Surrealism A nineteenth- and twentieth-century movement in art which included dreamlike, fanciful images which appear generated in the subconscious; images are usually variations on visual reality.

Symmetrical Balance The visual components on one side of a composition are mirror-imaged on the opposite side of the implied central axis of the work. May also be referred to as *axial* balance.

Technique Systematic use of tools and media to accomplish a task; the individual manner or style in which an artist manipulates a medium; the process by which a form is created.

Tectonic A three-dimensional form having no appendages or protrusions into space from the primary mass, emphasizing its mass and bulk.

Tenebrism Exaggerated CHIAROSCURO for dramatic effects.

Tension A strained relationship between the visual forces working in a composition and/or between the image and the viewer.

Tertiary Colors Pigments which are the result of the mix of a primary and a secondary color.

Texture The actual or implied tactile quality of a surface.

Three-Dimensional Arts Images which exist in three dimensions—length, height, and depth—usually including sculpture.

Tint The lightening of a color with a neutral.

Tool Any implement that will work in harmony with the selected medium to produce an image that is in harmony with the artist's expressive objectives.

Triad A relationship of three colors equidistant from one another on the color wheel. A connecting line between the three creates an equilateral triangle.

Trompe L'oeil Art Literally, "to fool the eye." A form of art that has as its object fooling the viewer into believing that what is painted is real.

Two-Dimensional Arts Images which exist in two dimensions—length and height—usually including painting and graphic arts.

Umbra The darkest part of the shade.

Undercuttings Recessed areas behind a forward-facing surface or plane in a relief sculpture.

Unity See EURYTHMY.

Value The relationship of light to dark.

Value Scale Stages of value changes between and including white and black.

Value Scheme The overall relationships of lights and darks on a form or in a composition. Syn.: VALUE PATTERN.

Vanishing Point An implied location on the horizon line where receding forms that lie parallel to the surface of the earth would, if extended to infinity, appear to diminish into a single dot.

Vantage Point Location from which something is viewed; bird's-eye, person's-eye, and worm's-eye views.

Variety A simultaneous recognition of similarities and differences of visual parts.

Vehicle See BINDER.

View See VANTAGE POINT.

Viewer Experience The entire response of an individual to the circumstances involved in viewing a work of art: intellectual, emotional, physical, and so on.

Visual Components of Art Observable elements of an art form, including dot, line, shape, value, color, and texture.

Void A penetration through a three-dimensional shape which yields a negative space/shape. Syn.: NEGATIVE SHAPE.

Volume The actual space or area a three-dimensional form displaces or circumscribes.

Volumetric Emphasizing volume.

Wash Media—such as oil paint, acrylics, and watercolor—applied in a diluted manner, creating a transparent film of a color or neutral.

Wavelength The measure from peak to peak or any other corresponding phases of consecutive cycles, as seen on an oscilloscope.

White Light The source of color; light that contains the visible spectrum. (In its purest form, it is sunlight. It may be artificial, but variations in the spectrum are usually noticeable.)

Selected Bibliography

The following represent selected references used in the writing of this text.

Adeline, M. Jules. *Adeline's Art Dictionary*. New York: Ungar, 1966.

Albers, Joseph. *The Interaction of Color*. New Haven: Yale University Press, 1963.

Arnason, H. H. *History of Modern Art: Painting, Sculpture, Architecture*. Englewood Cliffs, N.J.: Prentice-Hall, Inc.; New York: Harry N. Abrams, Inc., 1968.

Arnheim, Rudolf. "Visual Dynamics," *American Scientist*, 76 (November-December 1988), 585-91.

Art and Artists of All Nations. New York: Knight and Brown, 1900.

Bascom, William. *African Art in Cultural Perspective: An Introduction*. New York: W. W. Norton and Company, Inc., 1973.

Block, Jonathan, and Gisele Atterberry. *Design Essentials*. Englewood Cliffs, N. J.: Prentice-Hall, Inc., 1989.

Butler, Ruth. *Western Sculpture: Definitions of Man*. New York: Harper and Row, 1979.

Canaday, John. *Mainstreams of Modern Art*. New York: Holt, Rinehart, and Winston, 1959.

————. *The Lives of the Painters*, Vol. I. New York: W. W. Norton and Company, Inc., 1969.

————. *What is Art? An Introduction to Painting, Sculpture, and Architecture*. New York: Farrar, Straus and Cudahy, 1963.

————. *Embattled Critic*. New York: Farrar, Straus and Cudahy, 1962.

Carroll, Lewis. *Alice's Adventures in Wonderland*. New York: Random House, 1946.

Coleman, Ronald. *Sculpture: A Basic Handbook for Students*. Dubuque: Wm. C. Brown, 1980.

Copplestone, Trewin. *Art in Society: A Guide to the Visual Arts*. Englewood Cliffs, N. J.: Prentice-Hall, Inc., 1983.

de la Croix, Horst, and Richard G. Tansey. *Gardner's Art Through the Ages*. Washington, D.C.: Harcourt Brace Jovanovich, 1986.

Edwards, Betty. *Drawing on the Right Side of the Brain: A Course in Enhancing Creativity and Artistic Confidence*. Los Angeles: J. P. Tarcher, Inc., 1979.

Elsen, Albert E. *Purposes of Art* (4th ed.). Philadelphia: Holt, Rinehart and Winston, 1981.

Feldman, Edmund B. *Thinking About Art*. Englewood Cliffs, N.J.: Prentice-Hall, Inc., 1985.

————. *Varieties of Visual Experience* (3rd ed.). Englewood Cliffs, N.J.: Prentice-Hall, Inc.; New York: Harry N. Abrams, Inc., 1987.

Fichner-Rathus, Lois. *Understanding Art*. Englewood Cliffs, N. J.: Prentice-Hall, Inc., 1989.

Gilbert, Rita, and William McCarter. *Living with Art*. New York: Alfred A. Knopf, 1985.

Goldstein, Nathan. *Design and Composition*. Englewood Cliffs, N.J.: Prentice-Hall, Inc., 1989.

Guccione, Bob, ed. "First Communion," *Omni*, (December 1988), p. 110.

Hughes, Robert. *The Shock of the New*. New York: Alfred A. Knopf, 1981.

————. "Of Vincent and Eanum Pig," *Time* (April 13, 1987), p. 80–81.

"Italian Renaissance Frames," *New Yorker*, July 2, 1990, p. 9.

Itten, Johannes. *Design and Form: The Basic Course at the Bauhaus*. New York: Reinhold Publishing Corporation, 1963.

Janson, H. W. *History of Art: A Survey of the Major Visual Arts from the Dawn of History to the Present Day*. Englewood Cliffs, N.J.: Prentice-Hall, Inc.; New York: Harry N. Abrams, Inc., 1987.

Langland, Tuck. *Practical Sculpture*. Englewood Cliffs, N.J.: Prentice-Hall, Inc., 1988.

Lauer, David A. *Design Basics* (2nd ed.). New York: Holt, Rinehart and Winston, 1985.

Lucie-Smith, Edward. *The Thames and Hudson Dictionary of Art Terms*. London: Thames and Hudson, 1984.

MacCurdy, Edward. *The Notebooks of Leonardo da Vinci*. New York: George Braziller, 1954.

Mayer, Ralph, *The Artist's Handbook of Materials and Techniques*. New York: Viking Press, 1982.

McCarry, Charles. "Three Men Who Made the Magazine," *National Geographic*, 174, no. 3 (September 1988), 304.

Mueller, Conrad G., and Mae Rudolph. *Life Science Library: Light and Vision*. New York: Time Inc., 1966.

Myers, Jac Frederic. *The Language of Visual Art*. Philadelphia: Holt, Rinehart, and Winston, Inc., 1989.

Ocvirk, Otto G., et al. *Art Fundamentals: Theory and Practice* (5th ed.). Dubuque: Wm. C. Brown Publishers, 1985.

Rawson, Philip. *Design*. Englewood Cliffs, N.J.: Prentice-Hall, Inc., 1987.

Rennolds, Margaret B., ed. *The National Museum of Women in the Arts*. New York: Harry N. Abrams, Inc., 1987.

Richardson, John Adkins. *Art: The Way It Is* (3rd ed.). Englewood Cliffs, N.J.: Prentice-Hall, Inc., 1985.

————, et al. *Basic Design*. Englewood Cliffs, N.J.: Prentice-Hall, Inc., 1984.

Rubens, Melvin L., and Gordon Walls. *Studies in Psychological Optics*. Illinois: Chas. C. Thomas, 1965.

Russell, Stella Pandell. *Art in the World* (3rd ed.). Philadelphia: Holt, Rinehart and Winston, Inc., 1989.

Sagan, Carl. "The Unexpected Consequences of Our Expeditions to the Moon," *Parade* (July 16, 1989), p. 7.

San Lazzaro, G. di, ed. "Homage to Max Erns," *Siecle Review*, Special Edition (1971).

Shahn, Ben. *The Shape of Content*. Cambridge: Harvard University Press, 1980.

Shermer, Michael. "Master of My Fate," *Bicycling* (June 1989), p. 73.

Thompson, Sir Eric. "A Traveler's Tale of Ancient Tikal," *National Geographic*, 18, no. 6 (December 1975), 801.

Walker, John. *Glossary of Art, Architecture, and Design Since 1945*. Hamden: Linett Books, 1977.

———. *The National Gallery of Art, Washington*. New York: Harry N. Abrams, Inc., 1975.

Ward, Fred. "Images for the Computer Age," *National Geographic*, 175, no. 6 (June 1989), 737.

Wildenhain, Marguerite. *The Invisible Core: A Potter's Life and Thoughts*. Palo Alto, CA: Pacific Books, 1973.

———. *Pottery: Form and Expression*. Palo Alto, CA: Pacific Books, 1973.

Winokur, John, ed. *The Portable Curmudgeon*. New York: Penguin, Inc., 1987.

Young, Frank M. *Visual Studies: A Foundation for Artists and Designers*. Englewood Cliffs, N.J.: Prentice-Hall, Inc., 1985.

INDEX

Page numbers in italic type refer to art works. Titles of works are also in italics.

A